Accented Speech in Literature, Art, and Theory

Languages and Culture in History

The series *Languages and Culture in History* studies the role foreign languages have played in the creation of linguistic and cultural heritage, at the individual, communal, national and transnational level.

At the heart of this series is the historical evolution of linguistic and cultural policies, internal as well as external, and their relationship with linguistic and cultural identities.

The series takes an interdisciplinary approach to a variety of historical issues: the diffusion, the supply and the demand for foreign languages, the history of pedagogical practices, the historical relationship between languages in a given cultural context, the public and private use of foreign languages – in short, every way foreign languages intersect with local languages in the cultural realm.

Willem Frijhoff (1942-2024) was the co-founder of the series *Languages and Culture in History* and Professor of History at the Vrije Universiteit in Amsterdam, the Netherlands. He is considered "the most eminent historian of culture and mentalities of the last fifty years" (Boom). His extensive oeuvre covers a broad field of religious history, heritage studies, urban history, and the history of education, and he devoted many of his publications to the history of education, language acquisition, and multilingualism.

Series Editor
Karène Sanchez Summerer, Groningen University

Editorial Board Members
Federico Gobbo, University of Amsterdam
Gerda Hassler, University of Potsdam
Aurélie Joubert, University of Groningen
Douglas A. Kibbee, University of Illinois at Urbana-Champaign
Marie-Christine Kok Escalle, Utrecht University
Joep Leerssen, University of Amsterdam
Nicola McLelland, The University of Nottingham
Despina Provata, National and Kapodistrian University of Athens
Valérie Spaëth, University of Paris III: Sorbonne Nouvelle
Javier Suso López, University of Granada
Pierre Swiggers, KU Leuven

Accented Speech in Literature, Art, and Theory

Melodramas of the Foreign Tongue

Tingting Hui

Amsterdam University Press

This research was supported by funding from the Netherlands Institute for Cultural Analysis (NICA). I am deeply grateful for their generous support, which made this work possible.

Earlier and shorter versions of Chapter 1 and Chapter 4 were published, respectively, in *Bodies that Still Matter*, ed. Annemie Halsema, Katja Kwastek, and Roel van den Oever (Amsterdam University Press, 2021), 65–76, and *Tawada Yoko: On Writing and Rewriting*, ed. Doug Slaymaker (Lexington Books, 2019), 199–212. All these previous versions have been substantially rewritten and expanded.

Cover illustration: Cover art by Karen Zuo. *The scent* (2023). www.karenzuo.com

© Studio Karen Zuo. All rights reserved.
Cover design: Coördesign, Leiden
Lay-out: Crius Group, Hulshout

ISBN	978 90 4856 900 7
e-ISBN	978 90 4856 901 4 (pdf)
e-ISBN	978 90 4857 266 3 (accessible ePub)
DOI	10.5117/9789048569007
NUR	618

© T. Hui / Amsterdam University Press B.V., Amsterdam 2025

All rights reserved. Without limiting the rights under copyright reserved above, no part of this book may be reproduced, stored in or introduced into a retrieval system, or transmitted, in any form or by any means (electronic, mechanical, photocopying, recording or otherwise) without the written permission of both the copyright owner and the author of the book.

No part of this book may be used or reproduced in any manner for the purpose of training artificial intelligence technologies or systems.

Here is the central rhythm; here the common main spring. I watch it expand, contract; and then expand again. Yet I am not included. If I speak, imitating their accent, they prick their ears, waiting for me to speak again, in order that they may place me—if I come from Canada or Australia, I, who desire above all things to be taken to the arms with love, am alien, external. I, who would wish to feel close over me the protective waves of the ordinary, catch with the tail of my eye some far horizon; am aware of hats bobbing up and down in perpetual disorder.

— Virginia Woolf, *The Waves*

You're not French are you? No, you're right, I'm English. Half a sentence and already you've placed me: in a body with a mouth that can't help adding this peculiar signature as it speaks.

— Kate Briggs, *This Little Art*

You can become a virtuoso with this new device that moreover gives you a new body, just as artificial and sublimated—some say sublime. You have a feeling that the new language is a resurrection: new skin, new sex. But the illusion bursts when you hear, upon listening to a recording, for instance, that the melody of your voice comes back to you as a peculiar sound, out of nowhere, closer to the old spluttering than to today's code. Your awkwardness has its charm, they say, it is even erotic, according to womanizers, not to be outdone. No one points out your mistakes, so as not to hurt your feelings, and then there are so many, and after all they don't give a damn. One nevertheless lets you know that it is irritating just the same. Occasionally, raising the eyebrows or saying "I beg your pardon?" in quick succession lead you to understand that you will "never be a part of it," that it "is not worth it," that there, at least, one is "not taken in."

— Julia Kristeva, *Strangers to Ourselves*

Table of Contents

Introduction: The Return of the Speaking Body — 9

1. Accented Speech Acts — 39
2. Audiovisual Counterpoint — 67
3. From the Buccal Tribunal to the Buccal Theater — 105
4. Onomatopoeic Translation — 127
5. The Little Girl, the Schizophrenic, and the Exophonic — 155

Conclusion: For the Love of Literature — 185

Works Cited — 205

Index — 213

Introduction: The Return of the Speaking Body

Abstract: In response to Roland Barthes's *The Death of the Author*, which downplays the author's intentions in interpretation, this book calls for the return of the body to the literary scene. It rethinks the literary voice as embodied by centering on the accent. The foreign accent, in particular, raises questions about how a body inhabits a language and how language claims a body. This chapter examines whether literature privileges the mother tongue as its origin of life and validity, or if the literary voice can embrace a foreign body, whose sounds may seem out of tune. Is style, after all, not a form of translation between voice and writing, between body and language?

Keywords: non-native accent; literary voice; language and body; performativity; foreignness

> The day has been full of ignominies and triumphs concealed from fear of laughter. I [Louis] am the best scholar in the school. But when darkness comes I put off this unenviable body—my large nose, my thin lips, my colonial accent—and inhabit place.
> — Virginia Woolf, *The Waves*

In the late 1970s, Roland Barthes found in himself a curious desire to talk again about the author (*The Preparation of the Novel* 207)—and *again*, in the sense of *anew*, considering the fact that his iconic 1967 essay "The Death of the Author" seemed to have put a stop to such an approach and interest.

In this essay, Barthes famously proclaims that it is impossible to know whose voice it is that one encounters in a literary work, "for the good reason that writing is the destruction of every voice, of every point of origin" ("The Death of the Author" 142). Writing is thus defined as a "neutral, composite,

---

Hui, Tingting. *Accented Speech in Literature, Art, and Theory: Melodramas of the Foreign Tongue*. Amsterdam: Amsterdam University Press, 2025.
DOI: 10.5117/9789048569007_INTR

oblique space" where voices become indiscernible, and where the author loses his identity and meets his death. However, Kate Briggs, the English translator of two volumes of Barthes's lecture notes, observes in her book *This Little Art* (2017) that in the later stage of his life, Barthes, surprisingly, experienced a "renewed interest in the author, in the life lived by the author, in his or her biographical circumstances" (50).

How come, all of a sudden, Barthes seemed ready to welcome the return of the author to the literary scene? Why this change of position?

"But this is precisely the point: I'm not immobile," Briggs paraphrases Barthes's explanation (51). Barthes attributed the inconsistency to the mobile nature of desire. But in fact, before Barthes openly acknowledged in the lecture series his revived passion for the writing body, this idea had been fermenting early on since the publication of *The Pleasure of the Text* (1973/1975).

In this book, Barthes makes the distinction between the text of pleasure (*plaisir*) and the text of bliss (*jouissance*), with the former being associated with the classical narrative in which the pleasure of reading comes from a finely cultured taste and the latter with the modern text in which the bliss of reading is uncodified and unutterable. Laying out a theory of textual pleasure redeemed through the reader, this book, at first glance, picks up where "The Death of the Author"—which ends emphatically with the claim that "the birth of the reader must be at the cost of the death of the Author" (148)—left off. But there is more to it than that. Kaja Silverman argues, in her book *The Acoustic Mirror* (1988), that Barthes actually revised his proposition about the authorial death in *The Pleasure of the Text*—a book that showcases that "Barthes desires not so much the author's dissolution as his recovery in a new guise" (190). Silverman argues that for Barthes the author is dead as an institution and a biographical person, but *not* as "a figure inside the text," which the reader needs so as to produce an erotics of reading.[1] Barthes still does not approve of the author being the anchor of the text's meaning; yet, he finds it relevant and even necessary to attend to the author as a body that writes and that makes a certain work possible. The writer is an initiating force of a text and is retrospectively made and

---

1   In *Pleasure of the Text*, Barthes states clearly that "[a]s institution, the author is dead: his civil status, his biographical person have disappeared; dispossessed, they no longer exercise over his work the formidable paternity whose account literary history, teaching, and public opinion had the responsibility of establishing and renewing; but in the text, in a way, I *desire* the author: I need his figure (which is neither his representation nor his projection), as he needs mine (except to "prattle")" (27).

remade through the text. The writer and the text are independent but also undeniably interrelated.

But what exactly does the revival of the authorial figure mean for Barthes? One of the implications is, as Silverman observes, the exhumation of the *voice*: "Whereas 'The Death of the Author' attempts to deoriginate writing by severing its connection to the voice, *The Pleasure of the Text* argues passionately on behalf of what it calls 'writing aloud,' or 'vocal writing'" (190). Therefore, the voice, according to Silverman, is what remains after the proclaimed death of the author. Once disembodied and severed from the text, the voice is retrieved by Barthes in *The Pleasure of the Text* to give voice to writing as a creative practice.

Barthes proposes the notions of "writing aloud" and "vocal writing" at the very end of *The Pleasure of the Text*. Being fully aware that these notions can be misleading because they seem to conflate writing with speech, Barthes makes it clear that they have nothing to do with speech. Writing aloud, to use Barthes's own words,

> is carried not by dramatic inflections, subtle stresses, sympathetic accents, but by the *grain* of the voice, which is an erotic mixture of timbre and language [...] its aim is not the clarity of messages, the theater of emotions; what it searches for (in a perspective of bliss) are the pulsional incidents, the language lined with flesh, a text where we can hear the grain of the throat, the patina of consonants, the voluptuousness of vowels, a whole carnal stereophony: the articulation of the body, of the tongue, not that of meaning, of language. (66–67)

Barthes envisions that writing aloud is a literary practice that benefits from the conjunction of voice and body. This idea resonates deeply with another seminal essay that Barthes published around the same period—that is, "The Grain of the Voice," which appeared originally in the journal *Musique enjeu* in 1972. In that essay, Barthes theorizes vocal music as "the very precise space (genre) of *the encounter between a language and a voice*" (181). He takes the example of a Russian bass and proposes that the thrill of listening to vocal music is to hear the "grain" of the voice, with the grain being "something which is directly the cantor's body, brought to your ears in one and the same movement from deep down in the cavities, the muscles, the membranes, the cartilages, and from deep down in the Slavonic language, as though a single skin lined the inner flesh of the performer and the music he sings" (181–82).

I would argue, thus, that the way in which Barthes argues about the "grain" of the voice in music and in literature is similar: it has to do with the material manifestation of the writing and singing body within the art form in question. In this regard, Barthes's revived passion for the author in *The Pleasure of the Text* and in his lecture series is not as unexpected as it seems. It attests to his rather consistent desire to enjoy various types of media (music, cinema, theater, literature) as *voicing bodies*—bodies that are placed at the service of art and become eroticized through the particular art form.

In terms of literature, it has been rarely noticed that Barthes, in fact, openly muses on the idea of approaching the text as a bodily form. In *The Pleasure of the Text*, Barthes asks, "Does the text have human form, is it a figure, an anagram of the body?" (17). There are several of them, according to Barthes: first, the scientific body—"the body of anatomists and physiologists, the one science sees or discusses: this is the text of grammarians, critics, commentators, philologists"; second, the erotic body—"a body of bliss consisting solely of erotic relations, utterly distinct from the first body" (16). These two types of textual bodies correspond to Barthes's distinction between the text of pleasure and the text of bliss: one is anatomical and analytic, whose exemplary form is the linguist's articulation of a sentence, which is, for Barthes, "immutably structured and yet infinitely renewable: something like chess" (51); the other is unique and unconscious, whose exceptional object of desire cannot be sought outside itself and has no other way of representation than to "bring together all the texts which *have given pleasure to someone* (wherever these texts come from) and display this textual body (*corpus*: the right word)" (34).

Barthes, at this point, begins to adopt a critical attitude toward the linguistic approach to language, which he used to endorse by modeling his argument of the authorial death on the emptiness of the "I" of an utterance.[2] By reintroducing the voice and body into his theorization of textual pleasure, Barthes suggests a more nuanced way of understanding literature in relation to its material (i.e., language): unlike the structuralist model of language, which renders the speaker irrelevant and insignificant, literature is seen as the invention of a singular voice that mobilizes and entices the body.[3] In *The Pleasure of the Text*, Barthes proposes to understand this process via the concept of "figuration," which he distinguishes from "representation." "Figuration is the way in which the erotic body appears (to whatever degree and in whatever form that may be) in the profile of the text," writes Barthes (55–56). He further clarifies that the figure, as an embodiment of desire,

---

2   See Benveniste and Lacan for further discussion of the split of the speaking subject.
3   For more information regarding the postulates of linguistics, please refer to the conclusion of this study.

INTRODUCTION: THE RETURN OF THE SPEAKING BODY

can appear in the text at three different levels: the author, a character in a novel, or the text itself. Figuration, to Barthes, implies a blissful encounter with any one of them in the form of a body.

* * *

Taking my cue from Barthes, I argue that literature releases, by accident and by design, a voice that is in search of *a* body, *any* body, *the* body. Such a body does not constitute a focal point where notions such as identity, subjectivity, and presence converge. Instead, providing the literary voice with flesh and bone, the body prompts the understanding of literature as an embodied voice, and as—to borrow the term from Barthes—the "figuration" of language. And literary studies today, I propose, need to solicit and attend to the return of the body to language in literature, so as to allow the literary voice to granulate, rustle, and caress.

But still, what body, and whose voice?

"One entered French literature only by losing one's accent" (45), claims Derrida in *Monolingualism of the Other; or, The Prosthesis of Origin* (1996/1998):

> I think I have not lost my accent; not everything in my "French Algerian" is lost. Its intonation is more apparent in certain "pragmatic" situations (anger or exclamation in familial or familiar surroundings, more often in private than in public, which is a quite reliable criterion for the experience of this strange and precarious distinction). But I would like to hope, I would very much prefer, that no publication permit my "French Algerian" to appear. In the meantime, and until the contrary is proven, I do not believe that anyone can detect *by reading*, if I do not myself declare it, that I am a "French Algerian." (45–46)

Derrida does not want to let his accent be heard and betray his origin, so he turns to writing, which he perceives as accent-free, as a tactic of camouflage. Symbols mediated, audience absent, writing takes the place of speaking not just to dismantle the logocentrism and the metaphysics of presence that Derrida criticizes in his book *Of Grammatology* (1967/1997) but also to conceal the traces of an origin and to craft an intellectual voice free of accent. It is interesting to put these two books of his side by side; the temptation of a deconstructive reading is in full swing. Here is the disparity between theory and life (to destruct undauntedly and to suffer privately), the discrepancy between language and body (*différance*: the variation of meaning unmarked in sound; *accent*: words stretched and distorted because of the speaking body), and the gap between speaking and writing (to write against the logocentric privilege of voice and to speak in favor of a writing persona): all these have boiled down to accent. Does accent—I will not go into details with this line of thought but am just thinking aloud—perhaps, hold the key to deconstructing deconstruction?

Although the French obsession with linguistic purism is quite a particular case, whose influence cannot be properly analyzed without zooming in on its specific national, historical, and institutional contexts, I still think that Derrida's observation of the incompatibility between literary voice and accent has wider repercussions in general. Of course, there are literary works that use accents and dialects to depict particular regions, characters, and social groups in a convincing and recognizable way; examples are *The Adventures of Huckleberry Finn* by Mark Twain and *A Dictionary of Maqiao* by Han Shaogong. Yet, what Derrida suggests here has nothing to do with accent as a narrative device. The incompatibility between literature and accent is *not* at the technical level. It points to the implicit and unchallenged theoretical assumption of upholding the ideal of the literary voice as pure, sublime, and without accent.

While the literary voice seems to be on guard against the accent, it is rather the speaking body that is its target. Whereas accent, with its distinctive melody and intonation, persistently draws one's attention to a vocalizing mouth that swallows, drops, and transforms syllables and sounds, such an image—raw, coarse, too bodily and too sensational—never fails to put literature face to face with a rather primitive and regressive force of consumption and absorption. Anxiety about the admission of such an image is generated by the tension between the supposed sublimity of expression and the primitiveness of consumption. So, when will literature be ready to assume a "flawed" body—mouth open, tongue loose, voice tampered with an odd and foreign accent?

To argue for the return of the body in literature, I propose to rethink the literary voice by means of the accent, insofar as it spotlights the compatibility and oddity between body and language. It is the foreign accent, in particular, that provokes one to understand the mother tongue in relation to what is foreign, while enabling the literary voice to come into terms with its dimension of otherness. It raises questions such as: how does a body inhabit a language and how does a language lay claim to a body? Does literature, nevertheless, favor the mother tongue as its origin of life and vitality? Is the literary voice capable of accommodating a foreign body whose mutterings and noises are not always intelligible, not always well tuned? What, after all, is style if it isn't a translation between words and flesh, voice and writing?

INTRODUCTION: THE RETURN OF THE SPEAKING BODY

I am drawn to Louis, one of the characters in Virginia Woolf's novel *The Waves* (1931), the perpetual outsider who both commits and erases himself from the scene of poetry. With his Australian accent, Louis speaks of love in a language of fear and foreignness. He feels the urge to submerge himself in the flow of everyday life—to love, to live, to be a businessman. At the same time, he dreams of dwelling upon the infinite and the permanent—to write, to contemplate, to impose order on life. He wishes to be embraced by love but instead veers away from it for fear of his accent. Louis, always caught between irreconcilable desires, always at odds with his language and existence, arises from the pages and comes across to me as an embodied figure of the accented voice. His voice allures me to read on. I read so that my gaze can give shape to a bodily form, which will house and nourish his voice with tenderness and patience. I see an unenviable body, indecisive and half-veiled, slip into the waking hours: first the tight-bitten lips, the pricked ears, a pale face that blushes too easily, then a rigid body frame, inside of which an accented and hesitant voice is trapped.

In my reading, Louis can be approached as the figure of the accent, which holds the key to my understanding of the literary voice as embodied. In fact, when the figure of the accent is understood along the lines of Barthes's idea of the "figuration" of authors and characters, it is not rare to find in literature. Vladimir Nabokov's *Pnin* (1957) tells the story of a Russian-born professor whose English sounds like the murder of that language. Richard Rodriguez's autobiography *Hunger of Memory* (1982/2005) recalls the shame of a child upon hearing his parents' heavily accented English in public. Eva Hoffman's language memoir *Lost in Translation: Life in a New Language* (1989) depicts the painful awareness of how her face and voice are transfigured and undone by an accent. Last but not least, the narrators of Yoko Tawada's essays and short stories—for example, in "Portrait of a Tongue" or "The Bath"—are often foreigners who speak the language imperfectly and lack the common sense of an insider. However, before delving into these intriguing scenes and characters, I wish to address the following questions: What is an accent after all? Why is it relevant to literature and everyday life? Whereas it is easier to approach the figure of the accent as the "figuration" of the author and characters, how to understand the figure that gives a bodily form to the text?

* * *

A strange phenomenon: being able to speak a language is not a prerequisite for a person to fake it and give the illusion that the gibberish he or she just performed is Spanish, Korean, or Hebrew. What conveys credibility, at least from an initial impression, is not the legible reproduction of words and meaning but the accurate perception and imitation of the rhythmic and melodic patterns of a certain language. In his article "The Music of Language and the Foreign Accent," Robert Somerville Graham observes that each language has its own patterned combinations "of melody, rhythm, and timbre that give a language its characteristic sound," and he calls this dimension of the sound composition "the music of language" (445). Unlike pure music, the music of language is rarely listened to for music's sake; it is the undulating wave that runs beneath the vessel of messages, thoughts, and emotions, carrying it along while remaining unheeded all the same.

Graham's understanding of accent is precisely built on this theory of the music of language. He writes,

> Although accent is not the music of language, it derives from it. There are two basic kinds of accents, one foreign, the other native. A foreign accent comes from speaking one language with the music of another, usually of one's mother tongue. A native accent stems from certain minor variations in sound and rhythm patterns that differ from accepted and standard speech. (446)

He observes that some people, despite their extraordinary and native-like fluency in a foreign language, speak it with a foreign accent—all because they fail to acquire the right music, and the failure often results from the interference of the music of one's mother tongue. Therefore, it is supposedly easier to imitate and master the music of a foreign language, if it closely resembles the sound composition of one's mother tongue (449). From this perspective, accent foregrounds the music of language, and a foreign accent, in particular, tests and reveals the degree of the musical compatibility among different languages.

A more conventional definition of accent is given in the *Oxford English Dictionary*, which reads, "a way of pronouncing a language that is distinctive to a country, area, social class, or individual." An accent is, above all, a manner of speaking and a style of pronunciation that works at grammatical, phonetic, and prosodic levels. It can concern the infelicitous dropping of a syllable, an uncommon choice of words, or the idiosyncratic execution of the intonation and melody of a sentence. It can also be a social marker, a geographical revelation and an unwitting confession of one's origin. Do we not sometimes arrive at certain opinions—after detecting someone's accent—about a person's education, social class, country of origin, and even sexuality (for instance, in the case of the so-called "gay lisp")? Accent can betray the speaker, giving more information than what the speaker provides or intends to provide. Often perceived as a linguistic *deviation*, an accent seems to offer a "convenient" pretext for stereotyping and discriminating against someone. In this regard, it makes audible the ruling norms, melodies, and discourses that have so far surrounded accent with an aura of brokenness and indecency.

Indisputably, the regional, social, and educational differences registered in accents are not exclusively discriminative. Across cultures, there have always been literary traditions and subcultures which creatively appropriate the differences in the sound and tone of various accents for composing poems or for creating private, sometimes secret, societies. Daniel Heller-Roazen's book *Dark Tongues: The Art of Rogues and Riddlers* (2013), for instance, offers a fascinating account of rogue and riddling poets' masterful use and creation of slangs, obscure languages, and criminal jargons throughout European history. Another example is nüshu (女书), a secret syllabic script that, since the Song dynasty, has been used exclusively by women living in Jiangyong County in China and passed down from mother to daughter through songs and embroidered texts (Zhao 127; McLaren 382). These cases often lead to discussions about how accents create communities and when a "dialect" becomes a language. These are very interesting and important topics, and yet they fall outside the purview of this book. My approach to accent is very much grounded in the context of speech standardization in the emergence and popularity of nation-states.

Lynda Mugglestone, in *Talking Proper: The Rise of Accent as Social Symbol* (1995), has investigated the particular British obsession with accents within the context of the historical and ideological process of language standardization. In the late eighteenth and nineteenth centuries, observes Mugglestone, there emerged a normative and prescriptive zeal toward codifying a set of non-localized speech features, which ranges "from the [h] which it would be 'social suicide' to drop to the [iŋ] which 'polite speakers' all over the country might assimilate, alongside the vocalization of [r] in words such as *bird,* and the use of /ʌ/ rather than /ʊ/ in words such as *butter*" (264). The issue of "good" speech became a great preoccupation of phoneticians, writers, educators, while pronouncing dictionaries, handbooks on linguistic etiquette, and works on elocution were written to "level up" speech varieties and to infuse certain beliefs and attitudes in speakers' phonetic consciousness. "Propriety" and "impropriety," "elegancy" and "vulgarity" gradually and respectively evolved into distinctive implications pertaining to spoken Standard English and its variations.

While Mugglestone reviews the social movements and discursive constructions that have made the Standard English appear superior to its geographically variant forms, Friedrich Kittler notices a similar national obsession with speech standardization in Germany at the same period. His analysis of this trend in *Discourse Networks 1800/1900* (1985/1990), however, focuses on the myth of the mother tongue, which predicates the national ideology on a literal and fetishized constellation of language and the mother's body. Kittler argues that during the eighteenth century many primers were published to teach the mother to become a qualified instructor on pronunciation, while schools and institutions began to lay emphasis on the mother's mouth as an effective channel to "purify" sounds. This has created the *myth* of the mother tongue, which ceases to be a mere metaphor but a "natural" condition of attachment between the speaker and the maternal language. As a consequence, people who write in foreign languages and grow attached to languages other than their mother tongues can perceive themselves or be perceived as committing an act of betrayal.[4]

Another term, which equally draws scholarly and critical attention for undoing the mystique, is the native speaker. Sociolinguistic and educational scholars have pointed out that the native speaker, which has long been privileged as the most reliable source of language data, the frame of reference for correct language use, and the model for curriculum design and test, has shaped the field in terms of its scope, methods, and research objects (Paikeday; Ferguson; Braine). Applied linguist Alan Davies, in his book *The Native Speaker: Myth and Reality* (2003), lucidly unravels the central ambiguity related to the idea of the native speaker—that is, the uncritical and essentialized conflation of a person of flesh and blood and the idealization of certain attributes. In other words, the mystique of the native speaker lies in the fact that it is often used interchangeably yet unreflectively with the *ideal* native speaker. Although almost all the attempts at defining the native speaker—by language competence, birthright membership, insider knowledge, an unbroken oral tradition, etc.—end up being unsatisfying, Davies does not agree with Charles Ferguson's proposal to have this term "quietly dropped from the linguist's set of professional myths about language" (Ferguson vii). Neither does he sympathize with Thomas Paikeday's proposal, which Davies summarizes as a proposal to separate "the ideal and the operative meanings of native speaker, making proficiency the criterion for employment, and personal history the criterion for ideal membership"

---

4   *Lives in Translation: Bilingual Writers on Identity and Creativity*, edited by Isabelle de Courtivron, gives many examples of such a reading.

(Davies 6). Looking into the complexity and ambiguity of the native speaker concept in his book, Davies aims at a critical approach to this concept. On the one hand, he acknowledges the language and communication skills of the native speaker; on the other hand, he emphasizes that such attributes are not exclusively owned by the native speaker but attainable as well to the non-native speaker.

Terms such as native speaker and mother tongue can function in a way that weaves folkloric beliefs and linguistic knowledge into a discursive network, which encodes foreign accent as a barrier, leading to a situation in which the non-native speaker is excluded in advance from the linguascape domesticated by the native speaker. As far as language ideologies and discursive dynamics are considered, we are no longer dealing with accent in a purely linguistic sense. We are hurled into the everyday scene where accent is loosely referred to as any verbal and/or visual features that fail to conform to the ruling norms or to satisfy implicit expectations. "Every person has an accent," legal scholar Mari J. Matsuda states in her article about accent and antidiscrimination laws. "Yet, in ordinary usage, we say a person 'has an accent' to mark difference from some unstated norm of non-accent, as though only some foreign few have accents" (1330). In this sense, having an accent means being *unlike* someone else, someone "normal," familiar, and mainstream. Accent thus becomes associated with an "illegitimate" and even "pathological" form of speech that results from a speaker's "incomplete" acquisition of a certain language. As if it were a linguistic technique of chiaroscuro, we are ready to seize on it in the most ordinary and banal scene of encounter to sketch a portrait of the speaker that would fit into our biases and to create a contrast effect between insider and outsider. In fact, we do not even have to *hear* the accent in real. Visual traits alone are proven to be enough to conclude that the speaker has an accent. The following episode might give a glimpse of what I call visualized or imagined accent:

> A young woman of Asian Indian family, but a native and monolingual speaker of English, related a story in which a middle-aged man in a music store is unable to help her when she asks for a recently released Depeche Mode tape (Kapoor 1993). "You'll have to speak slower because I didn't understand you because of your accent," he tells her. She is understandably hurt and outraged: "I have no discernible accent. I do, however, have long dark hair and pleasantly colored brown skin. I suppose this outward appearance of mine constitutes enough evidence to conclude I had, indeed, just jumped off the boat and into the store." (Lippi-Green 226)

The perception of accent is no doubt ideologically saturated. However, in the scenario above, we are no longer in the realm of concealment and revelation where accent makes public the social status and the educational background of the speaker. Our understanding of the accent is shifted to the biased ears of the listener, who unwittingly translates visual foreignness into verbal incomprehensibility.

Recently postcolonial studies have witnessed a renewed interest in the relation among language, race, and ethnicity. Cultural critic Rey Chow, for instance, in her book *Not Like a Native Speaker* (2014), observes that "although much has been written in the field of Francophone studies on the connections between colonization and language [...] a comparable set of critical reflections on *languaging* as a visceral and emotional as well as intellectual limit experience is, to my knowledge, relatively lacking—and long overdue—in Anglophone postcolonial studies" (14). Taking a cue from Chow's observation, I contend that, on the one hand, accent enables us to reconceptualize race and ethnicity as an *audiovisual* spectacle, a concept that I shall develop in Chapter 2; on the other hand, the perception of one's race and ethnicity might influence our judgments toward one's accent.

In the contemporary globalized world, while the accent of the native speaker is tolerated or even promoted to reflect linguistic diversity, it is usually the accent associated with a foreign body that triggers concern and hostility.[5] Kenn Nakata Steffensen remarks that the foreign accent is made into a problem because it signifies and reinforces the outsider position of the speaker, who seems unable to master the linguistic nuances and cultural implications of a certain language (514). However, this account of the general outsider position fails to explain why certain foreign accents are perceived to be less favorable than others. Carina Bauman, for example, after conducting experiments on American listeners' attitudes towards various foreign English accents, concludes that Asian-accented English was rated significantly lower in terms of attractiveness, status, and dynamism, compared with mainstream US English and Brazilian Portuguese-accented English (15). As linguist Rosina Lippi-Green observes in her book *English with an Accent: Language, Ideology, and Discrimination in the United States* (1997),

---

5   A good exmaple is the changing attitudes toward native and non-native accented English on the BBC. When the BBC was first set up, announcers were required to equally elevate "standards of decorum and tone throughout the nation." Later the exemplary role of the BBC in promoting Standard English was gradually weakened; it attempted to broaden the varieties of native-accented English heard over the radio. However, the way the BBC presents foreign-accented English still tends to reinforce a hierarchy between Britain and other nations. See Mugglestone 324; Steffensen 511.

INTRODUCTION: THE RETURN OF THE SPEAKING BODY 21

"It is crucial to remember that it is not *all* foreign accents, but only accent linked to skin that isn't white, or which signals a third-world homeland, that evokes such negative reactions" (238). Compared with other indicators of foreignness (skin tone, religion, dietary habit, etc.), accent, which reminds one of a homeland and a mother tongue other than one's own, seems to be a more acceptable incitement to xenophobia.

To understand the dynamic interaction of foreignness and accent, the first two chapters will explore the cultural and political implications of a set of core terms such as "mother tongue," "native speaker," and "hate speech" while developing new terms and concepts—for instance, "accented speech acts," "the audiovisual counterpoint of face and speech"—that may contribute to the analysis and critique of individual and institutional practices that fall back on accent to perform racial and ethnic stigmatization and to "justify" social exclusion. Such practices range from the daily situations of name-calling and bullying[6] to the shibboleth incidences in history. Accent, in these cases, is not only the crux of the matter but also a springboard for theorizing pressing social and cultural issues—issues that speak to the current trend of globalization, migration, and multilingualism.

*　*　*

Whereas it is my intention to develop the accent from a linguistic and social phenomenon to a critical concept for cultural analysis and critique, my primary fascination with accent is rather of a theoretical and philosophical kind. The accent, as a *melodrama* of the tongue, highlights the bodily dimension of speech, and the pain and pleasure involved in the act of speaking. It is the relation between language and body that this study attempts to elucidate: Why and how is accented speech as such capable of acting on and against the speaking body, making it the object of desire and the accomplice of hostility? Being at once an alluring and undesirable linguistic performance of a speaking body, the accent showcases how the body demarcates the possibility of a language, and how, at the same time, a language may impinge on the bodily domain, transforming it into a concentrated articulation of seduction and animosity.

My use of the term "melodrama"—which also appears in the title of this study—may be confusing, as the term, in common usage, refers to

---

6   An accented speaker can be the target of bullying and mistreatment. "Ching chong chinaman" is one example of the name-calling that aims for the ridicule of a Chinese person through the pejorative imitation of his or her speech and accent. See Frumkin 317–31; Kristiansen 129–45.

a subgenre of drama that involves high sentimentalism and exaggerated characterization (Bentley 195). However, recent scholarship tends to trade melodrama for the *melodramatic*, expanding the scope of the term from a dramatic genre to a mode of expression (Brooks; Elsaesser; Straub; van Alphen). Peter Brooks suggests, in his book *The Melodramatic Imagination: Balzac, Henry James, Melodrama, and the Mode of Excess* (1976), that melodrama can be approached as a literary form of expression. Brooks explains that although *melos*—derived from Greek, which means "song, tune, melody"—is not directly applicable to literature, it is manifested in a different way in literary works. In his own words:

> The emotional drama needs the desemanticized language of music, its evocation of the "ineffable," its tones and registers. Style, thematic structuring, modulations of tone and rhythm and voice—musical patterning in a metaphorical sense—are called upon to invest plot with some of the inexorability and necessity that in pre-modern literature derived from the substratum of myth. (10)

The *melos* of literature, for Brooks, is related to the stylistic articulation that can be better grasped in terms of rhythm, voice, and tone—"the desemantized language of music," or, better still, the immanent music of language. While upholding a relatively broad conceptualization of the melodrama as a mode of literary expression that includes thematic and stylistic features, Brooks nonetheless confines his analysis to the "melodramatic emplotments" in literature (van Alphen, "Legible Affects" 26). It is Thomas Elsaesser and Ernst van Alphen who advance the applicability of the melodrama to cinema and visual arts, respectively. Elsaesser's discussion on the Hollywood family melodrama pioneers the research on the filmic melodrama as a distinguishable genre with consistent themes, techniques, and styles. Van Alphen, taking his cue from Elsaesser, close reads Andrew Wyeth's painting *Christina's World* by focusing on the dramatic mise-en-scène: instead of the implied, ambiguous narrative of the painting, his analysis centers on the melodramatic visual constellation, which embeds emotional resonances in visual and formal articulations.

My use of the term melodrama is derived from Elsaesser and van Alphen's conceptualization. The accent can be understood as the enactment of a melodramatic mise-en-scène of the speaking body in scenarios ranging from literature and performance to everyday life: the *drama* of speaking involves the peculiar orchestration of bodily parts (tongue, mouth, face), while the *melos* refers to the accented and varying patterns of speech that manifest the dramatic displacement of the speaking body in a new language and culture.

"This should have been my first clue that what I really wanted from André was language," writes Alice Kaplan in her language memoir *French Lessons: A Memoir* (1993):

> I can still hear the sound he made when he read my love letter: "T,t,t," with that little ticking sound French people make by putting the tips of their tongues on the roof of their mouths—a fussy, condescending sound, by way of saying, "that's not how one says it." What I wanted more than anything, more than André even, was to make those sounds, which were the true sounds of being French, and so even as he was insulting me and discounting my passion with a vocabulary lesson, I was listening and studying and recording his response. (86)

Love me, love my accent. However, what Kaplan alludes to is the opposite: I love you because of your accent.[7] The seduction of the body is the seduction of language. We are thus dealing with the entrapment and displacement of the body in the desire for a foreign language and the reconfiguration of a language into the physiognomy of speaking. The intersection between language and body—this is where the literary figure of the accent arises, enchanting literature with its sincere humor and overdone eagerness. After all, isn't literature a wholehearted flirtation between language and body? Doesn't the accent, as a corporeal style, entice the literary voice to granulate, to splutter, and to enjoy? Doesn't it give rise to an exploratory and transformative stage in which language and body probe the limits of reciprocity?

In her book *The Scandal of the Speaking Body* (1983/2003), literary critic and theorist Shoshana Felman notices that Molière's Don Juan has staged the convergence of the linguistic, the erotic, and the literary with the scandalous act of promise. Felman writes,

> The desire of a Don Juan is thus at once desire for desire and desire for language; a desire that desires *itself* and that desires its own language. Speech is the true realm of eroticism, and not simply a means of access

---

[7] It reminds me of a popular joke in China. One day a foreigner shouts over the phone on the street, "No, you never loved me! You were together with me only to practice your English!" Whereas this joke clearly puts language and desire at opposite poles, the relation of language, desire and sexuality is rather nuanced and complicated. See Cameron and Kulick.

to this realm. To seduce is to produce language that enjoys, language that takes pleasure in having "no more to say." To seduce is thus to prolong, with desiring speech, the pleasure-taking performance of the very production of that speech. (15)

In her book, Felman interprets the Don Juan myth of seduction based on Austin's theory of the performative utterance. On the one hand, for Don Juan, the art of seduction relies on a concentrated articulation of physical desire in speech. His language aims to deliver a feast of enjoyment that leads its prey to fantasize and react accordingly. To seduce, therefore, is to transform speech into a performance of sincerity and pleasure, with its force being transferred and enacted on the desiring body through activating a knowable but non-immediate future. On the other hand, if Don Juan's promise of marriage is ever erotic in nature, it is because its fulfillment is indefinitely postponed so as to prolong the pleasure of speaking and the fantasy of marriage. Hence the paradox of Don Juan's promise: it is performative insofar as it fails to sustain itself in reality.

Felman argues, however, that it is not Don Juan who abuses the faculty of promise but that the act of promise as such is scandalous—since no one can know and master the future beforehand. "[E]very promise is above all *the promise of consciousness*," says Felman, "insofar as it postulates a noninterruption, continuity between intention and act" (34). As a human, fallible, shunned from the unconscious, how can one promise anything but a particular state of mind at a particular moment? The scandalous nature of Don Juan's promise, as Felman observes, lies in the fact that consciousness and intentionality alone cannot exhaust the potentiality of the body and therefore fails to vouch for the consistency between speech and action, words and reality. The scandal of the promise is rather the scandal of the speaking body. Insofar as one is not fully aware and in control of one's desire and action, language and body are incongruously and indissolubly related to one another, each being at once the instrument and the blind spot of the other.

In the afterword of this book, Judith Butler encapsulates the significance of Felman's contribution as follows:

> Derrida recasts the speech act as a function of writing, not speech. Arguing against the presumption in Austin that subjective presence offers the spoken word a legitimate effect, he shows that the spoken word, to have performative force, must be subject to a logic of iterability that belongs to the transposability of the written word. Felman returns deconstructive

reading to the question of voice and of speaking, not to defend a "sovereign" subject as its guarantor, but to remind us that speaking is, in part, a *bodily* act. As bodily, the speech act loses its claim to sovereignty in a different way than it does when recast as writing. The speech act "says" more than it can ever intend or know. (114)

Here Butler situates Felman's book in the context of the heated debate over convention, meaning, and literary speech acts. In *How to Do Things with Words* (1962), Austin, after making the distinction between performative utterances and descriptive statements, proposes that the appropriateness in terms of the circumstances, procedures, and persons that are involved is essential "for the smooth or 'happy' functioning of a performative" (14). This implies that, for Austin, a major part of the performative force depends on the sovereign and accurate execution of established and formalized conventions. If the act of speaking amounts to doing anything at all, this effect, to a large degree, is due to authoritative repetition and felicitous recognition. Derrida, however, as Butler points out, argues that iteration or iterability is the condition of writing and speaking, which diminishes sovereignty insofar as it entails the breach from an original speaker and a fixed context. While Felman's understanding of the speech act is no less tuned into the fragility of the context and the speaker, she diverges from Derrida's arguments over citation and repetition, shifting the focus to the bodily and unconscious domain of speech.

An unkept promise, a slip of the tongue, or an overambitious resolution: everyday life is full of scenarios where words fail to foresee the oddity of the body. "What the myth of the speaking body, in other words, *performs*, is the very subversion of consciousness," suggests Felman (34). Indeed, no one knows better than an accented speaker about the bodily revolt against consciousness. Hoffman notes in her autobiography *Lost in Translation*,

> There is, of course, the constraint and the self-consciousness of an accent that I hear but cannot control. Some of my high school peers accuse me of putting it on in order to appear more "interesting." In fact, I'd do anything to get rid of it, and when I'm alone, I practice sounds for which my speech organs have no intuition, such as "th" (I do this by putting my tongue between my teeth) and "a," which is longer and more open in Polish (by shaping my mouth into a sort of arrested grin). (122)

It is an odd thing to speak with an accent. Often you think you know by heart the essential rules for producing the desired sounds—for example, the composition of the speech organs, the melodic procession of the syllables, or the tonal variation of different characters—then you open your mouth and the sounds go completely off track. What you meant to say might still be comprehensible, only the words sound like acts of defiance against your will and authority. However, while Felman restages the untenability of sovereignty by shedding light on the unconscious body (and accent, in a way, epitomizes how this unconscious body might sound), my fascination with accent lies in the fact that it allows me to rethink the relation between language and body from a perspective that is rather *literally bodily*. I am most enchanted by accent insofar as it acts out the drama of speaking in literary and everyday scenes—for instance, in terms of the physical orchestration of speech organs, the intrusion of the voice at the expense of meaning, and the different perceptions regarding how native and non-native accents become attached to the speaking body.

Elsa Triolet, as a native speaker of Russian who is also fluent in German and French, expresses antithetical attitudes toward her French accent and Russian accent. "It is in French, that I had, and still have, an accent," Triolet writes proudly. "People have offered to help me get rid of it, but I always refused: an accent is like a hump, and only death can take it away" (Triolet, qtd. in Beaujour 72). Despite being an "abnormality," Triolet's French accent does not bother her to the point of wanting to change it. Elizabeth Klosty Beaujour observes, in *Alien Tongues: Bilingual Russian Writers of the "First" Emigration* (1989), that it is because Triolet regards her French accent "as a hostage, a sacrifice to Russian, a constant proof that she had not really betrayed her first linguistic loyalty" that she prefers to keep it (72). In contrast, when it comes to her Russian accent, Triolet shows unusual frustration about not being able to "keep it [Russian] intact, as pure as when it was born in [her], without its being disturbed by any foreign accent" (71). As a native speaker of Russian, Triolet considers the accent a threat to her "natural" bond with the mother tongue. "My Russian accent embarrasses me," says Triolet, "like ugly teeth which keep one from smiling [...] an accent seems to me to be ugly. I don't want to inflict ugliness on others" (72).

Whereas in both narratives, Triolet compares accents to parts of her body, the similes suggest distinct ways in which accents are perceived to interact with the non-native and the native bodies. Like a hump, an accent clings to the non-native body in an obviously unnatural manner, yet it is an "abnormity" that the body cannot or does not need to get rid of. In contrast, for the native body, speaking with an accent is like revealing a mouth full of rotten teeth, which one should hide from others. Beneath the subtle distinction between these similes lies the myth of an organic and irreplaceable bodily intimacy with one's mother tongue. "My mother tongue, my irreplaceable language," Triolet claims, "You would think that no one would take a language away from you, that you carry it with you wherever you go, that it is alive with you—unforgettable, incurable, divine" (71). Here the fantasy of the mother tongue being one's ultimate belonging produces and discharges a non-native body, whose delimited intimacy with that language is and should be safeguarded by the presence of accent.

* * *

The undertaking of this study, therefore, is not a linguistic one. To start with, I consider an accent a distinct way of speaking that calls attention to how a speaker inhabits a language. This entails the uprooting of the notion of accent from its "native" soil of linguistic studies—not because the original setting is unfruitful, but because I like to think it would bear other strangely delicate fruits when grafted to other fields of study. Since speaking is a sensual way of being, whose scope and intensity exceeds the rationality of phonological assessment and linguistic analysis, there should be room for an equally *sensual way of knowing* when it comes to the physical event of speaking (with an accent). I wish to solicit the return of the speaking body to the scene of language—not as an instrument for making meaningful sounds, not even as a bearer of the unconscious mind, but as a cultural and political canvas where the face, the ears, the tongue, and the mouth are configured and reconfigured from time to time.

What makes the accent clash with the intention of the speaker is not only the unconscious but also, as banal as it seems, the speaker's muscles. While the mother tongue requires one to fall into a habitual composition of the speech organs, a foreign language unsettles the muscle memories and, through accent, conveys the incomparability of different languages and the gaps between language and body. Phonologist Francis Nolan, in the article "Degrees of Freedom in Speech Production: An Argument for Native Speakers in LADO," brings attention to this bodily aspect of speaking, arguing that "speech is produced at the interface between a discretised, abstract communicative system and a flesh and blood, gradient anatomical machine driven by neuro-motor commands" (266–67). The implication is that the biblical myth of words becoming flesh is, to some degree, literally what happens when one tries to acquire a language. A second-language learner, as Nolan explains, might comprehend and pronounce the individual vowels and consonants accurately but still sound unlike the native speaker, because the phonological traits of the mother tongue have tuned particular muscles into optimally coordinated structures, which will limit the potential articulatory combinations of vocal organs. Nolan writes,

> So, for instance—paraphrasing Honikman—for English the tongue need to be 'anchored' literally on the roof of the mouth allowing the tip and blade, tapered in shape, to swing up and down to make alveolars, whereas for French the tip is anchored behind the lower teeth and the blade and front of the tongue rise for most coronal sounds. (270)

To speak a foreign language is thus to accommodate an alien body. The strange transference from the craving for a certain language to the longing for a person who speaks that language, perhaps, is not as absurd as it seems to be. The protagonist of Chang-Rae Lee's novel *Native Speaker* (1995), who is Korean American, describes his passion for Lelia, a speech therapist who later becomes his wife, as follows: "But even before I took measure of her face and her manner, the shape of her body, her indefinite scent, all of which occurred so instantly anyway, I noticed how closely I was listening to her. What I found was this: that she could really speak" (10). And Kaplan in *French Lessons: A Memoir*: "What I wanted more than anything, more than André even, was to make those sounds, which were the true sounds of being French" (86). Last but not least, Hoffman in *Lost in Translation*: "Should you marry him? the question comes in English. Yes. Should you marry him? the question echoes in Polish. No" (199).

If the erotic and the linguistic converge here, and converge in a certain language, it is due less to, as Felman suggests, "[the] scandalous fact that the erotic is always linguistic" (78), as to the much more unheeded fact that the linguistic is always bodily. While Felman's understanding of the relation between language and body carries a distinct psychoanalytical undertone, this study aims at a *literal* reading of language as bodily, whose meaning and force are modified, distorted, or enhanced by the way in which a certain body speaks and shows it. The main sets of questions that I attempt to address—different from Felman's interest in the body as a linguistically performative vessel for erotic desire—are: In what way does the dynamic entanglement of body and speech play out in everyday and literary scenes? Why and how is accented speech able to trespass the linguistic domain, sustaining and threatening the speaking body simultaneously? When the literary voice is tinted with the (muscle) memory of the speaking body, can we speak of literary creativity in relation to or despite the primitive, almost obscene, opening of the mouth?

Ah, the mouth—Felman names it "the speech organ *par excellence*, even the organ of seduction" (37); Kleinian psychoanalyst Donald Meltzer calls it "the theatre of phantasy and play, a mid-point between external play and internal thought" (179). The myth of the mouth, other than being the locus of eroticism and phantasy, is that it houses a *rebel*—the tongue. It is reported that in Korea some clinics carry out lingual frenectomy, claiming that it is a miraculous cure for Korean children who cannot "speak English properly" (Parry). Indeed, the incongruity between body and speech may be registered at a more superficial and bodily level than the unconscious. The tongue exemplifies the vulnerability of our body, which is always already a battlefield of vying discourses, fantasies, and ideologies.

Readers who are familiar with Judith Butler at this point may be reminded of their brilliant essay "On Linguistic Vulnerability," an introduction to their book *Excitable Speech: A Politics of the Performative* (1997). This study is indeed inspired by Butler's claim of the human's linguistic vulnerability and survivability to language. "Could language injure us if we were not, in some sense, linguistic beings, beings who require language in order to be?" (1–2), I remember Butler asking at the beginning of that essay. It had a strange appeal to think of existential vulnerability and to link it to the heroic act of us surviving the wound of interpellation and name-calling. Yet another question, related but not quite the same, occurred to me: Am I invariably vulnerable in different languages? Speaking in Mandarin, which is my mother tongue, I find my words rarely strike people (except for foreigners) as weighty and authoritative. Why bother to be taken seriously, if you are a young woman with a sing-song voice? When I switch to English, however, it is less my gendered body, but the accent, that stands in the way of my claim to the intended social significance of my words. People say that I do not have a typical Chinese English accent—the kind of accent that adds tones to words, but I know as well that I still have difficulty distinguishing between "seen" and "sing," "feel" and "fail," "would" and "wound." I make my accent less audible by replacing the unpronounceable words. I try to avoid saying "I *feel* nervous," but instead "I *am* nervous." (Because I lack the word, the come-and-go state has the risk of becoming my identity.)

Indeed, as *linguistic beings*, we are vulnerable to language *per se*. However, as *speaking bodies*, our vulnerability may be expressed and experienced dissimilarly in different languages, and our survivability may lie in the sensitivity to the various situations in which we find ourselves. In Butler's essay, they speak of "resignification as a strategy of opposition" (38) when it comes to offensive name-calling and injurious speech. "The political possibility of reworking the force of the speech act against the force of injury consists in misappropriating the force of speech from those prior contexts" (40), says Butler. However, what if we are dealing with verbal wounds done to the speaker instead of the addressee? As I will discuss at length in Chapter 1, accented speech can become a source of vulnerability, which makes the speaker susceptible to discrimination and hostility. How to *talk back* when it is speech itself that is out of control? Since the very language will inevitably remain "accented," every act of speaking can be potentially wounding to the speaker.

This makes me think that *tactics*, rather than *strategies*, might be a much more appropriate term for discussing the survivability of the accented speaker. Michel de Certeau draws the distinction between the two in the introduction to his work *The Practice of Everyday Life* (1984). While a strategy implies "a subject of will and power" who can isolate and assume a proper place to develop an overarching and subversive scheme, a tactic, according to de Certeau, belongs to the weak and the ordinary, those who cannot but live within a physical and discursive force field initiated and controlled by others:

> The weak must continually turn to their own ends forces alien to them. This is achieved in the propitious moments when they are able to combine heterogeneous elements (thus, in the supermarket, the housewife confronts heterogeneous and mobile data—what she has in the refrigerator, the tastes, appetites, and moods of her guests, the best buys and their possible combinations with what she already has on hand at home, etc.); the intellectual synthesis of these given elements takes the form, however, not of a discourse, but of the decision itself, the act and manner in which the opportunity is "seized." (xix)

Comparable to a housewife's impromptu wisdom in the supermarket, tactics do not adhere to one single consistent principle but rather depend on one's sensitivity to the situation and the flexibility to adjust the plan accordingly. For the weak and the ordinary, there is no secluded and solid base from which to launch a large-scale revolt that would crush their enemies and competitors. Because it seems unlikely and even undesirable to destroy the enemies in one go, the weak and the ordinary have to improvise from time to time, seizing upon opportunities before they pass by.

Now, you may wonder, what are the tactics available to the accented speaker? Here I will attempt a few suggestions in a half-serious manner and without giving consideration to their political and social efficacy—since the aptness of a tactic can only be assessed in combination with the particular situation and context. The most thorough act of rebellion against language, as far as I can imagine, is what Julia Kristeva calls in *Strangers to Ourselves* (1991) "the silence of polyglots" (15). She playfully advises that "the foreigner can, instead of saying, attempt doing—house-cleaning, playing tennis, soccer, sailing, sewing, horseback riding, jogging, getting pregnant, what have you" (16). Although it sounds like a how-to book on becoming a practical person or a man of deeds, the lesson, if there is any, is about forging a different relation to silence. Yet, how difficult it is to reconcile with uncomfortable silence, even when we are with loved ones! What we can do is perhaps to be silent when silence occurs, making it pregnant with possibilities, letting it condense the air into vague echoes of the unsaid and the ineffable, adding to it layers of "impervious fullness: cold diamond, secret treasury, carefully protected, out of reach" (Kristeva 16).

Another tactic is to *camouflage* one's foreignness by, for example, adopting a different name. "I cast aside my long and unpronounceable name in favor of a short ordinary All-American nickname" (161), says Isabelle de Courtivron in her essay "Memoirs of a Bilingual Daughter." Jacques Derrida, when he started to publish, changed his name from Jackie to Jacques, "choosing something which was 'very French, Christian, simple'" (Still 153).[8] Indeed, no one wants to end up being referred to as the-foreigner-who-has-a-challenging-name. Nor does one wish to be associated with a name that prevents him or her from being taken seriously. Whereas de Courtivron and Derrida readily give up their names, there are some other cases where the person becomes "renamed" in an onomatopoeic fashion because the foreign name seems incompatible with the local tongue. The German poet Heinrich Heine was all too familiar with this:

> Here in France my German name, "Heinrich," was translated into "Henri" just after my arrival in Paris. I had to resign myself to it and finally name myself thus in this country, for the word "Heinrich" did not appeal to the French ear and the French make everything in the world nice and easy for themselves. They were also incapable of pronouncing the name "Henri Heine" correctly, and for most people my name is Mr. Enri Enn; many

---

8   Other than Jackie, Derrida's Hebrew name Elie (Elijah) is relatively unknown. Judith Still has an interesting analysis of Derrida's hidden names in relation to his work *Monolingualism of the Other*. Still observes, "Plain Jacques, the public and professional *nom de plume*, can be seen as just too eager to please and follow the rules. Jacques is so polite that the name is a little like a veil over his true (truly dangerous) identity—and veils of course connote difference to 'us', but in a way that can displease the metropolitan, both conservative and revolutionary, particularly in an educational context" (157).

abbreviate this to "Enrienne," and some called me Mr. Un Rien. (qtd. in Heller-Roazen, *Echolalias* 35)

I myself, having now lived in the Netherlands for twelve years, have started to respond to any sounds that would remotely resemble my name. I am proud to have managed to recognize it when in the waiting room the general practitioner, hesitantly, looked for "mevrouw Hui," pronounced in a manner comparable to the Dutch word *huis*. Ach, the foreigner, it is through witnessing other people struggle with your name that you are confronted with your untranslatability. This situation, which I consider to be "the onomatopoeic translation of names," will be discussed in detail in Chapter 4.

To come back to the subject, another example of camouflage is to pass as a *hyper-foreignized* foreigner—thus not to blend in—and to pretend speaking an "exotic" language that most people do not understand. This is what the artist Hetain Patel did in his stage performance *Who am I? Think Again* (2013). I will analyze this piece of work at length in Chapter 2. Here, for the purpose of reframing it in relation to tactics, I wish to provide a brief introduction to this work. This performance begins with the familiar scene of translation. We hear Patel speak Mandarin and see him squat on the chair in his kurta pajama. All these elements—his appearance, clothes, language, and posture—appear quite foreign and original to a Western audience, raising, as a consequence, the expectation of translation. Another performer, Yuyu Rau, who claims to be Patel's translator, plays along with this expectation, fittingly performing the translation in English at intervals. We are convinced that the translation is done for our benefit until the moment when Rau reveals that the artist himself is a native speaker of English:

> I [Patel] was born and raised near Manchester, in England, but I'm not going to say it in English to you, because I'm trying to avoid any assumptions that might be made from my northern accent. The only problem with masking it with Chinese Mandarin is I can only speak this paragraph, which I have learned by heart when I was visiting in China. So all I can do is keep repeating it in different tones and hope you won't notice.

Through manipulating visual and verbal elements, Patel's provocative attempt of camouflage aims at becoming a "drag foreigner," whose exaggerated manners question exoticism precisely by appearing to cater to such expectations. I will elaborate, in Chapter 2, on the way that Patel reconfigures the face-and-speech combination to loosen the often too tight imagination surrounding race, ethnicity, and gender. At this point, however,

I want to emphasize that such a goal cannot be achieved without the aid of translation. It is because the practice of translation is not motivated in a linguistic sense that it serves to shed light on the violence of the everyday practice of translating from someone's appearance and accent into his or her linguistic origin and ethnic background. Patel impersonates a Mandarin speaker so as to avoid being "literally" translated according to his northern English accent. Especially because his Indian guise seems incompatible with his native English accent, his ethnicity seems to stand in the way of claiming a righteous "ownership" of his speech. Patel has to find someone to translate for him, because his language, which clashes with his look, is not able to ascend to the status of the original.

The theoretical significance of works that reflect on speech patterns and habits—such as the one mentioned above, the *Aural Contract* trilogy (2012–14) by Lawrence Abu Hamdan, or "Say: 'Parsley'" (2001) and *Meddle English* (2011) by Caroline Bergvall, just to name a few—is that they suggest an alternative way of framing the issue other than through the politics of language and speech. In all the aforementioned works, the emphasis is not on speaking intelligibly and eloquently, adopting a mainstream accent that may pass easily, but on calling for the audience to listen differently and to tune their ears into the passions, desires, and longings registered in one's speech. I agree with these artists that the politics and ethics of listening require further critical attention and intervention. In the chapters to come, I will read Butler's understanding of speech acts and performativity together with some of these artworks, in the hope that it will shed new light on the speech act as a listening practice, whose felicity depends just as much on the listening modes in use as on particular circumstances and conventions.

* * *

Speaking of tactics and strategies, in this study, I employ a tactic of writing that involves traveling back and forth between theory and literary and visual objects, with the aim of putting literature and theory on an equal footing, allowing them to become mutually revealing, adding nuances and complexities to each other. Often, in literary studies, we tend to advise ourselves and students to use certain theories to analyze literary works, as in the example of applying Butler's performative theory of gender to Virginia Woolf's *Orlando: A Biography*. Literature is, in this way of understanding, treated as an object of study, whereas theory and the act of theorizing is at best a tool or a method, which promises fresh interpretations of the object of study by framing and positioning it from a new angle. There is nothing wrong about this approach, insofar as we allow the object—in this case literature—to "talk back," in the sense of us watching for occasions where the object of study overflows, challenges, and reconstitutes the territory and boundary that the theory initially delineates.

Cultural theorist and video artist Mieke Bal, at various occasions but mostly in the context of visual arts, advocated for the idea of approaching certain works of art as "theoretical object" (*Quoting Caravaggio* 46–48; "Narrative Inside Out" 104). This term is meant, as Bal argued, to foreground "both the theoretical thought and the articulation of that thought in visual objects" ("Narrative Inside Out" 104). In other words, art and images can be conceptually rich and theoretical shrewd, even though in art such theoretical thought manifests itself in a coded and artistic "language" that is alien to the one common in philosophical thinking. Bal's proposition, therefore, emphasizes the capacity of certain works of art to "become" theory or theory-like. The way that I mediate the dialogue among literature, art, and theory in this study is close to Bal's proposition. I see it as my major task to introduce the figure of accented speech as a critical concept in literary theory, by allowing diverse media including literary texts, visual arts, and live performances to form and surface theoretical thoughts about the incongruous relationship between language and the speaking body. My major interlocutor in this study is the state of literary theory, as it has been developed in the wake of the tumultuous 1960s, when philosophy became the primary inspiration for literary theorists. Although other developments have followed, in my view it is the state of literary theory in the 1960s to the 1990s that has had the greatest impact on the field internationally and therefore remains the primary discussant for my project.

Overall, this is a book about accents, stuttering, bilingual and multilingual sensibilities, the mixing of genres and codes, and the hybrid and unstable references and identifications in intercultural encounters. I want to foreground these emphases with the writing itself. As a genre, academic writing has its own norms, conventions, and expectations. What would be an accented piece of the academic writing? And most importantly, what are its promises and compromises? These are the questions that I aim to explore through stylistic experiments. If the language of science, marked by (or perhaps, in a way, rather unmarked by) objectivity and neutrality, can be considered the native tongue of academic writing, literariness, taste and sensuality are what gives it a jarring—yet to some ears also charming—accent.

Roland Barthes is an exemplary figure of such "exophonic" academic writing, whose bold, intimate, and eccentric style dares me to write this study with a literary accent. Each chapter begins with a short experimental piece of writing—a first-person prose, a fragment of a film script, a rewrite of Lewis Carroll's *Alice's Adventures in Wonderland* (1865), etc.—usually literary in nature and *performative* in relation to the overall topic of the chapter. These little pieces are laboratories of thought, which construct and produce what Gilles Deleuze and Félix Guattari call "*conceptual personae* [that] *show thought's territories, its absolute deterritorializations and reterritorializations*" (*What is Philosophy* 69). At the same time, they are meant to be served as appetizers and teasers for readers—or simply as edible words.

The comparison between knowledge and taste, between writing and eating, should not be taken lightly, for, as Barthes suggests in his inaugural lecture, "writing is to be found wherever words have flavor (the French words for *flavor* and *knowledge* have the same Latin root)" ("Lecture" 7). In *Empire of Signs* (1970/1983), he *de*-estranges and estranges the Japanese dinner tray through the aesthetics of painting:

> The dinner tray seems a picture of the most delicate order: it is a frame containing, against a dark background, various objects (bowls, boxes, saucers, chopsticks, tiny piles of food, a little gray ginger, a few shreds of orange vegetable, a background of brown sauce) and since these containers and these bits of food are slight in quantity but numerous, it might be said that these trays fulfill the definition of painting which, according to Piero della Francesca, "is merely a demonstration of surfaces and bodies becoming ever smaller or larger according to their term." However, such an order, delicious when it appears, is destined to be undone, recomposed according to the very rhythm of eating; what was a motionless tableau at the start becomes a workbench or chessboard, the space not of seeing but of doing—of *praxis* or play; the painting was actually only a palette (a work surface), with which you are going to play in the course of your meal, taking up here a pinch of vegetables, there of rice, and over there of condiment, here a sip of soup, according to a free alternation [...] (11)

If, for Barthes, eating is a way of seeing, reading, writing, and rewriting, can the reverse be held equally true? Are reading and writing compatible with a consumptive body that eats, digests, and makes noises? The writings of Barthes certainly whet my appetite. His language, sensuous and daring, speaks to me in the image of a body that enjoys itself and takes pleasure in the act of writing. Doesn't he feel exposed and unprotected, I sometimes wonder, by writing intellectual treatises without putting on the mask of impersonality and the tone of impassivity? With this study, I entrust this experience to you, hoping that this odd combination of a certain body, language, and genre will not turn you off completely. Please continue and be my guest. Words are waiting to be undone and redone—all depends on your own rhythm of eating.

But how precarious and unsettling it is to go against the grain, especially when one is dealing with a topic that seems incompatible with literature. I myself carefully make sure that the odd and alien taste of accent influences only the *style* of my writing—not grammar, not syntax, not anything that might give the impression that I lose control of this language. I will discuss this aspect of accent by relating it to "exophonic" literature in Chapter 5. Through a close reading of a philosophical treatise by Deleuze and the literary works of Tawada, I propose to understand exophonic literature as a mode of writing or a certain style that makes a language—whether it is the writer's mother tongue or not—sound foreign by re-embodying it. The accent, in this kind of literature, manifests itself in the text as a stylistic feature that gives language an edible form and a peculiar taste, resulting in what Barthes calls the "figuration" of the text (*The Pleasure of the Text* 56).

The exophonic, thus, can refer to writers such as Kafka, Beckett, Nabokov, Lispector… Kafka, Beckett, Nabokov, Lispector… A better way of understanding them as exophonic writers is to repeat their names until they stop making sense, until nothing is left but the voluptuous body of the sounds, lingering at the tip of your tongue like angels dancing on the head of a pin. They write in an untamed voice and with an unsatiated appetite. Their works, with tastes refined and images powerful, occasionally release a sudden explosive and primitive force. I get goose pimples when I read the works of the Brazilian writer Clarice Lispector.

"When I paint I respect the material I use, I respect its primordial fate. So when I write you I respect the syllables" (48), writes Lispector in *Água Viva* (1973/2012). Whereas the art of writing, with precision and vividness being at the heart of it, is usually associated with capturing and articulating thoughts with words, hers is a constellation of sounds; meaning emerges not as a consequence of the constellation but as a coincidence. What matters is the bodily and vocal measure of words. Lispector writes, "But I'm trying to write to you with my whole body, loosing an arrow that will sink into the tender and neuralgic centre of the word [...] I write acrobatics and pirouettes in the air—I write because I so deeply want to speak" (6).

To speak? And to borrow a foreigner's mouth?

"Paradoxically, the better one's Portuguese, the more difficult it is to read Clarice Lispector," comments Benjamin Moser in the introduction to this book. "The foreigner with a basic knowledge of Romance grammar and vocabulary can read her work with ease. The Brazilian, however, often finds her difficult" (xii). I have no knowledge of Portuguese and thus cannot comment on the accuracy of this judgment. Still, what a curious thing to imagine a piece of work that is easier for foreigners to read! Maybe one way of reading the exophonic literature is to allow oneself to drift away from the common sense and become a foreigner of one's own language. After all, it is all ultimately so. With texts that insist on the physical mechanism of speaking, the act of reading is to peer voyeuristically into a mouth that chews and grunts. Words release a poignant scent of food. You smell the dream-like memory of a minor incident of killing. Bite into it. I say bite into it. Devoured, devouring, the tongue is awakening in the middle of a clash between words and food.

And a piece of flesh is spat out.

1. Accented Speech Acts

When Language Meets a Non-Native Tongue

Abstract: This chapter explores the "tongue-tied" experiences of non-native speakers, drawing on Judith Butler's concept of linguistic vulnerability. It argues that language is not merely a tool but an agent capable of acting on or against the speaker. While Butler suggests that language wounding is a universal phenomenon, this chapter contends that not all speakers are equally vulnerable. Accented speakers, in particular, are disproportionately subjected to linguistic violence. Through case studies of Amy Tan's "Mother Tongue," Richard Rodriguez's *Hunger of Memory*, and Maxine Hong Kingston's *The Woman Warrior*, this chapter examines how the ideological construction of the "mother tongue" and the "native speaker" shapes the violence inflicted on accented speakers and whether resistance is always possible.

Keywords: linguistic vulnerability; mother tongue; native speaker; resignification; Judith Butler

Monologue I

Admit it—you're held hostage by the tongue. A few months have passed since you arrived here; but still, your tongue bosses you around at its whim. You talk when being talked to. You open your mouth because the tongue needs fresh air. Even when silence becomes dense and suffocating, you don't know how to jump into a conversation. Sometimes you do wish to participate, yet you give up easily—since you notice people have eased into another topic as you were busy preparing your tongue for its debut.

You learned English in your home country. Initially, this language fascinated you. Each letter had its curves and angles: V was a valley deep and narrow. C decided to end her world trip halfway. H borrowed a ladder from his neighbor. Together these letters promised a novel landscape where words were free and undomesticated. Now you are finally inside the frame of that landscape; yet the tongue, ironically, wishes to be locked in its dark chamber. Tongue-tied, you blame yourself whenever the conversation goes wrong: "Is it because of my accent and mispronunciation?" There are, as your rationality tells you, many reasons why a conversation dries up. You *believe* the problem lies in your tongue, regardless.

You have an accent. There is nothing shameful about it. Who, after all, doesn't have an accent? It is just—let me put it this way—inconvenient. You cannot, for example, separate /l/ from /r/ without efforts. It is a minor innocuous mistake, but *not* so when a successful election, according to the way you pronounce it, becomes a hormonal response. People correct you with good intention; or, sometimes, they simply laugh at you. You are the tongue's hostage; its ambition and self-importance, as people tell each other behind your back, clearly shine through in the word "e[l/r]ection." The hassle of having an accent is that you lose the ease of being an anonymous deliverer of words. You become duty-bound to the words, especially the mispronounced ones, that pass through your mouth. Little by little, it becomes unimportant whether people notice these. You are on the alert for the slightest trace of an accent.

You show generosity by accommodating an alien tongue in your mouth. However, your ungrateful guest abuses it and plays tricks on you. You remind the tongue to observe the rules: with /l/, the tip of the tongue touches the gum ridge; with /r/, the tongue should be pulled back without touching the top. The rules are simple, but it is not easy to teach the tongue to respect them. Ignorant of your counsels, it runs wild in the mouth, shattering your dream of peace and order. You have a Medusa living in your mouth. It seduces you, teases you, but always somehow eludes you. But you are a good host who does not give up easily. To reassure yourself of the humanity of your guest, you hold a mirror close and open your mouth. Instead of the tongue, you see a head half-covered by snakes, whose forked tongues are hissing in the air. Maybe they're right, you tell yourself, to complain that you are here but can't even speak their language well.

Monologue II

No justification is required for the intricate movements of native tongues. Lips dance, the tongue leads, air vibrates, and the voice sings along. It seems the natural talent of native speakers to orchestrate the delicate symphony of the mother tongue. No one approaches a speaker, blonde and white, with a heavy British accent, and inquires, "Hey, how come you speak such good English? You've got the perfect accent!" In contrast, if you are not bestowed a face that is not obviously or even typically English, a face that unfolds naturally according to the English syntax, and yet you happen to speak that language very well, it is highly probable that you may encounter such a question.

You behave like native speakers of English and dream in English. You know no other languages than English; it is your mother tongue but not the tongue of your mother. Compared to your parents, you have a better accent—better in the sense that people cannot pretend they do not understand you. However, it is better but—how to put it—not quite right. You know this because people are frequently fascinated by your excellent command of English. They ask you, "So how long have you been here? I almost couldn't hear your accent." Because they are native speakers, they have—as you learn from occasions like this—the last word about your accent.

You are slightly annoyed. What bothers you is that your intimacy with English appears false and unjustified. However, instead of complaining that it hurts your feelings, you tell people your family history. Your parents moved here when they were young and ambitious, giving up everything except their language. The beginning was, as you are told again and again, no less difficult than that of most immigration stories. Sometimes they became disheartened. And you, as a child, felt but did not quite understand the melancholy tone of the lullaby your mother sang to you. You have not learned to speak their language, partially because your parents wished you to talk pretty. They sent you to a white school and always made sure that you passed your English exam. They gave you the native-like accent that sometimes made them feel uneasy. But still, they are proud of you, and have wished that you never know how painful it is to talk like them.

Non-Native Accented Speech

These monologues sketch out the psychological landscapes of two types of non-native English speakers.

The first type is the foreigner, whose mother tongue, not being English, interferes with the speaker's accent. Among all the bad names that plague the image of the foreigner, the complaint about the alienness of the foreigner's mother tongue is a typical one. In one of his seminars on hospitality, Jacques Derrida compares the foreigner to the sophist, saying that "[i]t is as though the Foreigner were appearing under an aspect that makes you think of a sophist, of someone whom the city or the State is going to treat as a sophist: someone who doesn't speak like the rest, someone who speaks an odd sort of language" ("Foreigner Question" 5). The mother tongue of the foreigner is seen as a linguistic veil that isolates the speaker and masks his or her transparency. At the same time, to be a foreigner means to uproot the mother tongue and graft it onto a new language. The non-native accent, as a symptom of "transplant rejection," thus appears as a "defensive" reaction of a tongue whose "immune" system alerts the speaker to the invasion of alien and potentially harmful substances. Thus, to the foreigner, the accented tongue is at once the veil and the revealer, the protection and the obstacle.

The second type is rather unconventional. It has to do with people—for instance, the second-generation immigrants—whose mother tongue is different from that of his or her mother: people whose native-like accent is repeatedly put into question and subjected to justification. This group does not strictly belong to what we commonly associate with the definition of the non-native speaker. However, as inquiries about the accent reveal the implicit but commonplace assumption that a native speaker has to belong to a certain ethnicity and inherit the language from the mother, it constitutes a critical category for understanding what one takes for granted with the notion of the native speaker. Whereas the native speaker is perceived to have an organic bond with the mother tongue, the native-like accent typically exposes an intimidating body that appears to blend in but still carries the stigma of foreignness.

These everyday experiences of the non-native English speaker—be it the tongue-tied condition of the foreigner, or the "unjustified" native-like accent—encode the non-native accent as a barrier, which prevents the speaking body from claiming ownership of his or her language. In these scenarios, language is not simply a tool ready for use but almost like an agent, able to act, to be out of control, and even to act against the speaking body.

That having an accent can expose the speaking body to peril can operate on two levels: first, even if the speaker is aware of it, an accent can be difficult to get rid of. It can appear in places where the speaker drops his or her guard or fails to pay attention, revealing the speaker as no longer in sufficient charge of his or her tongue. That the foreign tongue is able to make the speaker insecure and embarrassed, therefore, demands a closer look at the odd relation between speech and the body: how come that certain words and syllables are able to get by the speaking body, and even elude the conscious intervention of the speaker? Second, the imperilment may come from the outside. In today's globalized world, accent is a salient way of marking the distinction between insiders and outsiders. Speaking with a non-native accent can sometimes trigger hostility or, in extreme cases, provoke bodily attacks.

Caroline Bergvall and Ciarán Maher's language-sound installation *Say: "Parsley,"* first exhibited in the Spacex Gallery in Exeter in 2001, for instance, critiques the social and cultural phenomenon of distinguished speech patterns and accents that "brings about" verbal abuse or physical assault. The installation took place in a bare and minimally decorated space, in which a mono recording of fifty voices saying the phrase "rolling hills" was repeatedly played. Bergvall, compiling twelve poetic text installations that derive from her off-page performance works into a book titled *Fig* (2005), writes in the chapter on *Say: "Parsley,"*

> In the culturally pluralistic, yet divided, and markedly monolingual society of contemporary Britain, variations in accent and deviations from a broad English pronunciation still frequently entail degrees of harassment and verbal, sometimes physical, abuse, all according to ethnic and linguistic background. (51)

Thus, as Bergvall explains, accent is more than a piece of communicative noise or residue. It constitutes a particular form of speech—which I refer to as "accented speech"—that appears to trigger, invite, and even "justify" acts of hostility and violence. Such violence typically performs a gesture of othering based on the conflation of ethnicity and language, and further raises the question of how to undo the violence with a speech that remains accented and is therefore always already in the locus of that violence.

What does it mean to claim that one is hurt by one's own speech? How to understand the susceptibility of the accented speaker to humiliation and discrimination? Is it possible to talk back with an accented foreign tongue? To answer these questions, I will first discuss Judith Butler's take on linguistic vulnerability and agency, showing that Butler's politics of performativity lays great emphasis on humans' fundamental dependence on language, which constitutes, for Butler, a "scene of enabling vulnerability" (*Excitable Speech* 2) that makes it possible for a person—when being called a name, for instance—to respond and talk back. Second, I will examine accented speech as a case of linguistic survivability, which not only challenges Butler's generalized account of linguistic vulnerability but also raises the question of how to respond to the kind of violence that exploits precisely the incongruity between body and speech. I will perform a close reading of Maxine Hong Kingston's memoir *The Woman Warrior: Memoirs of a Girlhood Among Ghosts* (1976), Amy Tan's essay "Mother Tongue" (1996), and

Richard Rodriguez's autobiography *Hunger of Memory*, all of which provide philosophical insights into understanding the relation between language and body, while also drawing attention to the ideological and political construction of the so-called mother tongue and the native speaker—notions that, to a large extent, shape the linguistic vulnerability and survivability of the accented speaker.

Language Wounds

In the introduction to their book *Excitable Speech: A Politics of the Performative*, Butler poses the following question: "When we claim to have been injured by language, what kind of claim do we make? We ascribe an agency to language, a power to injure, and position ourselves as the objects of its injurious trajectory" (1). The kind of linguistic injury that here concerns Butler is hate speech, as exemplified by racial epithets, sexual slurs, pornography, and gay self-declaration in the military. Instead of asking which words wound, under which circumstances, and who gets to decide on this, Butler frames hate speech as showcasing humans' primary vulnerability to language. They ask, "Could language injure us if we were not, in some sense, linguistic beings, beings who require language in order to be?" (1–2). Butler explains that we, as linguistic beings, depend on language. We are able to recognize ourselves through being addressed in the terms of language, which, as a consequence, constitutes the linguistic and social condition of our existence. Even when we claim to be hurt by language, we have to do so by using language. Our *a priori* dependence on language is a linguistic condition that needs to be foregrounded before engaging in any discussion on linguistic survivability and agency.

That language can wound and act against us, according to Butler, can be manifested at the bodily level. For instance, the overlap between linguistic and physical vocabularies in words and phrases—for example, "tongue-lashing," "words wound," and "words cut deeper than knives"—demonstrate that, first, it is "difficult to identify the specificity of linguistic vulnerability over and against physical vulnerability" and, second, that the somatic dimension is crucial to our description and understanding of linguistic injury (5). Even though some of these phrases do not explicitly refer to the body, they function to invoke a physical sensation of pain so as to articulate the violence done and assisted by language.

However, the interrelatedness between language and body is far more profound than a metaphorical connection. To Butler, the connection between the two is crucial for understanding how social norms rule and prevail. Drawing on Pierre Bourdieu's notion of the habitus, which refers to the way in which a given culture inhabits and produces the body in the form of ingrained behaviors, habits, and dispositions, Butler understands the body as the site of an incorporated and sedimented history, which not only participates in the social field and reproduces sets of beliefs but also embodies and normalizes ritualized activities through gestures and bodily stylistics. In other words, the norms demand the body be lived and experienced in a way that is reducible and equivalent to a codified, legible language. Butler explains,

> One need only consider the way in which the history of having been called an injurious name is embodied, how the words enter the limbs, craft the gesture, bend the spine. One need only consider how racial or gendered slurs live and thrive in and as the flesh of the addressee, and how these slurs accumulate over time, dissimulating their history, taking on the semblance of the natural, configuring and restricting the *doxa* that counts as "reality." (159)

Butler uses the example of hate speech to illustrate how discourses of racism and homophobia are given a life of their own by not only "regulat[ing] the subject of speech [but] also seek[ing] to inhabit and craft the embodied life of the subject" (142). Indeed, hate speech produces a culturally stylized and historically crafted body, whose limbs and spine have to become bent and unnatural so as to stand in stark contrast to the "natural" and "normative" body, and to reinforce the distinction between what the culture and society deems proper and improper.

While acknowledging the capacity of social conventions to animate and reproduce the body, whose obviousness, naturalness, and predictability becomes an effect of the incorporation of social norms and rituals, Butler nonetheless criticizes Bourdieu's understanding of the bodily habitus as conservative and limiting, because it overlooks the fact that the discursive formation of the body is not always successful. Butler thinks that Bourdieu fails to address what happens when an interpellation misses its target, a possible scenario that they develop as follows:

> If that constitution fails, a resistance meets interpellation at the moment it exerts its demand; then something exceeds the interpellation, and this excess is lived as the outside of intelligibility. This becomes clear in the way the body rhetorically exceeds the speech act it also performs. (155)

Indeed, the *excess*: it points to Butler's view of the body as irreducible and even incongruous to its statement and intention. In other words, the body can say something other than what it intends and do something different from what it says. The disjuncture of intention, utterance, and action is what constantly brings forth a crisis of meaning, making it unlikely for the utterer of hate speech to vouchsafe the subordinate constitution of the addressee.

Butler's understanding of the bodily excess is influenced by Shoshana Felman, who formulates the relation between speech and body as at once indissoluble and scandalous. In her book *The Scandal of the Speaking Body*, Felman offers a reading of Don Juan's promise of marriage as exemplifying (the crisis of) J. L. Austin's speech act theory. Austin holds that not every instance of speech can be evaluated in terms of truth and falsity; some utterances are performative in the sense that they do not simply state a point of view but rather, through the act of speaking, perform actions that transform the reality. The declaration of marriage is one of such examples: the saying of "I do" in the course of the marriage ceremony performs the act of marrying. Felman's reading of Don Juan, however, complicates the issue. Don Juan's repeated promise of marriage is a kind of doing to the extent that it succeeds in seducing those being addressed; but it is, at the same time, a misfire of the performative, since it is a promise that he never materializes nor intends to materialize. Felman points out that Don Juan's parasitic relation to the speech act is not only due to his lack of intention to bring out what he has promised but more significantly a consequence of the unpredictability of the human act. She explains, "The scandal consists in the fact that the act cannot *know what it is doing*, that the act (of language) subverts both consciousness and knowledge (of language)" (67).

Butler believes that the strength of Felman's reading of Don Juan is that it introduces the speaking body into the speech act theory. While Austin's formulation of performative utterances implies a conscious and sovereign subject, whose words and deeds are considered inaugural and singular, Felman draws attention to the bodily dimension of the speech act, arguing that the body, being the conduit and the organic condition of speech, signifies, on the other hand, "what is *not* admitted into the domain of 'intention,' primary longings, the unconscious and its aims" ("Afterword" 119). Both for Butler and for Felman, the unconscious body, or the body as the unconscious, is what problematizes and scandalizes the efficacy of performative utterances. "And insofar as a speech act knows not what it does," says Butler, "the claim is a kind of performative, a form of doing, that is clearly not the product of the sovereign 'I,' a doing at odds with an intending, in persistent divergence from itself" (120–21). Therefore, the example of Don Juan is more than a random failed case of promising; it demonstrates the constitutive failure of the performative, which presumes that the speaking body, together with its aims, intentions, fantasies, and actions, is knowable, representable, and consistent in language and speech.

Butler holds that the performative's capacity of failure results less from the improper or insufficient execution of certain felicity conditions than from the fact that the position of an intentional and sovereign "I" that the utterer of the performative speech is supposed to occupy is largely unattainable and unsustainable. This is the major point where their approach to hate speech differs from that of Catharine MacKinnon and Mari Matsuda, who advocate the removal of pornography and racist speech from being legally protected as freedom of expression, on the grounds that these forms of speech are themselves wounding acts, which constitute the addressee in a socially subordinate and degrading position (MacKinnon 21). Butler agrees with MacKinnon and Matsuda that hate speech is an enactment of social hegemony in the broad sense; they insist, at the same time, that it is ill-judged to assume that such enactment consequentially and successfully subordinates the addressee in reality. Butler criticizes MacKinnon's and Matsuda's understanding of hate speech for, first, confusing representation with conduct and collapsing the distinction between the verbal act and the physical action of harm and injury and, second, mistakenly holding the utterer of the hate speech chiefly accountable for the injurious effects of words, whereas this causative connection itself is a legal and grammatical fabrication that functions to render a legally culpable subject. The danger of MacKinnon's and Matsuda's approach to hate speech, which champions legal remedies and state interventions, is that it allows the state to decide what is speakable and what is not, which, in a way, gives censorship a free pass. The result is that the hate speech appearing in rap and film becomes censored and prohibited as injurious and unresignifiable, whereas the legal speech's repetition of injurious terms is conceived of as contextual and resignifiable.

Tying their reflection on speech and body to hate speech, Butler proposes that the key to countering the wounding force of hate speech is not to seek legal regulations relentlessly but to realize that the speaking body, insofar as it implicates the unconscious, cannot foreclose the gap between meaning and intention, and between speech and act. Furthermore, the addressee can respond to the injurious name-calling precisely by deploying the openness of meaning and by foregrounding the immensurability between the name itself and the person being named. In *Excitable Speech*, Butler does not give any example that would illustrate the addressed body's subversive response at the scene of being called a name. However, in an interview with Gary A. Olson and Lynn Worsham, Butler does mention such a response. They say,

> I remember once walking on a street in Berkeley and some kid leaned out of a window and asked, "Are you a lesbian?" Just like that. I replied, "Yes, I am a lesbian." I returned it in the affirmative [...]. To the extent that I was able very quickly to turn around and say, "Yes, I am a lesbian," the power of my interrogator was lost. My questioner was then left in a kind of shock, having heard somebody gamely, proudly take on the term—somebody who spends most of her life deconstructing the term in other contexts. It was a very powerful thing to do. It wasn't that I authored that term: I received the term and gave it back; I replayed it, reiterated it. (760)

Butler's politics of performativity, in a way, can be construed as the performativity of the body, which accentuates the capacity of the addressed body to resist the temptation of lending itself to incorporating the injurious and interpellative call, restaging, confounding, and subverting the hate speech by resignifying and misappropriating it for one's own purpose. Butler stresses that using the term "lesbian" affirmatively is not tantamount to authorizing the term. In this way, they make it clear that their politics of performativity is not predicated on a sovereign subject whose speech act can be considered authorized, original, and inaugural. Instead, Butler envisions both the speaker and the addressee as actors who neither write the script nor originate the performance of words and actions; they belong to the category of what Butler calls "the postsovereign subject," whose agency is delimited and derivative from the outset (*Excitable Speech* 139).

However, before celebrating the kind of linguistic agency that does not rest on sovereignty, I want to ask: Is postsovereignty a universal condition? Do we have equal access to any and all languages? What makes a certain type of speech—for example, Standard English—at least *appear* more authoritative and efficacious than accented speech? If, for Butler, the unconscious body promises the disjunction between speech and act, which makes it possible to diffuse and counter the injurious force of hate speech, how does one respond to the kind of violence that exploits the incongruity between body and speech, i.e., violence triggered by accented speech?

Tongue (Un)Tied

It is said in Judges 12:6 that around the eleventh century BC, after the inhabitants of Gilead defeated the tribe of Ephraim, the Gileadites who guarded the fords of the Jordan forced people who attempted to cross to say "shibboleth." Because of the phonetic difference in the pronunciation of /sh/, those who pretended to be Gileadites were quickly identified; 42,000 Ephraimites were killed at the passages of the Jordan (Speiser 85).

The word "shibboleth" originally derives from the Hebrew word *shibbolét*, which, as Jacques Derrida explains, literally means "river, stream, ear of grain, olive twig" ("Shibboleth" 22). However, in the biblical story, "shibboleth" was used not as a linguistic sign that signified a corresponding referent but as a code word that indexed the differences of the speaking body. It prefigured the act of killing. It rendered the accented speaker as the one that gives rise to meaning but falls prey to sound. It portrayed the speaking body as either congruous or incongruous with the intended sound, making life and death a matter of lip and tongue gymnastics.

I suggest we can understand the effect of the word "shibboleth" as implicating the speaker in the logic of *différance*, a term coined by Derrida in a different context to highlight and to combine the mutually exclusive meanings of the verb "to differ" (*différer*), which, in French, indicates difference as either distinction or deferral (*Speech and Phenomena* 129). Derrida deliberately misspells the word "difference" as "*différance*," playing with the fact that the silent spelling mistake is not discernible in speech; and the difference between the two becomes delayed and postponed until the moment of writing. "The *a* of differance, therefore," says Derrida, "is not heard; it remains silent, secret, and discreet, like a tomb. It is tomb that (provided one knows how to decipher its legend) is not far from signaling the death of the king" (132). On the surface, *différance* and shibboleth imply antithetical strategic deployments of words: one draws on the sameness in sound, while the other manipulates the difference of pronunciation. Yet, seen in a different light, the biblical shibboleth is in itself the embodiment of *différance*, which, according to Derrida, "could be said to designate the productive and primordial constituting causality, the process of scission and division whose differings and differences would be the constituted products or effects" (137). The shibboleth test thus marks the occasion where the meaning and relevance of the speaking body becomes differed and deferred, where the act of speaking produces the difference between life and death.

The biblical shibboleth is not an exception in history. In her book *Fig*, Bergvall remarks that her installation *Say: "Parsley"* is inspired by the mass killing of Haitians, during which *perejil* (parsley) was used as a shibboleth word:

> Speaking is a give-away. My tongue marks me out. It also trips me up, creates social stuttering, mishearing, ambiguities. Say what. The shibboleth provides an extreme case of speech as gatekeeper. The massacre of tens of thousands of Creole Haitians on the soil of the Dominican Republic during the dictatorship of Trujillo in 1937 is still perhaps the most recent documented example of such a shibboleth at work. For failing to roll the /r/ of "perejil" (parsley). This familiar, anodyne word makes the horror all the more disturbing. (51)

These shibboleth incidents showcase how a particular word is chosen to decide whether a speaking body may pass or not, becoming, as a consequence, an instrument of violence that manipulates variations in pronunciation. The speaking body comes into play not only as a receptacle of violence but also as an organic condition of speech that registers and betrays the foreignness of the speaker. No wonder there is a belief that accented speech is a physical condition that can be corrected early on through, for example, the act of tongue-cutting.

With an intricate blending of voices and genres, often contradictory and ambiguous, Maxine Hong Kingston, in *The Woman Warrior: Memoirs of a Girlhood Among Ghosts*, portrays the social and linguistic displacement faced by her family and other Chinese immigrants who lived in a closed community in San Francisco. In the last chapter of this book, Kingston reflects on her preference for staying silent in her childhood, and the ensuing anxiety at school that pressured her into speaking. She traces her struggle with speech to the event of tongue-cutting that her mother claimed to have performed on her:

> She pushed my tongue up and sliced the frenum. Or maybe she snipped it with a pair of nail scissors. I don't remember her doing it, only her telling me about it, but all during childhood I felt sorry for the baby whose mother waited with scissors or knife in hand for it to cry—and then, when its mouth was wide open like a baby bird's, cut. The Chinese say "a ready tongue is an evil."
>
> I used to curl up my tongue in front of the mirror and tauten my frenum into a white line, itself as thin as a razor blade. I saw no scars in my mouth. I thought perhaps I had had two frena, and she had cut one. I made other children open their mouths so I could compare theirs to mine. I saw

perfect pink membranes stretching into precise edges that looked easy enough to cut. (164)

The whole event is based on the storytelling of Kingston's mother, which has been refabricated in Kingston's imagination with complementary and contradictory details. A sense of mystery and disquiet hovers above Kingston's narration. Although neither her memory nor the scarless tongue confirms her mother's words, the tongue itself becomes for Kingston an alien, unknowable, and fetishized object. It grows into an uncanny space where she confronts the desirability and undesirability of the speaking body.

Kingston's mother explained, "'I cut it so that you would not be tongue-tied. Your tongue would be able to move in any language. You'll be able to speak languages that are completely different from one another. You'll be able to pronounce anything. Your frenum looked too tight to do those things, so I cut it'" (164). Being a crucial nexus where the body meets its voice, the tongue is the battlefield of two connotations: it is at once the speech organ and the language. The powerful act of cutting the tongue, as her mother explains, is carried out with the conviction of bodily adaptation for desired speech. It is supposed to function like the removal of the lingual umbilical cord, which will loosen up the mother tongue and make it possible for other languages to become part of that tongue.

Here the tongue is imagined to be a site that accommodates a primordial incongruity between speech and body, and an organ that entails preventive interventions. Recalling the effect of tongue-cutting on her speech, Kingston comments that her mother should have cut more or not cut at all, because when she had to speak English in kindergarten, a stubborn dumbness still broke her voice up and made her fall into silence: "A dumbness—a shame—still cracks my voice in two, even when I want to say 'hello' casually, or ask an easy question in front of the check-out counter, or ask directions of a bus driver. I stand frozen, or I hold up the line with the complete, grammatical sentence that comes squeaking out at impossible length" (165).

To avoid the pain of speaking, the instinctive reaction would be, naturally, to fall silent. Quite often silence is interpreted as an absence of speech through which the social power relations that codify the ineffable and the unacceptable becomes tolerated and reproduced. In *Articulate Silences: Hisaye Yamamoto, Maxine Hong Kingston, Joy Kogawa* (1993), King-Kok Cheung explains that "[s]ilence can be imposed by the family in an attempt to maintain dignity or secrecy, by the ethnic community in adherence to cultural etiquette, or by the dominant culture in an effort to prevent any voicing of minority experiences" (3). The silent speaker is seen not only as a passive victim of the discursive domination but also as an accomplice whose submission in the face of suppression gives rise to self-marginalization. In the opening chapter of *The Woman Warrior*, Kingston tells a story of her no-name aunt, who became a taboo topic after she betrayed the family by committing adultery and suicide. The familial silence about the no-name aunt served, in Kingston's eyes, as a beyond-death punishment that not only consigned her aunt to oblivion but also made Kingston aware of the destructive power of the taboo—"I have believed that sex was unspeakable and words so strong and fathers so frail that 'aunt' would do my father mysterious harm" (16). However, with lips sealed, Kingston found herself becoming a ghost harboring a memory that denied her own existence: "But how can I have that memory when I couldn't talk? My mother says that we, like the ghosts, have no memories" (167). Silence, on this account, is not only enforced upon the no-name aunt through the elimination of her existence from the memories of the whole family but, more crucially, displaces those family members who participate in silencing her.

"Not just prohibition against speech," however, as Cheung observes, "but also coercion to speak can block articulation" (169). Cheung takes issue with the vocal mandate prevalent in the United States that tends to invest "blanket endorsements of speech and reductive perspective on silence" (3). By endorsing speech as opposed to silence, the American mainstream discourse overlooks the "more salient, less verbal" nuances of Asian cultures, resulting in an indiscriminate renouncement of silence and a deliberate reversal of the stereotypical image of quiet and obedient Asians among some Asian American male critics. There is no doubt that the practice of silence does contribute to the marginalization of Kingston and the other Chinese girls: when the class did a play, "the whole class went to the auditorium except the Chinese girls" as their voices were "too soft or nonexistent" (Kingston 167). However, equating silence with negativity and passivity, while relating speech to agency and subjectivity, may pressure one to speak out by renouncing the rich connotations of silence. In her childhood Kingston did not interpret silence as an absence of meaning and speech but, as she puts it metaphorically, as a black curtain through which multiple meanings and possibilities could emerge, as a gesture of a dignified reserve, and a protective cover for her exclusive relationship with the unexpressed:

> My silence was thickest—total—during the three years that I covered my school paintings with black paint. I painted layers of black over houses and flowers and suns, and when I drew on the blackboard, I put a layer of chalk on top. I was making a stage curtain, and it was the moment

before the curtain parted or rose [...] I spread them out (so black and full of possibilities) and pretended the curtains were swinging open, flying up, one after another, sunlight underneath, mighty operas. (165)

"It was when I found out I had to talk that school became a misery," Kingston writes, "that the silence became a misery" (166). Kingston suffered from her silence not only because of the failed IQ test and punishments from her teacher but, more crucially, the feeling of shame that she came to associate with silence. "I did not speak and felt bad each time that I did not speak," Kingston writes, "I read aloud in first grade, though, and heard the barest whisper with little squeaks come out of my throat" (166). Her anxiety about producing comprehensible speech was made worse under the pressure to undo silence and to speak out. It prompted her, as Kingston recounts, to project the oppressive feeling on a Chinese girl by forcing and seducing her to talk:

> "You're going to talk," I said, my voice steady and normal, as it is when talking to the familiar, the weak, and the small. "I am going to make you talk, you sissy-girl." [...] I looked into her face so that I could hate it close up. She wore black bangs, and her cheeks were pink and white. She was baby soft. I thought that I could put my thumb on her nose and push it bonelessly in, indent her face [...]. I stared at the curve of her nape. I wished I was able to see what my own neck looked like from the back and sides. I hoped it did not look like hers; I wanted a stout neck. (175)

Kingston associated the silent Chinese girl with "the familiar, the weak, and the small," whose softness and fragility, as Kingston claims, seduced her into violence. The repulsion toward the soft weak body of the silent girl reflected her struggle with her self-image: the fear of being mute, dumb, and invisible. At first, along with squeezing and pinching the Chinese girl's face, Kingston tried to make her say basic words, like "no" or "hi," or her own name. Then later, when Kingston's "well-intentioned" efforts turned out to be in vain, Kingston began to blame the girl for triggering the violence:

> "Now look what you've done," I scolded. "You're going to pay for this. I want to know why. And you're going to tell me why. You don't see I'm trying to help you out, do you? Do you want to be like this, dumb (do you know what dumb means?), your whole life? [...] And you, you are a plant. Do you know that? That's all you are if you don't talk. If you don't talk, you can't have a personality. You'll have no personality and no hair. You've got to let people know you have a personality and a brain." (180)

Kingston promised the girl that she would stop abusing her as soon as the girl talked. Associating her own violence with the Chinese girl's silence, Kingston wanted to make the girl understand that her silence was an open invitation to assault. Speech, on the other hand, was promoted by Kingston as the cure for dumbness and brainlessness.

However, to what extent can we associate speech with agency? Is the claim to agency invariably true for any form of speech?

Performative Contradiction

In her essay "Mother Tongue," Amy Tan describes how her mother, a first-generation Chinese immigrant in the United States, was treated as inferior, because she spoke a kind of English that people usually labeled as "broken" or "fractured":

> I was ashamed of her English. I believed that her English reflected the quality of what she had to say. That is, because she expressed them imperfectly her thoughts were imperfect. And I had plenty of empirical evidence to support me: the fact that people in department stores, at banks, and at restaurants did not take her seriously, did not give her good service, pretended not to understand her, or even acted as if they did not hear her. (323)

Young Tan mistakenly believed that her mother's "broken" English reflected the limitation of her thoughts, yet correctly observed that it made her mother invisible to American society and vulnerable to mistreatment. Like in the shibboleth tests, Tan's mother's accent was deployed as a marker of difference, which further made her social existence irrelevant and insignificant. On the other hand, unlike the shibboleth tests, the scenario depicted above did not rely on a particular word chosen beforehand to tell the speaker apart. Tan's mother's "broken" English amounted to a voluntary, instead of forced, confession of foreignness, revealing a condition of the foreign tongue as being not completely at home in that language.

Here my discussion about the violence triggered by accented speech resonates with Butler's view on hate speech, to the extent that these two modes of speech draw attention to the possibility of language to act on and against the body, raising the question of linguistic vulnerability and survivability. Accented speech *acts*, and it acts at different levels. First, as a vocal trace that bears one's ethnic origin and linguistic background, accented speech can amount to a confession or performance of bodily difference. Second, whereas the utterance of accented speech seems to reveal or confirm the undesirability and inferiority of the speaking body, the hateful reaction, verbally or physically, often "justifies" itself as purely a symptomatic or metonymic response to the "hateful" body.

On the other hand, my analysis of accented speech diverges from Butler's account of hate speech: first, hate speech aims to transform the addressed body into a receptacle of violence, whereas in the scenario of accented speech, it is the *speaking* body, instead of the addressed one, that becomes betrayed and stigmatized. Second, these two modes of speech implicate the speaking body in the scene of linguistic violence in an opposing manner. While the utterer of hate speech often employs a mode of address that sounds imperative and sovereign, the accented speaker tends to hesitate and look for words. Third, they seem to convey disparate sensitivities to language and meaning. That an accent has the power to offend people has little to do with the content of the utterance. Rather, it is often the variations in pronunciation, intonation, rhythm, pitch of the voice that evidence one's foreignness while causing discomfort. Even though Butler makes it clear that, regarding hate speech, "linguistic injury appears to be the effect not only of the words by which one is addressed but the mode of address itself" (*Excitable Speech* 2), the difference is that in hate speech the phonetic and prosodic dimension of speech does not stand apart from what is said, but consolidates and intensifies the intended meaning of offensive words.

Above all, the rationale for bringing these two modes of speech together is that I believe accented speech, in a way, exemplifies what Butler calls "the degraded speech situation" (86) that the addressee of hate speech often finds oneself in: that is, one has to respond to a speech act that purports to silence the one being addressed and disentitle him or her to the claim of a proper and sensible speaker. In other words, hate speech aims at portraying the addressee as deviant from social norms, whose response is, from the outset, discredited as illegible, unworthy, and, in a way, "accented."

This complicates Butler's idea of subversive resignification and misappropriation, for whether or not the social subordination targeted at the addressee of hate speech is successful, he or she, to talk back, has to effect changes and transformations in a social context that marginalizes and disregards his or her capability to use words effectively. One example is given by the Russian writer Zinaïda Schakovskoy, who, looking back to her early days in Paris, recalls,

> Badly dressed, with a foreign accent, and looking younger than I was, I was robbed right and left [...]. In cafés, they would never give me my

change. I tried to protest, but my stuttering made my protest ineffectual and only provoked jeers. "She doesn't even know how to talk and she still wants to complain!" (Schakovskoy, qtd. in Beaujour 126)

Here Schakovskoy's debilitating stutter and foreign accent are exploited to enforce an unfavorable image of the incompetent speaker and to dismiss her appeal for justice. Even though failure is always a possibility—and the only way to foreclose failure is to relinquish all action—the type of failure faced by the accented speaker, as is the case for the addressee of hate speech, is rather specific: he or she has to respond with a tongue commonly denounced as "broken" and "illegitimate."

Butler is not unaware of the linguistic and social constraints facing the addressee of hate speech. Similar arguments, as Butler notes, have been made by McKinnon, who draws on the example of Anita Hill to show that pornography deprives the addressee of the power to speak in a convincing and authentic manner. In the Senate hearings of 1991, Hill's testimony about the sexual harassment she faced was received as confessing her shame and complicity. In analyzing this case, Butler says, "This is what some would call a performative contradiction: an act of speech that in its very acting produces a meaning that undercuts the one it purports to make" (84).

Even though Butler admits that hate speech may result in silencing and stigmatizing the speech of the addressee, they wonder if such linguistic vulnerability is rather a universal linguistic condition. Butler asks, "If pornography performs a deformation of speech, what is presumed to be the proper form of speech?" (86). By posing this question, they shift the discussion of "the degraded speech situation" facing the addressee to a rather general reflection on the open and polysemous nature of communication. According to Butler, the testimony of Hill, whose intended "no" was systematically taken as a "yes," is not at all a unique case; the reversal of meaning is a risk that everyone has to take if one wants one's voice to be heard. Butler disagrees with the idea of grounding politics in consensus, which is supposed to be achieved through creating an ideal and proper communicative situation in which meanings are univocal and pre-established. That one cannot know for sure in advance what one says will be received univocally, for Butler, is what makes language a potential site of contestation and resistance. Since no one is able to claim total ownership of language, even those whose speech is de-authorized and discredited can cite, restage, and respond to the injurious words so as to create a shift in meanings and contexts.

However, does Butler's politics of performativity that insists on the disjuncture between utterance and meaning come at a price?

By framing the powerlessness of the addressee's speech to convey and perform intended meanings as a fundamental linguistic vulnerability, Butler disregards the fact that not everyone has equal access to any and all language. The degree of our linguistic vulnerability varies, depending on whether we are dealing with a language we are familiar with or a foreign language (which does not have to be literally foreign—think, for example, of the legal language that Socrates claims he is foreign to), and on whether we are socially and politically recognized as being "entitled" to that language.[1] The risk of naturalizing the incommensurability between words and meaning, and between speech and body, is that we fail to do justice to those ones whose linguistic vulnerability is not so much a human condition as it is a discursive construction. It is worth noting that my argument about the constructed nature of certain linguistic vulnerability does not imply that such construction is static, unchangeable, or final. Instead, precisely because it is constructed, we can analyze it, restage it, and even transform it. However, the process is perhaps not as simple as resignifying and expropriating certain words and names, while hoping that one day the social and discursive field will be recontextualized and reformed. Rather, the task is to give hopefulness a concrete shape, by struggling for the right to say what one means and to mean what one says, even if meaning is, in the end, always a matter of negotiation and translation.

The Proper Speech and the Mother Tongue

Tan's mother also realized that, because of the limitations of her English, people turned a deaf ear to her requests and complaints. She thus often asked Tan, who was born in the US and spoke "perfect" English, to talk on the phone, to yell at people who treated her unfairly, and even to bargain with the stockbroker. Tan recalled one particularly stressful occasion in which the hospital lost her mother's CAT scan but did not apologize, even though, as her mother told Tan, "she had spoken very good English, her best English, no mistakes":

> She said they did not seem to have any sympathy when she told them she was anxious to know the exact diagnosis since her husband and son

---

[1] Jacques Derrida writes that Socrates defends himself by emphasizing that "he doesn't know how to speak this courtroom language, this legal rhetoric of accusation, defense, and pleading; he doesn't have the skill, he is *like* a foreigner" ("Foreigner Question" 15).

had both died of brain tumors. She said they would not give her any more information until the next time and she would have to make another appointment for that. So she said she would not leave until the doctor called her daughter. She wouldn't budge. And when the doctor finally called her daughter, me, who spoke in perfect English—lo and behold—we had assurances the CAT scan would be found, promises that a conference call on Monday would be held, and apologies for any suffering my mother had gone through for a most regrettable mistake. (324–25)

It is astonishing to see how Tan's perfect English effectively changed the doctor's attitude, intervening in the case that had initially appeared disadvantageous to Tan's mother. With her accented English, Tan's mother was positioned to both suffer from and to take responsibility for the mistake of the hospital. Her welfare concerned no one, while her protest was not taken seriously. In contrast, as soon as Tan spoke over the phone on behalf of her mother, the doctor admitted the mistake and promised to compensate.

Butler's rhetorical question "What is presumed to be the proper form of speech?" (86), in this case, does have a positive answer. It is the Standard English that is perceived to be the proper form of speech, which has the power to make the voice heard and things done. That such propriety and performativity is constructed is indisputable. Yet, it is inaccurate to assume, like what Butler's line of argument suggests, that the constructed nature of the proper speech can be equated with or reduced to the proposition that there is no proper speech as such. Instead, it asks for a closer scrutiny of how the discursive field that differentiates the proper speech from the "broken" speech operates and comes into being.

One of the concerns that prevents Butler from pinpointing and analyzing the discursive and contextual embeddedness of hate speech is that they believe contexts are dynamic and unfixable. Butler considers Austin's proposal regarding the felicity conditions of the performative speech—which involve the proper invocation of the relevant *convention* by an *authorized* person in an appropriate *circumstance*—precisely such a fruitless effort to understand the performative force of speech by fixing a total speech situation. I want to suggest, instead, that the felicity conditions are productive in analyzing the performative force of the proper speech: the efficacy is constructed to rely on the mother tongue as an appropriate convention and the status of the native speaker as an entitlement to authority.

Lynda Mugglestone, as I mentioned in the introduction, in *Talking Proper: The Rise of Accent as Social Symbol*, observes that a standard of "proper" speech, having an aura of being superior to its variant forms, prevailed in the eighteenth century. At that time, a clear sense of an emergent standard of spoken English became perceptible owing to the extensive works on the articulation and classification of speech sounds by phoneticians (13). The emerging paradigm of received pronunciation of the time strived for adopting a geographically neural accent through eradicating what Thomas Sheridan, a major proponent of the elocution movement, proclaimed to be "those odious distinctions between subjects of the same King, and members of the same community, which are chiefly kept alive by differences of pronunciation" (316). Sheridan considered accent the main cause of social stratification and thus envisioned and promoted elocution and standardization as a national project contributing to social equality. In fact, as Mugglestone argues, contrary to Sheridan's belief, in the eighteenth century, due to the normative and prescriptive zeal of the age, accent was manipulated by the framing ideology of the institutional discourse to "foreground its nuances as a prime determiner of social, cultural, and even intellectual acceptability" (255). In other words, the unequal social status of the speaker was not a result of accent itself, but of the stigmatizing of the speech variations that the national movement of standardization had led to. One illustrative example is the "fatal" letter [h], whose "presence in initial positions associated almost inevitably with the 'educated' and 'polite,' while its loss commonly triggered popular connotations of the 'vulgar,' the 'ignorant,' and the 'lower class'" (107). With the attempted imposition of "proper" speech, phoneticians and theoreticians placed the speaker in a binary opposition of "right" and "wrong," "elegant" and "vulgar," "deviant" and "mainstream." The difference in accent was thus perceived in terms of aberrance, deficiency, and incompetence.

One of the consequences of the historical and ideological process of standardization is the gradual conjunction of nation and language, which, as Yasemin Yildiz observes in *Beyond the Mother Tongue: The Postmonolingual Condition* (2012), further gives rise to the prevailing narrative of the mother tongue as engaging with an affective investment in the maternal body. Yildiz argues that the emotional connotation surrounding the mother tongue began to take shape following a trend of linguistic socialization in the late eighteenth century in Europe. At that time, large social and political transformations, according to Yildiz, "produced new and interrelated conceptions of family, kinship, motherhood, nation, and state" (10). The bourgeois mother, owing to a renewed emphasis on affective care toward the child instead of physical care alone, became a crucial figure in terms of the reorganization of public and private spaces (11). The discourse on the mother tongue emerged against the backdrop of the political linkage of nation and language, drawing on the literal meaning of "mother" and "tongue" to emphasize the physical closeness to the maternal voice and the organic relation to the mother's language.

The mother tongue, for Yildiz, can be read as a shorthand term for the literal and fetishized constellation of language and the mother's body. In her introduction, Yildiz aligns this reading with Friedrich Kittler's account of the discourse network of the eighteenth century in Germany, during which the phonetic reading instruction was introduced and predicated on the mother's affectionate mouthing and voicing of "pure" sounds.[2] In *Discourse Networks 1800/1900*, Kittler argues that the eighteenth century witnessed the invention of the mother as primary instructor for teaching children how to read (26). This role was enforced on the mother through the proliferation of a new type of book that appealed to the mother for performing elementary acculturation. Kittler further quotes one of these books, *Primer for Children of Noble Education, Including a Description of My Method for Mothers Who Wish to Grant Themselves the Pleasure of Speedily Teaching Their Children to Read* (1807), written by Heinrich Stephani: "In order to provide you with a correct view [of my method], I must ask you from now on to consider *our mouth* with its different constituent parts *as an instrument upon which we are able to play certain meaningful tones* that together we call language" (Stephani, qtd. in Kittler 33). The novelty of this method, Kittler explains, consists in its reconfiguration of bodily parts. "This body has eyes and ears only in order to be a large mouth," Kittler writes, "The mouth transforms all the letters that assault the eyes and ears into ringing sounds" (33). Relying on the mother's mouth, books such as this one acquire a renewed "textuality," which manifests itself not primarily in letters and words but through voice and sound. These books, correspondingly, have aimed at a new reading experience: the mother is supposed to explore her own oral cavity, so as to compose the language music as precisely as possible with the aid of "the mouth instrument," whereas the child is instructed to "read" the mother's mouth for meaning, and to relate to the visual form of the letter *through and as* the mother's pointing finger (34).

---

2   Yildiz observes that the contemporary feminist scholarship varies in terms of the complex imbrication of mother and language: "Some feminist critics celebrate the 'mother tongue' as bearing residues or traces of the maternal body [...] Yet, other feminists, working within a psychoanalytic framework, stress the divergence between the maternal and the linguistic" (11). Yildiz, instead, following suit of Kittler, proposes a third strand that links language and the maternal body with male authority and considers the mother's mouth the central conduit for male ventriloquism.

Stephani's primer is meant to instruct the mother to become a qualified instructor. "The mother's pleasure," comments Kittler, "is at once the methodical production *and* the methodical purification of sounds. An accomplished Mother's Mouth at the end of its self-education no longer works in an empirico-dialectical manner but becomes the mouthpiece of an 'original voice sound' that generates all others" (35). Being at once the instructor and the instructed, the mother paves the way for the promoted language ideology by feeding purified sounds into the child's mouth. The phonetic method lays claim on the mother's voice to carry out the campaign against dialects and speech variations. However, Kittler observes that while the method gives rise to an affectionate and transcendental mother tongue, the mother's voice itself has lost the articulatory dimension of speech. The mother's voice marks "the hesitant beginning of articulation and signification" (49), whose unfinished act of speaking is to be repeated and completed in the child's mouth. As an example, Kittler mentions the psychologist Dieterich Tiedemann's experiment of having the mother pronounce the syllable *ma*, whose meaning becomes tangible only after the child's vocal repetition of *mama*. In order to make the child speak, the mother refrains from speaking herself. She is instructed to compose her speech organs in a way that solicits and generates, but by no means possesses and masters, meaning and discourse.

Yildiz, in *Beyond the Mother Tongue*, argues that the historical account of Kittler shows that the modern notion of the mother tongue is more than a metaphor. The discursive construction of the proximity between the mother tongue and the maternal body gives rise to the collective imagination of, according to Yildiz, "one predetermined and socially sanctioned language as the single locus of affect and attachment and thus attempts to obscure the possibility that languages other than the first or even primary one can take on emotional meaning" (13). Yildiz's argument raises the following questions: What if one's intimacy with the language of the mother is thought to be illegitimate? What if one's mother's language is not socially approved to play the affective role?

From "Broken" Speech to Intimate Speech

The mother tongue, exploited as ventriloquism of the national ideology of speech standardization, is gradually detached from the singular voicing of the mother. This homogenized experience of the mother tongue is mediated, on the one hand, by strengthening an "organic" verbal bond among the mother, the child, and the nation and, on the other hand, by cultivating a normative form of intimacy that undercuts the child's bond to the mother's language when it differs from the standardized language of the nation. Tan, for instance, recalls an unexpected clash between her mother tongue and the language of her mother as she was giving a public speech about her book:

> The talk was going along well enough, until I remembered one major difference that made the whole talk sound wrong. My mother was in the room. And it was perhaps the first time she had heard me give a lengthy speech, using the kind of English I have never used with her. I was saying things like, "The intersection of memory upon imagination" and "There is an aspect of my fiction that related to thus-and-thus"—a speech filled with carefully wrought grammatical phrases, burdened, it suddenly seemed to me, with normalized forms, past perfect tenses, conditional phrases, all the forms of standard English that I had learned in school and through books, the forms of English I did not use at home with my mother. (321–22)

In Tan's case, as it is in many immigrant families, the mother tongue, which is a discursively constructed, collectively imagined, and affectively loaded entity, does not overlap with the language that the mother of the immigrant family speaks. In fact, the language of the immigrant mother is often denounced for being a "hindrance" to the child's assimilation to the mother tongue of the nation. The mother is blamed not only for lacking language skills and qualifications to prepare the child for socialization outside the family but also for splitting the child's sense of integrity and widening the gap between public and familial spaces.

What Tan experienced was a clash of private and public spaces whose distinction, to Tan, had been unconsciously marked out by the different accents of English. Language, in general, does play a significant role in creating the sense of place. It is especially so in immigrant families, where the language spoken at home is often different from the language shared by the public. In his autobiography *Hunger of Memory*, Richard Rodriguez writes,

> In public, my father and mother spoke a hesitant, accented, not always grammatical English. And they would have to strain—their bodies tense—to catch the sense of what was rapidly said by *los gringos*. At home they spoke Spanish. The language of their Mexican past sounded in counterpoint to the English of public society. The words would come

quickly, with ease. Conveyed through those sounds was the pleasing, soothing, consoling reminder of being at home. (11)

With accented English and tense bodies, the public image of his parents, in Rodriguez's eyes, was burdened with the difficulty of speaking and listening. Spanish, on the other hand, resounded at home along with bodily ease and emotional closeness. His parents' experiences of bodily displacement in public were soothed and compensated by sticking to Spanish as their family language, which helped to transplant the sense of home from the past to the present.

This childhood memory of a particular language being attached to a particular place, as Rodriguez recalls, taught him to experience these places as neatly divided and as either threatening or secure, alien or intimate. It taught him, moreover, to relate to his parents in an ambivalent and differentiating manner. On the one hand, the parents *at home* were tender and irreplaceable. Rodriguez writes affectionately,

> At dinner, we invented new words. (Ours sounded Spanish, but made sense only to us.) We pieced together new words by taking, say, an English verb and giving it Spanish endings. My mother's instructions at bedtime would be lacquered with mock-urgent tones. Or a word like *sí* would become, in several notes, able to convey added measures of feeling. Tongues explored the edges of words, especially the fat vowels. And we happily sounded that military drum roll, the twirling roar of the Spanish *r*. Family language: my family's sounds. (17)

For Rodriguez, the sounds that made them publicly alienated were the sounds that bound the family together. Spanish separated them from the world outside; yet, it united them by making each other the immediate and *sole* channel of recognition and intimacy. Together they celebrated new sounds and words. They invented a private version of Spanish that made home different not only from the English-speaking world outside, but also from the homeland of Mexico. The "bastardized" verbs developed into codes of intimacy, whereas the Spanish *r*, which is difficult to pronounce for most English speakers, became the token of their alliance. On the other hand, the parents in public, because of their accents and insecure manners, appeared rather awkward and ashamed—an image that made it impossible for the child to uphold the fantasy of magnificent and powerful parents. Rodriguez says, "But it was one thing for *me* to speak English with difficulty. It was more troubling for me to hear my parents speak in public: their high-whining vowels and guttural consonants; their sentences that got stuck with 'eh' and 'ah' sounds; the confused syntax; the hesitant rhythm of sounds so different from the way *gringos* spoke" (13).

Compared to their parents, the second-generation immigrants are usually rid of the stereotypical accent. This "neutral" way of speaking makes it easier for them to assume a mainstream public persona and to take part in social life. However, as Yildiz observes, although the second-generation immigrants themselves do not experience migration, they "continue to be conceived under the sign of this phenomenon rather than as fully belonging in the new home as fellow citizens" (170). What concerns the second-generation immigrants, as I will address in the next chapter, is that their speech is not "matched" with their faces. Even though they speak unlike their parents, they still look like their parents. Since only certain facial features and skin tones are socially approved to express and confirm the native status of the speaker, the second-generation immigrants, despite the fact that English is their mother tongue, do not belong to the "natural" and "unproblematic" category of the native speaker. The notion of the mother tongue, in the case of the second-generation immigrants, becomes divorced from that of the native speaker: that a person is monolingual, having the "right" accent and an intuitive knowledge of the language, does not make him or her a native speaker. The native status entails not only that the person speaks the language as his or her mother tongue but also possesses facial and bodily traits that comply with the mainstream image of the native speaker.

Accented speech, therefore, constitutes a critical dimension for conceptualizing the relation between first- and second-generation immigrants. However, is it true that the articulation of intimacy is limited to a particular language? Is it true that the adoption of a foreign language hinders the expression of love and affection? Rodriguez recalls that when he first attended school, he was timid and silent, unable to express himself in English. The school was intimidating because it was the opposite of what he had experienced at and *as* home—the lively sounds of Spanish, the immediate recognition of each other, and the voice of singularity and intimacy. The consolation of home disappeared, however, when teachers came to visit his parents, bringing home what he thought to be the public language:

> With great tact the visitors continued, 'Is it possible for you and your husband to encourage your children to practice their English when they are at home?' Of course, my parents complied. What would they not do for their children's well-being? And how could they have questioned the Church's authority which those women represented? In an instant,

they agreed to give up the language (the sounds) that had revealed and accentuated our family's closeness. The moment after the visitors left, the change was observed. 'Ahora, speak to us *en inglés*,' my father and mother united to tell us. (20)

The young Rodriguez saw the visit of his schoolteachers as an intrusion into his private life and space, which marked the beginning of the gradual diminution of familial closeness. It was then, as Rodriguez explains, that he decided to speak up at school, adopting a public persona as it was expected from him.

Initially, Rodriguez mourned the loss of Spanish as an intimate family language. As Rodriguez became more fluent in English and acquired the standard accent from school, his parents, in contrast, grew more and more silent, trying not to attract attention to their thick English accent. English— or to be more precise, the difference in accents—divided them. As he grew up, however, Rodriguez started to realize that intimacy *"is not created by a particular language, it is created by intimates*. The great change in my life was not linguistic but social. If, after becoming a successful student, I no longer heard intimate voices as often as I had earlier, it was not because I spoke English rather than Spanish. It was because I used public language for most of the day" (32).

Intimate speech soothes and heals the wound torn open by language. In her essay, Tan makes a similar point: even "broken" English can become a perfect vehicle for love and affection, used among people who are capable of speaking "perfectly." A telling moment occurred when Tan unconsciously accommodated her mother's speech, saying "'Not waste money that way.'" (322). The interesting part is, as Tan explains, that her husband was also present but did not realize what she did to her language. Reflecting on it, Tan observes, "It's because over the twenty years we've been together I've often used the same kind of English with him, and sometimes he even uses it with me. It has become our language of intimacy, a different sort of English that related to family talk, the language I grew up with" (322). Still upset by the image of brokenness that people tend to associate with her mother's language, Tan has nonetheless developed an alternative way of relating to her mother tongue: it is a tender and nuanced way of listening that, instead of being on the lookout for errors and mistakes, is sensitive to the expressive quality of words. "But to me, my mother's English is perfectly clear, perfectly natural," writes Tan. "It's my mother tongue. Her language, as I hear it, is vivid, direct, full of observation and imagery. That was the language that helped shape the way I saw things, expressed things, made sense of the world" (323). For Tan, it is not *the* mother tongue—which is constructed as the collective skin of the nation state—that is singular and irreplaceable; it is rather the "broken" mother tongue, the language that her mother speaks daily, that generates a bond with loved ones.

2. Audiovisual Counterpoint

Because Your Face Voices a Different Accent

Abstract: This chapter addresses the intersection of race, speech, and the visual politics of face and body. It shifts the focus of postcolonial discourse from the visual to the aural dimension of racialization. Recent scholars like Rey Chow and Pooja Rangan argue that voice and language in the context of racism and postcolonialism have been underexplored. This chapter introduces the concept of face/speech dissonance, where the voice or accent of a speaker is perceived as incompatible with their physical appearance. It analyzes Hetain Patel's performance *Who Am I? Think Again* using Michel Chion's concept of "audiovisual counterpoint" to show how dissonant face and speech amplify racialized experiences.

Keywords: faciality; racialization; face-speech dissonance; sound-image disjunction; Hetain Patel

Scenario

It is summer—hot, moist, and bright. The massive heat rests its head on the shoulders of passersby; everyone on the street pauses after a few steps to wipe off the sweat. This is the maddest season of the year: no one seems clear-headed; everything is speaking in tongues. Inside a café, a Japanese woman is casually leaning against the edge of the cashier's desk.

The camera, shaky but determined, is hovering over her upper body. As soon as it captures her inanimate gaze, it moves along with the gaze, turning toward the direction of the door, as if it is anticipating a scene.

The door opens, and the sheer brightness is suddenly unlocked, melting into a white moving dot. The camera draws back as the dot approaches. Since the image is blurred, we cannot identify what or who it is, until the voice breaks the "silence" of the image.

Hui, Tingting. *Accented Speech in Literature, Art, and Theory: Melodramas of the Foreign Tongue.* Amsterdam: Amsterdam University Press, 2025.
DOI: 10.5117/9789048569007_CH02

We hear a man's voice. What a strange sound: as unintelligible as the groan of a wounded animal, as harsh as the white noise of an old machine.

Against the background noise of the soundtrack, the image becomes clear, identifiable. A white man's face (perhaps Caucasian) overtakes the screen. The lips, as we could see, continue moving with rigor, whereas the soundtrack falls silent.

Now we hear the Japanese woman's voice.

She says something. We hear passion in her voice. But we are not sure what language it is. It does not sound like Japanese or English. In fact, it does not sound like a language at all. As the face of the Japanese woman is off-screen, we cannot tell whether she is speaking or eating aloud.

Confused, the white face leans forward.

The camera discovers his hands. His index finger is dancing and pointing to his mouth.

Again, the camera scans the white face closely, zooming in on those dry, moving lips. So far, the camera is keen on anatomizing the body at hand. We see lips, hands, ears, postures. The fragmented images, intensified through the close-up, incite a sense of hallucination.

Man: このカフェは開いていますか？ちょっと聞いて！[His finger is pointing at his mouth.] 私はあなたに日本語で話しています。このカフェは開いていますか？

[Subtitle: Is this café open? Listen! I am speaking Japanese to you. Is this café open?]

The camera moves sideways. For the first time, we are able to see both interlocutors within one frame.

Demystified, the image pacifies and bores us at once.

Woman: はい。おかしいですね。私は、あなたが日本語で話していることに気づきませんでした。

[Subtitle: Yes. How strange! I did not realize you were speaking Japanese.]

Hearing the Face, Seeing the Speech: A Filmic Experience of Accent

Tomasz was from Poland. He was tall and lean, and had a typical white face accentuated by a pointing nose. To my surprise, he happened to speak Japanese—a language that did not readily rise from by his facial landscape.

Facing him while hearing him speak Japanese, my eyes were arguing with my ears. I could not help but draw to his speech, wishing to detect some traces of a foreign accent. He looked Polish but spoke Japanese. Was it because his face seemed to suggest and portray a different linguistic reality that my unconscious expectation of what I saw and what I heard was temporarily unsettled? His accent consoled me—not due to its nature of hybridity, which might conveniently enable a patronizing attitude in me, but to the fact that it allowed me to navigate my perceptive cognition when his linguistic traits did not map his facial landscape "faithfully."

I confessed my momentary disorientation to Tomasz, adding that it might result from my lack of exposure to Caucasians who spoke non-alphabetic languages. It was not something new to him, of course. He had some other "extreme" experiences, he told me. When he traveled in Japan, he once spoke Japanese to a shopkeeper, asking if the café was open. That person returned his speech with a mumble that in no way resembled any language but sounded more like a barbaric manner of chewing and swallowing. To make her realize that he was speaking Japanese, Tomasz had to silence the language of his face by "kidnapping" her attention and redirecting it to his mouth and moving lips—the physical source of his vocal emission.

What makes speech intelligible? What makes it leap from noise to language?

In the narrative of Tomasz, it entails visualizing a mouth, making it stand out from the framing effect of the face. Strange as it may seem, this story is not at all uncommon. What I am trying to depict here is an everyday scene that tends to slip away without notice, a scene that is slightly political in nature, since it unwittingly reveals our implicit bias. This chapter aims to freeze the initial moment of encounter where one's face and speech strike the listener as being at odds with one another. Quite often, with continuous or frequent exposure to such phenomena, the discomfort caused by this audiovisual discrepancy, as it is in the cinema, is inclined to be smoothed over, adapted, and forgotten. However, I propose to let our critical attention linger and caress this nascent and transient stage, because it is pregnant with possibilities, which, when attended to carefully, will illuminate how speech can be visualized and imagined, how the relation between face and speech may be configured differently, and how ethnicized and racialized encounters should be comprehended as an audiovisual scene. What fascinates me is not only that sometimes the mouth speaks a different language or speaks with a different accent than the face readily signifies, but also its peculiar effect on the listener, who seems to be invited to engage his or her visual and auditory perceptions asynchronously. This phenomenon constitutes a rare occasion in which hearing and seeing cease to proceed in an unreflective and complementary fashion.

When Tomasz narrated his story, I was translating the scene into a filmic language, which has become the scenario in the beginning of this chapter. As the vocal impression fails to resonate with the echo of his facial landscape, Tomasz's experience may correspond to a filmic scene in which sound and image are temporarily unresponsive to one another. This particular mode of real-life encounter, I suggest, could be understood in terms of an "audiovisual counterpoint" (11), a filmic concept that Michel Chion has developed in his book *Audio-Vision: Sound on Screen* (1994). This book argues that sound film has transformed cinema into an audiovisual medium where sound and image interact in such a way that impacts the audience's perceptions and sensations as a whole. Very often, in films, sound and image complement each other. When the woman in the beginning of *Hiroshima Mon Amour* (1959) says in a flat voice, "I saw everything. Everything [...]. The hospital, for instance, I saw it. I'm sure I did," it is followed with shots of patients, stairs, endless corridors. A man's voice denies it, "You did not see the hospital in Hiroshima. You saw nothing in Hiroshima." Without knowing it, we are ready to believe the woman; images of the hospital trick us to side with what she has said. Here the viewing experience is not about seeing pictures plus hearing sounds and does not generally attest to a neat division of audiovisual perceptions. We proceed without making perceptive distinctions between auditory and visual stimulants, until the moment where the very consistency of the two is challenged and cannot be sustained "naturally." In the case of the film in question, don't we start to reassess the authenticity both in terms of the woman's narrative and of the appalling images, as we repeatedly hear the man's voice offering plain denial and rejection of everything?

Chion, in his book, understands the relation between image and sound as a contract in the context of cinema, which is reciprocal in nature but can be put in danger or breached at certain moments. These moments of rupture—which Chion aims to comprehend with the term "the audio-visual counterpoint or dissonance"—are where filmic scenes refrain from stimulating and naturalizing the sensory completeness of the viewer while pushing filmic expressions to the limits. One such film that Chion has analyzed is Andrei Tarkovsky's *Solaris* (1972). In the resurrection scene of the hero's former wife, while her body violently twitched and convulsed, "[o]ver these images Tarkovsky had the imagination to dub sounds of breaking glass, which yield a phenomenal effect. We do not hear them as "wrong" or inappropriate sounds. Instead, they suggest that she is constituted of shards of ice; in a troubling, even terrifying way, they render both the creature's fragility and artificiality, and a sense of the precariousness of bodies" (Chion 39). Here the sound of breaking glass and the image of body shaking are initially grasped as irrelevant or even contradictory; yet, as the audiovisual dissonance is prolonged and recurred, it suggests a resurgence of meaning that is found precisely in the gap between image and sound.

Having sketched out its conceptual origin, I propose to transplant this term from film theory to a critical reading of a particular mode of encounter where one's speech or accent is not "synched" to one's face at the outset. Instead of addressing the audiovisual dissonance as a unique filmic expression, I use this term to look at instances where one's speech ceases to be a flat illustration of the face, and to see how it might incite an "instantaneous perceptual triage" (*The Voice in Cinema* 3) on the listener, who either prioritizes "hearing" the face or "seeing" the speech. Interestingly, the lack of correspondence between face and speech is often perceived initially in an appearance of falsehood: one is confronted and overwhelmed with a split of subjectivity and a loss of consistency; either the visual or the vocal reality will elude the listener for a moment, etching in his or her perceptive impressions asynchronously. How is it possible to proceed with the cult of reading and the cultural imperative of decoding, when face foretells and dictates how speech should be heard, while speech intrudes on the dialogue and invalidates the history of face? What sorts of "sacrifice"—the painful letting-go of our cultural habits of reading? the renouncement of the desire to know and to master?—shall we be making so as to have face and speech synched? Or, is the synch point itself an illusion of meaning and a tyranny of interpretation, and we should instead prolong the moment of dissonance and contradiction?

Reading the interpersonal encounter as an audiovisual spectacle, my emphasis is not on grasping face and speech as separate phenomena. Quite the opposite: I aim to show that face does not appeal to vision alone; it possesses an auditory dimension that works through activating an imagined and visualized speech. Similarly, speech is not only heard but also seen. When speech outflows its physical container, it redoes the face by anchoring it to or disentangling it from the facial image invoked by that speech. Disney's feature films, for instance, are exemplary in maneuvering the voice (by having the characters speak with a certain accent or in an idiosyncratic way) to build up and enrich the animated sketch of the characters. While images themselves—the Evil Queen with dark eye shadows, Snow White with plump face and innocent blushes—often already suggest the desired and appropriate moral attitudes from the audience, the voice intensifies the dramatic potential of the face and the image. In a way, the voice is what anchors the interiority (and sometimes the ethnic and cultural origin) of the character to its face. Isn't the cheerful Italian accent of Tony in *Lady and the Tramp* (1955) enough to convey that he is a comic figure; has dark hair and moustache; and cooks well?[1]

The questions that this chapter aims to address are the following: How does speech and voice sound when it comes not from the depth of the mouth but from the surface of the face? How does the imagined voice act on the actually heard voice? How is the face made to speak? Such questions had raised little concern until film started to talk. Chion observes in his book *The Voice in Cinema* (1999) that "Greta Garbo's voice was hoarse and had a Swedish accent, the producers of her first talkie, Anna Christie, wondered whether audiences would put up with it. John Gilbert's somewhat high and nasal voice spelled the ruin of his career" (12). Chion uses these instances to say that it is voice, rather than speech or language, that accounts for the lure of talking film, considering the fact that speech and language was already integrated in silent cinema through intertitles. Here I wish to add that the transition from silent cinema to talking film is not equal to a passage from silence to sound or from visualized speech to heard voice. The filmic image is "the talking picture" (1) throughout; it is only after the soundtrack was put into use that the image could be silent or speak otherwise. If the voice and accent of an actor turns out to be the spoiler of his well-received face, this disappointment is not only owing to the "harsh" reality of his vocal attributes but is also brought about by the viewer's experience of having to silence the visualized voice. For some people, the disappointment of talking film is rather that it finalizes the voice while leaving very little room for imagination.

On the other hand, the visualized voice and speech can also "shroud" the real one. To study how non-language factors affect American undergraduates' evaluations of non-native teaching assistants, Donald L. Rubin has carried out several sociolinguistic studies throughout the years. In one study, the participants were presented with a slide photograph of either a Caucasian or an Asian (Chinese) woman, while listening to a tape-recorded lecture. The models, Rubin explains, "were similarly dressed, were of similar size and hair style, and were photographed in the same setting and pose (standing at a lecturn [sic] in front of a chalkboard)" (514). And the lecture was "recorded by a single speaker, a doctoral student in speech communication, a native

---

[1] In *English with an Accent: Language, ideology, and discrimination in the United States* (1997), the linguist Rosina Lippi-Green gives a detailed analysis of the language use in Disney's animated feature films released in the years 1938-1994. She argues that in these films various languages, dialects, and accents are deployed to conjure up and reinforce linguistic and social stereotypes, and, as a consequence, to teach children how to discriminate. See Lippi-Green 79-103.

speaker of English raised in central Ohio." In other words, the participants were listening to *the same tape record* (and therefore the same voice and speech), whereas the different images of instructors from Caucasian or Asian background were intended to make them believe that the speech was issued from that person. Afterwards, the participants were asked to complete the homophily instrument, which contained items to check ethnicity manipulation and to measure the participants' impressions of the instructor's accent and teaching competence (515). The result showed that the accent of the Asian instructor were rated as "more foreign and less standard" (518), and the listening comprehension of the participants was undermined as well "simply by identifying (visually) the instructor as Asian" (519).

Interestingly and ironically, the foreign accent, in this case, is more visually configured than actually heard. It seems as if the visual clues have too strong of impacts that they short-circuit the auditory perception of the participants. Rubin's analysis demonstrates that the perceived ethnicity of the instructor is correlated with the perceived foreignness of the accent. However, Rubin offers no explanation of how the slide photograph manages to manipulate participants' perceptions of ethnicity. I suggest that since the models have the same dress, hairstyle, and posture, their ethnicities are primarily manifested and grasped through their facial traits. The face is imbued with signifying possibilities. It condenses prominent features that might encode ethnic and racial differences—the color of the skin, the shape of the eyes, the angle of the nose (pointed or flat), the thickness of the lips...

In her scholarly and autobiographical book *On Not Speaking Chinese* (2004), the cultural theorist Ien Ang observes as well that there is an intimate link between one's facial/bodily features and perceived ethnicity. Ang writes,

> This experience in itself then was a sign of the inescapability of my notional Chineseness, inscribed as it was on the very surface of my body, much like what Frantz Fanon (1970) has called the 'corporeal malediction' of the fact of his blackness. The 'corporeal malediction' of Chineseness, of course, related to the 'fact of yellowness,' identifiable among others by those famous 'slanted eyes'. (28–29)

For some people, Ang's Chineseness is a superficial fact conveyed through her yellow skin and slanted eyes, although her personal trajectory does not have much to do with China. Ang mentions that she was born in Indonesia, was raised and educated in the Netherlands, and later moved to Australia. She is only, to use Ang's own words, "inescapably Chinese by descent" (36). However, the slanted eyes, conceived as a corporeal revelation of her ethnicity, constantly undo the complexity of her transcultural and translingual trajectory, making her personal history a deviant compared with her facialized ethnic origin.

Later in that book, Ang writes, "The typical conversation would run like this, as many non-whites in Europe would be able to testify: 'Where are you from?' 'From Holland.' 'No, where are you *really* from?'" (29; emphasis added). How could Ang come from somewhere else other than her facial landscape? Implicit in this inquiry accentuated by the word "*really*" is an unquestioned presumption of origin and originality as a facialized ethnicity, which appears to rule out the possibility for Ang to use the Netherlands as the starting point of her narrative and to seek different modes of intimacy in relation to her history and origin. Ang offers another version of this encounter: "Despite my perfect Dutch and my assimilated lifestyle, people wanted to know 'where are you from?', and were never satisfied when I answered simply, 'from Holland'" (10–11). This time, even though her perfect Dutch *sounds* like a valid testimony to the place of origin that Ang chooses to reference, she is not *seen* as a convincing "*eye*witness" to this claim. Her eyes are too "slanted" to pass, too "slanted" to dispute with the listeners who pinpoint the place of origin in her bodily and facial features.

Ang's experience illuminates how one's origin and ethnicity can appear as a mystery and a problem, as one's speech counterpoints her facial image. "I look Chinese. Why, then, don't I speak Chinese? (23)"—this is the question Ang is constantly invited and even made to ruminate on. Ang recalls,

> So it was one day that a self-assured, Dutch, white, middle-class, Marxist leftist, asked me, 'Do you speak Chinese?' I said no. 'What a fake Chinese you are!', was his only mildly kidding response, thereby unwittingly but aggressively adopting the disdainful position of judge to sift 'real' from 'fake' Chinese. (30)

I argue that this "disdainful position of judge" becomes even more convenient when one's language and accent fail to be merged with the visualized speech stated by one's face. As Ang's perfect Dutch, with no trail of a foreign accent, cannot sustain her obvious non-Dutch appearance, "Do you speak Chinese?" becomes a question that aims to verify an anticipated co-incidence between her face and speech. However, to that man's disappointment, the synch point refuses to come. Labeling her as "a fake Chinese," the man seems to suggest that Ang's ethnicity is merely a visual trap, whereas her speech is nothing but a lame dub.

The question is, will it help if Ang "chooses" to narrate an ethnicity and origin that is more "faithful" to her face? Will the incongruence of her face, speech, and ethnicity cease to give her a hard time if Ang is relocated to a place where her foreignness does not stand out immediately? Regarding this issue, Ang recounts her experience of being invited to a conference in Taiwan:

> Imagining my Taiwanese audience, I felt I couldn't open my mouth in front of them without explaining why I, a person with stereotypical Chinese physical characteristics, could not speak to them in Chinese [...] I expected much questioning, which turned out to be more than warranted: again and again, people on the streets, in shops, restaurants and so on were puzzled and mystified that I couldn't understand them when they talked to me in Chinese. So my decision to present a semi-autobiographical paper on the historical and cultural peculiarities of 'not speaking Chinese' resonated intimately with this experience. It was the beginning of an almost decade-long engagement with the predicaments of 'Chineseness' in diaspora. In Taiwan I was different because I couldn't speak Chinese; in the West I was different because I looked Chinese. (vii)

The dilemma of Ang is that there is perceived to be a mismatch between her face and speech, and it does not resolve even when she goes "back" to the place where people from the other part of the world often think she should come from. When she seems to visually blend in, her inability to speak Chinese equally poses a problem: Ang has to respond to people's "innocent" and persistent curiosity while offering a piece of explanation to justify her English. Why, then, doesn't she speak Chinese, the language that resounds across her facial landscape, that testifies to her origin, and that is made to determine whether her ethnicized face is "real" or "fake"?

Dynamics of the Audiovisual Configuration: Three Modalities

A Facial Treatment of Speech: Does It Pass or Not?
What is the face? When we envisage the face, we speak of the eyes, the nose, the mouth, the chin, the forehead, the cheeks. Yet, do these elements configure the face as a flat surface that is potentially exhaustible by the visual perception? Or, is the face also bound to an internal depth from which gazes are averted and voices are resonated?

"Oddly enough, it is a face: the *white wall/black hole* system. A broad face with white cheeks, a chalk face with eyes cut in for a black hole," comment Deleuze and Guattari in "Year Zero: Faciality" (167), a less-discussed chapter from their philosophical book *A Thousand Plateaus: Capitalism and Schizophrenia* (1987). Here the rhetoric of the white wall/black hole system divides the face into two mechanisms: On the one hand, we see the forehead, the cheeks, and the chin, gently rippling over the smooth surface of the face. On the other hand, there are the eyes, the nose, and the mouth, swimming away from the regime of perception governed predominantly by vision, and diving deep into dark and invisible internal organs of the body. For Deleuze and Guattari, the different ways in which these two mechanisms are combined— "either black holes distribute themselves on the white wall, or the white walls unravels and moves toward a black hole combining all black holes, hurtling them together or making them 'crest'"— have manufactured the face into "*an abstract machine of faciality (visagéité)*" (168). No faces are ready-made. No faces can be comprehended and grasped a priori. The face is indecisive before the pattern of the "holey surface" (170) becomes clear or traceable. Hence, Deleuze and Guattari cry out, "*The face, what a horror.* It is naturally a lunar landscape, with its pores, planes, matts, bright colors, whiteness, and holes: there is no need for a close-up to make it inhuman; it is naturally a close-up, and naturally inhuman, a monstrous hood" (190).

Noticeably, for Deleuze and Guattari, the face is a horror story insofar as it registers madness and hallucination *in* vision. Their concern of the horror of the face is not *beyond* vision: what creeps in through holes and ruptures and what repels vision and luminosity do not find their way into their visualized imagination of horror. Unlike Edvard Munch's screaming figure, the face that concerns Deleuze and Guattari barely screams, let alone becomes contorted and screwed because of the scream. It is so because their rhetoric of the black hole is modeled on the eyes instead of the mouth—"a chalk face with eyes cut in for a black hole" (167). Later in their book, Deleuze and Guattari extend the metaphor of the white wall/black hole system in cinematic terms. The white wall is hollowed out into a "frame or screen" upon which "a suggestive whiteness" is dancing and flickering, whereas the black hole is specified as "the camera, the third eye" that captures and imparts visual impressions (168).

Throughout their discussion, Deleuze and Guattari never completely forgo the idea of viewing the face as "a visual percept" (168). The face sees and is being seen. The white wall/black hole system is centered on the eyes and thus, as Deleuze and Guattari imply, should be efficiently approached through the visual perception. Although when they turn to the face in terms of the mother/child relation, they seem to suggest that another set of sensations other than the visual—namely, the "manual, buccal, or cutaneous proprioceptive sensations"—may also play a role in the operation of the faciality machine, it does not make them hesitate to call it a "four-eye machine" (169). Because "the mother's face appears for the child to use as a guide in finding the breast," Deleuze and Guattari comment, "[t]his perception very quickly assumes decisive importance for the acting of eating, in relation to the breast as a *volume* and the mouth as a *cavity*, both experienced through touch" (169–70; emphasis added). Since Deleuze and Guattari explicitly propose not to mistake the surface-hole system of the face with "the volume-cavity system proper to the (proprioceptive) body" (170), the infantile mouth, at least in this scenario, is not a hole but a cavity and, therefore, belongs not to face but to head and body.

In his solo-authored chapter on faces in *The Machinic Unconscious* (1979/2011), Guattari narrows down the functionality of the face to a "facializing eye-nose-forehead triangle that collects, formalizes, neutralizes, and crushes the specific traits of the other semiotic components" (75). In this formulation, the mouth is obviously precluded from the triangular center and is rendered secondary to the abstract machine of faciality. In a sense, if the face does possess the quality of a cinematic experience, it is rather from the silent cinema that Deleuze and Guattari seem to draw inspiration. Like in the silent cinema where sounds and voice appeal to eyes alone in the form of intertitles and images, Deleuze and Guattari's face "speaks" the words of a flat screen, which possess no such potential to be disrupted and invalidated by the outflow of voice and speech from the dark holes.

The faces of the silent cinema, as I have mentioned, do have languages—although they are not explicitly vocalized and heard. Deleuze and Guattari, with no intention of integrating the mouth into the face, have attended to the relation between face and language:

> The face is not an envelope exterior to the person who speaks, thinks, or feels. The form of the signifier in language, even its units, would remain indeterminate if the potential listener did not use the face of the speaker to guide his or her choices ("Hey, he seems angry…"; "He couldn't say it…"; "You see my face when I'm talking to you…"; "look at me carefully…"). A child, woman, mother, man, father, boss, teacher, police officer, does not speak a general language but one whose signifying traits are indexed to specific faciality traits. (167-168)

I would say that Deleuze and Guattari consider the simile of the envelop inadequate and misleading because: first, face does not form a concrete and traceable enclosure that gives thoughts, speeches, and feelings a sense of unity and uniqueness. Second, the relation between face and thoughts, speeches, and feelings is not separable as it is in the case of the envelope and the letter, which more or less retains a distinction between form and content. For Deleuze and Guattari, face is rather within the signifying possibilities of language: it not only gives words a visually portable and tangible context, which guides the listener through the ambivalent unfolding of meanings, but also contributes to what Mikhail Bakhtin considers to be the heteroglossia of language that is "shot through with intentions and accents" (Bakhtin 293). "A child, woman, mother, man, father, boss, teacher, police officer": isn't the stratification of languages indexical to the specific facial features of various social groups? Doesn't it explain why linguistic passing, when not accompanied by facial and bodily attunements, can be easily picked up as uncanny or "fake"? This is why, in the film *Pygmalion* (1938), even before Professor Henry Higgins begins to train the flower girl Eliza to get rid of her "dreadful" Cockney accent—in order to pass her off as a duchess, he orders Mrs. Pearce to "take and clean her. Take off all her clothes and burn them." In the scenes that follow, Eliza is taught to waltz and to articulate the letter "h" at the beginning of a word; she has to learn to address people by their title and to drink soup silently; she will refrain from using slang words and use the spoon to clink her teacup. To pass as a duchess, it is not enough to "talk grammar" or to "talk like a lady." She has to transform herself in its entirety, which, in the end, has left her with the questions "What am I fit for? What have you left me fit for? Where am I to go? Where am I to do? What has become of me?" Her newly acquired body and accent, as Eliza painfully realizes, make her unfit for anything but a lady.

Deleuze and Guattari observe that not all the signs with which the face is entangled are of a linguistic nature. The repercussion between face and signs resounds in all types of "constellation of significances and interpretations," which range from non-linguistic interchanges to coded iconographic images. However, what makes the face crucial to language is that it anchors words and expressions against the endless chain of signification and therefore constitutes the "condition of possibility" for language to arise from noise (180). Deleuze and Guattari write, "Moreover, it is absurd to believe that language as such can convey a message. A language is always embedded in the faces that announce its statements and ballast them in relation to the signifiers in progress and subjects concerned" (179). Deleuze and Guattari do not view communication as an intrinsic value of language, which makes their philosophy partake in the linguistic turn arising from the early twentieth century. At the same time, their philosophy of language is distinct from the trend of structuralism during that period, which aims to situate meaning primarily in the circulation of signifiers. Assigning face to language, Deleuze and Guattari "burden" language with its social weight and have words circulate in a much bigger chain that is composed of discourses, fields, subjects, and various social groups.

Guattari, in his book *The Machinic Unconscious*, gives a thorough reflection on the implications of the entanglement between face and language:

> [I]t is primarily through its facial substance that language escapes itself, fleeing in all directions. Every proposition only receives its social weight of truth insofar as a "service" faciality takes charge of it. Every segment of signifying discourse is a tributary of faciality traits that "manages" its morphemes, that supports them in relation with dominant significations or deprives them of their sense. Iconic faciality does not depend on signifying binary machines that would have to account for it; it is on the contrary signifying linguistics that comes to be stabilized by calling on the binary machine of faciality. (84)

What concerns Guattari here is not only that faciality traits might contribute to linguistic signification; above all, he is fascinated by how the binary machine of faciality manages to impose on language a similar bipolar structure—a structure that can be condensed into the question "Does it pass or not, is it made of signification?" (95).

Similarly, in their collaborative work *A Thousand Plateaus*, Deleuze and Guattari point out that there is a "yes-no" structure implicit in the face. "The face is not a universal. It is not even that of the white man; it is the White Man himself, with his broad white cheeks and the black hole of his eyes. The face is Christ. The face is the typical European, what Ezra Pound called the average sensual man, in short, the ordinary everyday Erotomaniac" (176). It is clear here that the claim of the face being an abstract machine does not imply that the face is abstract and neutral. Quite the opposite: Deleuze and Guattari pinpoint White Man, the face of Christ, and the typical European face as the proto and supreme type for all faces; and all the other constellations of facial traits are merely tolerated and measured by "degrees of deviance in relation to the White-Man face." Based on this observation, Deleuze and Guattari argue that racism is not a simple matter of otherness and alterity that is statically found. The logic of racism is not difference but sameness: it happens whenever the spread of sameness meets a strain of resistance—"[t]here are only people who should be like us and whose crime it is not to be" (178).

In his single-authored book, Guattari proposes a distinction between *face-types* and *face-occurrences* (78). According to him, the *face-type* possesses a quality of tranquility and reassurance (82). It is closely tied to the feeling of everydayness, since it "functions as an indicator of 'normality'" and emphatically conveys the message that "nothing happens" (78). In contrast, the *face-occurrence* refers to singular and idiosyncratic facial traits that turn out to be incompatible with the desired reality of averageness. Its deviation is often taken as senseless. It leaves a touch of fear and anxiety on the face itself, which occasionally incites a similar sensation on the beholder. These two modalities betoken the logic of "faciality as binary signifying machine" (83), which "intervenes to delimit what is legitimate from what is not" (75). This point, as I have mentioned, is hinted in Deleuze and Guattari's collaborative piece. Yet, it is Guattari who expands this binary logic of faciality to the functionality of linguistic signification. Aware of (and partially embracing) Ferdinand de Saussure's structuralist linguistic theory, Guattari is more interested in pushing the issue of language in another direction: If language is a formal system that consists of differential signs referencing to one another ad infinitum, how exactly does the social stratification of language happen? At what point does the indifferent flow of signs become imbued with binary value judgments, bifurcating into the mainstream of the standard and the "deviant" branch of the vulgar?

To reconcile conflicts between the circular and the ramifying momentum of language, Guattari introduces the binary signifying machine of faciality into the mechanism of linguistic signification, saying that "[t]hrough the bias of consciential components of faciality, a semiotic production can always be reduced to the state of normalized signification. Signifying power nods its head; that's ok for a signification! It raises its eyebrows: this means that there is a danger of nonsense, or that of a previous meaning being annulled" (84). For Guattari, the ramification of value judgments follows after the installation of the supreme signifier, which is validated by the "transcendental referential faciality" (81). Interestingly, here Guattari's choice of phrases is thought-provoking: "nodding the head" guarantees the continuity of conversation and the passage of signifiers through the facial sieve, whereas "raising eyebrows" is a visual echo of senselessness that indicates that the outflow of signification is blocked. The response to the question "does it pass or not" is embodied in and reduced to a series of facial movements. "With the infinite range of facial movements," writes Guattari, "facialized consciousness will only retain the significative passages in extreme cases, the threats of crossing the deviant-types" (96). To put it differently, Guattari believes that the faciality machine should be accessed through its product, "the infinite range of facial movements"; and the operation of the faciality machine will become identifiable as soon as the deviant-types are found with multiple layers of deviance. For instance, as Guattari observes, "tan skin, beyond a certain threshold, will spark mistrust ("it's a foreigner, an Arab, a Jew, a gipsy"), especially if it is associated with a "deviant" linguistic accent" (96). The audibility of the deviant speech magnifies the effect of the faciality machine and interferes with how the facial image is received and interpreted.

It is at this point, I argue, that Guattari temporarily "deviates" from a silent cinematic reading of face and speech. His vision is not restricted to a "facial treatment of speech" (99) but expands to a linguistic reading of face. However, the way in which Guattari deploys the audiovisual devices of face and speech is still quite conventional. In the spirit of a realist director, his analysis features a synchronization of face and speech (tan skin and a "deviant" accent), which aims to intensify the dramatic revelation of the deviant facial types. Besides this conceptualization of face being the visual logic of speech, I will add two other modalities to spell out the dynamics of the audiovisual configuration of face and speech, which, I contend, are no less significant and compelling to understand how deviant-types are produced.

A Vocal Treatment of Face: How I Am Heard, How I Am Seen

To begin with, this modality reverses the formulation proposed by Deleuze and Guattari. Instead of giving a facial treatment of speech, it centers on the role of speech in animating and inscribing face in a sensory continuum. The Polish American writer and academic Eva Hoffman, in her memoir *Lost in Translation: Life in a New Language*, notices that her experiences of learning to speak a new language and settling down in another country have put her in situations in which she finds her speech either mobilize or cancel out her face. She writes,

> Because I'm not heard, I feel I am not seen. My words often seem to baffle others. They are inappropriate, or forced, or just plain incomprehensible. People look at me with puzzlement; they mumble something in response—something that doesn't hit home. Anyway, the back and forth of conversation is different here. People often don't answer each other. But the mat look in their eyes as they listen to me cancels my face, flattens my features. The mobility of my face comes from the mobility of the words coming to the surface and the feelings that drive them. Its vividness is sparked by the locking of an answering gaze, by the quickness

of understanding. But now I can't feel how my face lights up from inside; I don't receive from others the reflected movement of its expressions, its living speech. People look past me as we speak. What do I look like, here? Imperceptible, I think; impalpable, neutral, faceless. (147)

Hoffman implies that speaking is a face-bestowing or face-rebuffing activity. The very audibility and answerability of her speech is decisive in rendering her face visible to others. Because her speech fails to forge a smooth way to the ears of others, she feels that her face cannot imprint any visual or sensuous impressions. Moreover, how she experiences her face is mirrored through the facial and vocal responses of others: not only is the "sickness" of her speech diagnosed by a mumbled response but also the faceless state of her appearance is symptomized by the puzzled look on other people's faces. Hoffman says, "I can't feel how my face lights up from inside. I don't receive from others the reflected movement of its expressions, its living speech." If Hoffman's usage of the phrase "light[ing] up" implies that the face remains a visual percept for her, the visuality of the face is at least partially mediated and manifested through its vocal resonance in another person, which, according to Hoffman, constitutes the "living speech" of the face.

By having the face "synched" not only to its own speech but also to that of others, this modality gives the face away to a passive discursive construction. This subtle shift leads to a set of questions different from the ones that Deleuze and Guattari address. It asks: How does the speech of others—which is often emitted from the locus of discourse and ideology—contour and formalize the face, sharpening certain features while effacing others? If the other's speech can be conceived as an echo of one's face, is there a certain syntax and grammar from which the face originates? Here I will turn to the artist Lorna Simpson's work *Twenty Questions (A Sampler)* (1986), which offers a fine conceptual model for theorizing the relation between face and discourse.

Twenty Questions (A Sampler) showcases a series of faceless portraits, probably of the same black young woman. No clear clues are given to tell whether the portrait is about the back of a head or a face covered by thick black hair. Whereas each portrait seems to repeat one another identically, five questions beneath the portraits are mounted—"Is she pretty as a picture," "or clear as a crystal," "or pure as a lily," "or black as coal," "or sharp as a razor." Although all these questions follow a similar sentence structure, the variations of words reinscribe the series of identical figures into a linearized refrain. The title of this work, *Twenty Questions*, references the popular spoken parlor game in which players take turns to ask questions that can be simply answered by "yes" or "no."[2] While the face of the figure remains hidden throughout, the differentiating questions are mounted into a crescendo one by one, which gradually unmasks the face and makes its revelation a matter of proximity and contradiction in relation to the verbal inquiries.

Combining static, faceless portraits with non-identical polar questions, this piece introduces a way of reinterpreting the binary signifying machine of faciality proposed by Deleuze and Guattari as a linguistic and discursive issue. As we have mentioned, for Deleuze and Guattari, it is the face—with its facial traits split into transcendental prototypes and phenomenal divergence-occurrences—that imposes a binary signifying structure on language. In contrast, Simpson's work suggests the other way around: when the face is not readily accessible (and thus remains more or less inhuman), it is the speech of others, whose inquiries amount to what Hoffman calls "the reflected movement of its [the face's] expressions, its living speech" (147), that lends an imaginary face to the figure. Noticeably, what structures "its living speech" of the face, in this scenario, is a yes-no question that instructs one to hinge the face on a series of other things—a picture, a crystal, a lily, coal, and a razor. The selection of these things might be random, yet they are nonetheless composed into a frame of reference against which the quality of the face—is it pretty, clear, pure, black, or sharp—is measured and manifested.

Can the face be pretty, even though not as pretty as a picture? Can the face be black, although not as black as coal? The yes-or-no structure of these questions makes the subtlety of the face largely diluted and irrelevant. It is beside the point to ask whether or not the face has intrinsic values and qualities—since even if it has something that resembles essence and singularity, it will not be surfaced unless together with other objects, statements, discourses. Face is a word. It, too, circulates in a chain of signifiers, whose meanings become tangible through the mechanism of *différance*. *Twenty Questions*, therefore, adds the dimension of the other's speech into Deleuze and Guattari's discussion of face and language. Since the emergence of the face is partially dependent on the speech of others, it is more than a static entity or a fixed context from which one can take clues to navigate through the ambiguity of words and to complete the intention of the speaker. The face is a matter of becoming that takes form from words. It is sustained by the back-and-forth movements of speech and articulated within or beyond the locus of discourse and ideology.

2   For a description of the rules and origin of this parlor game, see Walsorth (1882).

In another piece of work from Simpson, *Easy for Who to Say* (1989), again, we notice a repetition of identical faceless figures. Yet this time, a series of vowels—A, E, I, O, U—have taken the place of the face, which reminds one of an exaggerated opening of the mouth that is about to outgrow the size of the face. Here the act of speaking and voicing stands very much in tension with the face. The vowels reconstitute the face into a vocal cavity, whereas its depth is flattened out into sheer whiteness. The image of speaking and the speaking of image become interchangeable. Although these vowels may point to multiple words beginning with the same voiced letters, the matching words beneath the figure—AMNESIA, ERROR, INDIFFERENCE, OMISSION, UNCIVIL—propose a way of lip-reading, if not the only way. To some extent, these labeling words threaten to enable a vocal enclosure of the face, making it circulate in terms of a negative *acoustic image*: she becomes the one who mumbles monosyllables, who talks unintelligibly, who is defaced by her speech. Unlike the attentive face-reader that Deleuze and Guattari have in mind, when confronted with an inarticulate speaker, the listener does not always try to pick up facial clues to contextualize the utterance. On the contrary, the listener might take advantage of it and string the dismantled syllables in a way that is agreeable to his or her own narrative impulse.

The face is generated and sustained by speech—not only the speech of oneself, but also the speech of others. This aspect is crucial to understanding the production of deviant-types. When Deleuze and Guattari talk about racism, the parameter is shifted from the difference of the skin color to "degrees of deviance in relation to the White-Man face" (178). This is not to undermine the role of the skin tone in triggering racial bias and discrimination. The skin tone, for Deleuze and Guattari, is what stands out from the body and works along with other facial traits to communicate racial deviance and to "justify" injustice. However, be it bound to face or skin tone, here, racism appears to be grasped primarily as a *visual drama*. This way of looking, I suggest, is convenient to explain the content of the expression—"Look, a Negro!" (93), a racist comment that Frantz Fanon mentions in *Black Skin, White Masks* (1952/2008). Yet, it is inadequate to account for the utterance itself and its relation to visual dynamics. Indeed, this offensive address is meant to activate a specific way of looking and to transform the person in question into a visual and racial object. Racism is a visual scheme, but when one says "a Negro," it is speech that shovels off the ambiguity of vision by prescribing not only what to see but also how to see it. Therefore, I propose to look at racism as an *audiovisual* spectacle, whose operation depends upon a triangular movement among face, speech, and discourse.

First of all, face and speech do not work separately to convey racial difference. If the color of one's skin is seen as a deficit, it can be more or less compensated by vocal and linguistic approximation to the speaking manner of the "right" skin tone. As Fanon observes, "The Negro of the Antilles will be proportionately whiter—that is, he will come closer to being a real human being—in direct ratio to his mastery of the French language" (8). Here the skin tone is clearly being heard. It can be "corrected" and "elevated" through feeding the ears with "uncorrupted" native-like sounds. Fanon says, "In any group of young men in the Antilles, the one who expresses himself well, who has mastered the language, is inordinately feared; keep an eye on that one, he is almost white" (11). For people of the Antilles, to speak French well means to put on a white skin and to distance oneself from the local community. Language contours corporeal features, from which the dramatic play of self and other, intimacy and hostility, faith and betrayal is set out.

Secondly, the racialized type of faciality is nonetheless an acoustic image. The "guilt" of being unlike *us* concerns not only how one looks but also how one speaks. It is the color of the tongue—the "dark" tongue, "corrupted," "unintelligible"—that makes us flinch. Fanon writes, "For the Negro knows that over there in France there is a stereotype of him that will fasten on to him at the pier in Le Havre or Marseille: 'Ah come from Mahtinique, it's the fuhst time Ah've eveh come to France.' He knows that what the poets call the *divine gurgling* (listen to Creole) is only a halfway house between pidgin-nigger and French" (10). The "Negro": he is the "divine gurgler," the one who claims our language without our consent, the one who ruins our language by cutting his tongue loose, the one who tinges our language with the color of his skin—and he dares to speak to us with that tongue!

Of course, he does not mean to offend people by speaking this way. He himself also wants to be a good "nigger"—which means, to talk "properly," to talk what Léon-G. Damas calls "the French of France/the Frenchman's French/French French" (Damas, qtd. in Fanon 10). If his skin is unlikely to undergo drastic transformation, he could, at least, declare war against his tongue:

> The Negro arriving in France will react against the myth of the *R*-eating man from Martinique. He will become aware of it, and he will really go to war against it. He will practice not only rolling his *R* but embroidering it. Furtively observing the slightest reactions of others, listening to his own speech, suspicious of his own tongue—a wretchedly lazy organ—he will lock himself into his room and read aloud for hours—desperately determined to learn *diction*.

> Recently an acquaintance told me a story. A Martinique Negro landed at Le Havre and went into a bar. With the utmost self-confidence he called, "Wait*errr*! Bing me a beeya." Here is a genuine intoxication. Resolved not to fit the myth of the nigger-who-eats-his-*R*'s, he had acquired a fine supply of them but allocated it badly. (11)

From the *R*-eating man to the *R*-supplier: Does his tongue have a sense of decency? What can it do save for eating, gurgling, making noise? Well, it can perform *white*face. It can put on an exaggerated curl and perform the white over the top. All in all, since the color of his skin makes his racial difference visible, his tongue expressively tells what he is "lacking" and what he wishes to proliferate without restraint. His skin may have something to do with *race*, whereas his tongue—teemed with an outspoken desire of being otherwise and making it "right"—stages the audiovisual spectacle of *racism*.

Here we arrive at an acoustic image of the "Negro." He is a "divine gurgler," an *R*-eater, and, we should also add, a "jabberer." Fanon writes, "It is said that the Negro loves to jabber. In my own case, when I think of the word jabber I see a gay group of children calling and shouting for the sake of calling and shouting" (15–16). This acoustic image of jabbering, compared with the plain "fact" of the skin color, seems to offer one a scientifically justified claim to racism. Fanon explains, "The Negro loves to jabber, and from this theory it is not a long road that leads to a new proposition: The Negro is just a child. The psychoanalysts have a fine start here, and the term *orality* is soon heard" (16). Here psychoanalysis gives the acoustic image of the "Negro" its ready-made ideology: he who loves jabbering is a child, a mentally and physically underdeveloped being. His "inferiority" is not as superficial as his skin. And jabbering is a neurosis symptom of being a "Negro," who is obsessed with oral stimulation, incapable of moving beyond the primitive oral organization of libido.

Lastly, racism invents deviant facial and acoustic images either by disregarding and misinterpreting one's words and speech or by ventriloquizing the visualized speech of that face. With Simpson's work *Easy for Who to Say*, I have shown how the speech of others may appropriate one's attempts of voicing, weaving them into a web of discourse that arrests meanings before they become polyphonic. The acoustic images of the "Negro" listed by Fanon attest as well to this point. However, how does the visualized speech come to discourse's aid? Here again, Fanon has an acute awareness:

> To speak pidgin to a Negro makes him angry, because he himself is a pidgin-nigger-talker. But, I will be told, there is no wish, no intention

> to anger him. I grant this; but it is just this absence of wish, this lack of interest, this indifference, this automatic manner of classifying him, imprisoning him, primitivizing him, decivilizing him, that makes him angry. (20)

> To make him talk pidgin is to fasten him to the effigy of him, to snare him, to imprison him, the eternal victim of an essence, of an *appearance* for which he is not responsible. (22)

Face-to-face with a "Negro," the white man begins to speak pidgin. He is not a racist, the white man claims. Indeed, he is only a "realist" filmmaker who tries to give a faithful representation of the sound of an image. He sees a "Negro," so he talks "black." He expresses what he sees in a vocal and acoustic register. In fact, talking pidgin to a black person is "to make him talk pidgin," even though he might not "naturally" speak that way. It is to stuff his mouth with pidgin, to impose the "deviant" speech on him. The implicit message is this: this is what is expected from you; this is how you should sound; this is your acoustic *appearance*. Do not even try to fool me.

Face and Speech Unsynched: "I Expected a Different Accent"

The following modality has to do with a situation I have mentioned at the beginning of this chapter. It aims to crystalize the moment where the expected correspondence of face and speech does not happen instantly and smoothly. The facial image flickers on the screen of perception, whereas the sound and speech seem to oscillate both inside and outside the image. In *Audio-Vision: Sound on Screen*, Michel Chion writes,

> But when we say in disappointment that "the sound and image don't go together well," we should not blame it exclusively on the inferior quality of the reproduction of reality. For this situation merely echoes a phenomenon we are generally blind to. In concrete experience itself, independent from cinema, they sometimes don't go together either.
>
> The most familiar example is the "mismatch" of an individual's voice and face when we have had the experience of getting to know one of them well before discovering the other. We never fail to be surprised, even shocked, when we complete the picture. (97)

Here Chion gives an example of a real-life audiovisual counterpoint. As one knows a person first by voice (over the phone, for example), one may find that upon meeting her, the concurrence of her voice and face seems peculiar or unexpected. The effect of perceptive disjunction, in this case, results from the asynchronous exposure to voice and face. What this chapter aims to say, however, is that such effect may take place even when face and speech are not subject to a linear unfolding. One can be seen and heard at the same time, yet the speech may still sound at odds with the face, or simply becomes silenced by the "visualized" speech.

Regarding this modality, I have recounted the experience of Tomasz. Admittedly, what happened to him is absurd and amusing—this is where our interpretation usually stops. His white Caucasian face tames our reading, making it impossible to elevate the audiovisual counterpoint to a point of critical theory. Therefore, I wish to add another case recorded by Lucille Lok-Sun Ngan and Chan Kwok-bun in their book *The Chinese Face in Australia* (2012):

> Don, whose family has resided in Australia since the late 1800s, pointed out, "when people meet me at the church I go to, which is mainly Anglo-based, they may not say it straight away but after a while they always say 'I expected a different accent.'" Most people, including both Anglo-Australians and Chinese, usually do not expect him, a person with a Chinese face, to speak in fluent English, with Australian accent, because of his physical appearance. (136)

The reality of having a Chinese face, as Don's experience shows, seems to be incompatible with the linguistic reality of his Australian accent. When these two conflicting realities are perceived to merge, it provokes confusion and curiosity. In this case, the verbal and visual realities march through one's perception in uneven paces, hinging the racialized and ethnicized encounter precisely upon the audiovisual counterpoint of face and speech.

With this concept of the audiovisual counterpoint, I wish to reconceptualize racialized and ethnicized encounters as *audiovisual spectacles* that can be approached through mapping out the perceptive triage between face and speech. Recently, scholars like Rey Chow and Pooja Rangan observe that politics of racism and postcolonial experiences are predominantly depicted in terms of visual dynamics. Racial alterity is often thought to manifest itself on the surface of the skin, which is picked up and retrospectively projected in the psyche of the racialized/ethnicized other through "a paralyzing gaze that 'fixes' the other in the manner of an object: a mere thing, fetish, or spectacle" (Rangan 95). While acknowledging the importance of this visual dimension, both Chow and Rangan propose to move beyond an ocular-centric reading by turning toward voice and language, which has received little critical attention in current debates on racialization and ethnicization. In particular, Rangan points out that the dominant vocal prototype serves to trivialize other types of voice, in the sense that they are often measured in terms of their degrees of deviance to the dominant one. Rangan says, "Taking stock of the dominant vocal attributes of the radio anchor (clear, articulate, eloquent, factual, informative, newsworthy, sober, articulate, knowledgeable), Dyson observes that a 'proper voice' is frequently equated with an authoritative male voice, especially one with a deep pitch and Euro-American accent" (Rangan 103). Taking cues from Chow and Rangan, I aim to highlight the vocal and linguistic dimension of racialization and ethnicization, whose effects, especially when they are produced under the situation where face and speech seem decoupled from one another, have so far remained under the radar. However, unlike Chow and Rangan, I do not take racialized and ethnicized encounters purely as a drama of vision or a drama of voice and language. It is at the conjunction and disjunction between face and speech, I want to emphasize, that we initiate an encounter with an ethnicized/racialized other and that we learn to encode intimacy and bias into bodily forms. The audiovisual counterpoint, which uncovers and unsettles the implicit "collusion" between vision and hearing, therefore, deserves more critical attention so as to undo the violence of interpretation that is often smoothed out by the "innocence" of perception.

Incorporating filmic terms into my discussion, I intend to shift the terrain of conceptualization regarding face and speech from painting to film. In a sense, Deleuze and Guattari's illustration of the faciality machine is primarily modeled on painting, whose flatness and muteness have led the face to an absolute visual experience. Although their discussion of face and language hints at a conceptual model of the silent cinema, their line of thinking falls under the debate of *image and word* that fascinates disciplines like art history, linguistic and semiotic studies, and literary theory. As a shorthand name for the division of the visual and the verbal, the term *image and word* is often invoked to discuss questions such as whether visual representations are subject to the semiotics of language, or whether perceptions of visual images border on that of linguistic signs. In a similar vein, Deleuze and Guattari interpret language as a system composed of mute linguistic symbols, whose regime is installed through the binary logic of the faciality machine. In the end, neither image nor word will win the battle between face and speech; it is semiotics that holds on to the trophy by dematerializing face and silencing language.

The concept of the audiovisual counterpoint, therefore, reflects my overall intention in rethinking the relation of face and language under the rubric of *image and sound*. A mute face is a silent image: even when it indexes expressions and emotions that temporarily unsettle the still surface, a mute face remains flat and far away, whose call for engagement rarely combats its imposed distance except in extreme cases (intimacy, danger, anguish, etc.). In contrast, the sounds emitted through the mouth—the murmur, the groan, the mundane speaking voice—give the face an immersive effect and an elusive depth, which urge the listener to interpret and to respond to visual traces indexed on the face. To shift the terrain of discussion from *image and word* to *image and sound* means to give language back its "voice," the voice that makes language a concrete and unique instance of happening, the voice that brings the speaker back to the scene of enunciation, the voice that allows image and word to outgrow a semiotic reading of both. When face speaks and language resounds, encounters of all kinds—be it ethnicized, racialized, everyday, etc.—become an audiovisual scene where different modalities of face-and-speech configuration are played out. I will end this chapter by looking at a piece of a stage work entitled *Who Am I? Think Again* so as to explore and showcase how this concept can contribute to a critical engagement not only with everyday face-to-face encounters but also with artworks. This analysis builds on a previous discussion of the performance in *Third Text*, where I examined how the performance of failure can be productive as a translational strategy (Hui 237). Here I shift focus to explore how the artists exploit the dissonance between face and speech to investigate the implications of speaking and performing as an audiovisual spectacle.

The Spectacularity and Everydayness of the Audiovisual Scene

This stage performance is delivered at the 2013 TED Global conference in Edinburgh. The performers include Hetain Patel, a conceptual artist based in London, and his translator Yuyu Rau. Addressing an audience whose majority is composed of English speakers, Patel begins the performance by speaking Mandarin, while having Rau do the translation for him at intervals. At first glimpse, there seems to be nothing special or dubious regarding this scene of translation. Patel speaks Mandarin fluently in various tones, while looking at the audience confidently and assertively; his hands move emphatically, which confirms and completes his utterance in a visual register. Above all, Patel's appearance suggests that he might be someone who needs a translator, since his "exotic" face and costume do not readily state Englishness but are more likely to invoke the image of India. Against this backdrop of verbal and visual jigsaw puzzle, Rau starts to translate for him, "Hi, I'm Hetain. I'm an artist. And this is Yuyu, who is a dancer I have been working with. I have asked her to translate for me. If I may, I would like to tell you a little bit about myself and my artwork." The "minor" face, the strange kurta pajama, the unfamiliar speech, the presence of a translator, and the name of the artist that is hard to pronounce and remember: together they cultivate an audiovisual scene of being presented to someone who is supposedly an unassimilated *foreigner*, while fermenting the expectation of a cultural testimony from an *ethnic* artist.

The turning point occurs when Rau makes public the hypocrisy and artificiality of this "exotic" scene. Rau says, "I [Patel] was born and raised near Manchester in England, but I'm not going to say it in English to you. I'm trying to avoid any assumptions that might be made from my northern accent." To one's surprise, Patel speaks English and could even be said to be a *native* speaker of English—of course, it depends on how one defines "native." "*But I'm not going to say it in English to you*," says Patel. Generally speaking, a shared language may help the artist to communicate his message efficiently and to strengthen the bond with the audience. Especially when it comes to the so-called "ethnic" artist, whose artworks do not take root and blossom in Western art traditions, the ability to articulate his artistic intentions and life stories in English is no doubt advantageous for the artworks to reach out to a bigger audience. This is not only about the effect of familiarity created by the linguistic bond, since the language barrier can easily be overcome by translation; more importantly, knowing the language implies that the artist at least has some awareness of Western art canons and practices and thus is able to address and play with expectations that the Western audience may embrace. Yet, by deliberately not speaking English, which happens to be his mother tongue, Patel rejects playing the role of the "authentic" and immediate interpreter of his artwork. He refuses to harmonize the foreign elements that make his performance a morning India bazaar. Estranging himself linguistically from his audience, Patel makes his face and speech amount to a spectacle of exoticism. He caters to it while making it audibly strange.

Besides this explicit message about Patel's deliberate and peculiar choice of language, this moment of revelation surfaces the absurdity and redundancy of translation. Why does Patel need a non-native speaker of English to translate for him if he speaks perfect English himself? What makes him want to hide his northern English accent? "*But I am not going to say it in English to you*," proudly claims Patel through his translator. What identity tags does he want to tear up by making this point? Is it about him being an "ethnic" artist? Is it about being an assimilated Indian who speaks the former oppressor's language without a distinguishable accent? Or, maybe the northern accent sounds unpleasant for him and he does not want to recycle the image of being a snobbish English gentleman? Or, perhaps, he just wants to avoid being accused of putting on a native accent, which may be interpreted as an embarrassing attempt to blend in?

Later in his performance, Patel explains, "so my artwork is about identity and language, challenging common assumptions based on how we look like or where we come from, gender, race, class. What makes us who we are anyway?" Patel interprets his artwork and the problematics of language mainly in line with stereotypes associated with one's gender, racial, and social identities. However, in spite of Patel's willingness to pin down his artistic intention, I argue that his performance suggests more nuances and possibilities than what he claims to do. Seen from the audiovisual perspective, his performance problematizes the discourse on the relation between the "ethnic" artist and his artwork and on the ideology that separates the native from the non-native speaker.

At large, his artwork speaks directly to the audience members who are ready to surrender to an "ethnic" artwork. With his traditional Indian costume and the presence of a translator, Patel intensifies the contextualizing effect of his face, while visually presenting himself as an expected and authentic "ethnic" artist. Yet, before the audience indulges itself in the visual celebration of exoticism, the translator Rau suddenly "unsynches" Patel's speech from his face and discloses the fact that the foreignness of his speech is merely a linguistic mask that the artist puts on. It is at this moment that Patel's speech is disembodied from his face and facialized performance. The audiovisual counterpoint crystalizes into a queer spectacle of over-played—and thus fake—foreignness.

Is it possible for an artwork to migrate? Can it travel and thrive beyond the national and cultural boundary? Patel might give a positive answer, since his performance demonstrates that an artwork can draw inspiration from different cultural backgrounds and artistic traditions. Nevertheless, Patel makes it clear that it is not something one can take for granted. The polyphonic possibility of an artwork—both in terms of its artistic representation and style, and of its interpretation and reception—is a crucial dimension of art practice and criticism that the artist can and should explore.

Inevitably the artwork bears a face or many faces. The facial landscape of the artwork can be intimately entangled with the concrete physical face of the artist, which often contextualizes and embeds the artwork in a discursive map of race, ethnicity, gender, etc. This explains why Van Gogh's ear continues to be an obsession for the public. In a way, his paintings are all about the act of cutting off the ear; the vibrant and sometimes ferocious colors are knives that cut his subject open. Most of his paintings are not still. They move and limp heavily, and bleed without stop. His damaged ear finds its way into his paintings and incites a deeper and longer repercussion. The madness of his ear situates his paintings in the aesthetics of modern art. On the other hand, the face of the artwork can also be an imagined or visualized image drawn from the artwork—for instance, from its theme, technics, and artistic style. An artwork is a faciality machine. To encounter it is to navigate through these many faces, and to reach a more or less stable, definable, comprehensible facial image.

What usually haunts the so-called "ethnic" artist is that her physical face tends to predetermine the overall facial image of her artwork. This attentive care given to the face of the artist often makes the artwork a blind spot of vision. As Ernst van Alphen observes in "Exoticism or the Translation of Cultural Difference," while the critical dimension of an artwork remains the most common criterion in contemporary Western art, the artwork from a non-Western artist is instead being judged by a different aesthetic criterion that is more attentive to her cultural background and identity. Van Alphen writes, "Whereas Chinese, Nigerian or Mexican writers are supposed to produce their cultural difference and specificity in their works; Dutch, French or American writers and artists are still judged on the basis of the critical dimension of their work" (2). I would suggest terming this approach a practice of "face-reading," which moors the faciality machine of the artwork alongside the facial image of the artist. Indeed, viewing experiences and approaches are inescapably facialized, but not all of them are "face-reading." The significance of Patel's performance, therefore, is that it shows that the artist can "dismantle" or "escape" that face, and one way of doing it is through unleashing speech and voice from the tyranny of face.

"But I'm not going to say it in English to you." This statement is not singular; writers in particular can easily fall prey to this language dilemma. For a bilingual or multilingual writer, before she decides on what to say, she has to settle on the question of in which language and sometimes in which accent she is going to write. This is not an easy choice to make. On the one hand, English has more capital and market value, which promises bigger readership and wider reception. Language becomes a battlefield to fight for whose experiences have more social relevance and in which form they are permitted to circulate and be related to. Sometimes writers do insist on writing in their indigenous languages or in their own versions of English, for they believe that Standard English is not the most expressive tool to convey their experiences. Often

it is about which language can have the status of being a literary language or a language per se. It is precisely in response to the legitimacy of a certain language that James Baldwin, an American novelist and social critic, exclaims, "If black English is not a language, then tell me, what is?" (5).

On the other hand, writers who are burdened with colonial heritage are particularly susceptible to these language politics, since the act of narrating one's most intimate self in English can be accused of being a form of betrayal. In his essay "English and the African Writer," Chinua Achebe, a Nigerian novelist, poet, and critic, formulates the question in the following way. Achebe says, "The real question is not whether Africans could write in English, but whether they ought to. Is it right that a man should abandon his mother tongue for someone else's? It looks like a dreadful betrayal and produces a guilty feeling" (348). Here Achebe emphasizes that the choice of language is not merely a question of in which language he feels mostly comfortable expressing himself; it is neither purely a literary choice nor a private decision. Choosing a language is to choose sides—whether she wants to be called a patriot or a betrayer, an "ethnic" writer or a global citizen. It might be easier if the so-called "ethnic" writer is monolingual, but still, her claim to English is rarely uncontested or overly celebrated.

Being a British of Indian descent, Patel is inescapably caught up in the politics of language. Although language is not as essential and integral for arts as for literature, his face nevertheless "implicates" his language and speech in his artworks, making it hard for him to speak beyond a "face-reading" of his artistic voice. In the performance, Patel recounts one episode:

> A few years ago, in order to make this video for my artwork, I shaved off all my hair so that I could grow it back as my father had it when he first emigrated from India to the U.K. in the 1960s. He had a side parting and a neat mustache.
>
> At first, it was going very well. I even started to get discounts in Indian shops.
>
> But then very quickly, I started to underestimate my mustache growing ability, and it got way too big. It didn't look Indian anymore. Instead, people from across the road, they would shout things like—*Arriba! Arriba! Ándale! Ándale!*
>
> Actually, I don't know why I am even talking like this. My dad doesn't even have an Indian accent anymore. He talks like this now.

The artwork Patel refers to is called *It's Growing on Me*, a video installation he made in 2008. This work has lasted nearly four months. During this period (and in other times as well), he wears the same face around: he "carries" it to his studio, home, the street, and the supermarket. The face traverses the boundary between his personal life and his artworks. As his moustache grows day by day, the face brings him to a head-on confrontation with people's visualized expectation in terms of his ethnic origin. Initially Patel uses the face, in particular his facial hair, to approximate the image of his father as a fresh Indian immigrant. It works at some point, as he jokingly implies, in Indian shops: his face becomes a currency, whose value increases because of the facialized intimacy with the shop owners. Curiously, in the performance, while narrating this episode, Patel puts on a distinguishable Indian accent. Later he comments on his accent: "Actually, I don't know why I am even talking like this. My dad doesn't even have an Indian accent anymore." That accent, as Patel implies, has little to do with how his father speaks; the accent comes almost as natural to him, as if it were a faithful dubbing of his "Indianized" face.

However, the face can go "mad" and be out of control. As his moustache grows beyond the limit of being recognizably "Indian"—a limit that is impossible to pinpoint—his face accidentally transgresses into another ethnic deviant-type that is verbally embodied through the call "*Arriba! Arriba! Ándale! Ándale!*" For many people, this phrase, which means "Up! Up! Go! Go!", immediately brings back the childhood memory of watching the animated cartoon of *Speedy Gonzales*, the fastest mouse in Mexico who wears a yellow sombrero and speaks with an exaggerated Mexican accent. Speedy's pet phrase, in a way, sketches out an acoustic image for the Mexican: foreign, comic, and not always intelligible. *Arriba! Arriba! Ándale! Ándale!* This outcry on the street, it seems, is an acoustic superimposition on Patel's overgrown moustache. The conjunction and disjunction of acoustic and facial images vividly stage the production of ethnic deviant-types as an audiovisual spectacle that relies on face and speech to produce a drama of revelation, solidarity, and stigma.

As an artist, Patel consciously overplays with his art objects and concepts, stretching them beyond certain limits so that they do not appear "normal" anymore. His experiment with the moustache and the "excessive" accent stands as a convenient example. The same goes for his play with the idea of foreigner and foreignness. With his native English accent and Indian face, Patel can more or less be seen as a *half* foreigner, an in-between figure. What he does is to transform into a *"drag* foreigner" by passing as a non-native speaker and by implicating his speech in the scene of translation. I propose that three components—the act of translation, the impersonation of a Mandarin speaker, and the deployment of the voice—are crucial to mobilizing his face-and-speech configuration and reception, and to moving beyond the common practice of "face-reading."

The deployment of translation momentarily and strategically caters to the expected consistency of foreignness embodied in Patel's face and speech. Yet the very exposure of this intention makes the "naturalized" and anticipated combination queer. *"But I'm not going to say it in English to you."* Through speaking via his translator Rau, Patel ushers the face into the debate on language by slightly shifting the emphasis of this sentence from *"English"* to *"I"*: *I* am not going to say it in English to you. In this way, the language issue shifts its terrain of discussion from the question of "in which language and accent" to that of *"who* is speaking."

Because the practice of translation is not motivated in a linguistic sense, it intervenes in the audiovisual scene that makes his ethnicity stand out. Patel chooses to impersonate a Mandarin speaker so as to avoid being literally translated according to his northern English accent. Especially since his *foreign* look seems incompatible with his *native* English accent, his ethnicity stands in the way of claiming a righteous "ownership" of his speech. The practice of translation, therefore, is manipulated to accentuate the tension between his face and accent—although it is done under the disguise of "appeasing" the tension. It provokes one to think: What has prevented Patel from addressing the audience directly? Whose innocent and unconscious practice of translation has silenced Patel's claim to his mother tongue? At the very moment that Rau reveals the fact that Patel not only speaks English but also is born into that language, the audience laughs hard. Indeed, the laughter does more than communicating the message "I understand your humor." It is through the laughter that the audience recognizes one another as the biased and laughable reader of the audiovisual scene of Patel's face and speech. If the accent and the laughter have very often engaged with one another metonymically—remember how often one makes fun of the other's accent—it is through unveiling the redundancy of translation and the dissonance of his face and accent that the laughter is able to be translated backwards. Suddenly it is not the accent of the speaker that is laughable but the "accented" ears that become embarrassingly absurd.

In this performance, Mandarin is used as a camouflage to safeguard Patel from the practice of "face-reading" his English accent. It is like a soundtrack added to his face in order to give the false impression that the image and sound go together well. The audiovisual counterpoint is dramatized when Rau explains, "The only problem with masking it with Chinese Mandarin is I [Patel] can only speak this paragraph, which I have learned by heart when I was visiting in China. So all I can do is keep repeating it in different tones and hope you won't notice. Needless to say, I would like to apologize to any Mandarin speakers in the audience." The paragraph that Patel keeps repeating in Chinese remains untranslated during the performance, which roughly says, "We can learn about different cultures by learning different languages. Besides accent and intonation, it is also important to feel motivated. What matters more is [to imitate and adopt] body language, habits, and gestures." His words certainly do not match Rau's translation. Yet they stand as a concise summary of what he is *doing* at that moment—that is, becoming a Mandarin speaker by adopting certain tones, accents, and gestures.

What Patel says here, on the other hand, points to the meta-level of language learning, which—because it is untranslated—is beyond the comprehensibility of the audience members who do not speak Mandarin. Does he aim to imply that such meta-level reflection and sensitivity regarding language is more accessible to multilinguals? His message and the lack of correspondence between Patel and his translator are only immediately accessible to a selected group of people—those who speak both English and Mandarin. This selective process could be read as a meta-message of Patel's words. Many people consider the experience of learning to speak a foreign language as a process of *translating* one's mother tongue and one's existence into that language. However, the mechanism of translation is often hidden and not audible to every listener. Only when the interlocutors share a similar linguistic background and trajectory can the listener easily "diagnose" which words the speaker is wrestling with, and can thus understand him or her even if the speaker is not as precise as the language allows one to be. The luxury of conversing with someone who has similar linguistic packages is that they do not have to limit themselves to one parcel of language and one set of rules. They can be "lousy" speakers. They can mix up words of different languages in one sentence, without worrying that they may fail the listener. They can keep the hybrid form of languages through which their thoughts manifest themselves. They can also relate to one another when it comes to the feeling of loss or excitement in regard to language. They are constantly reminded of the limit of one language over another. They come to notice that one language allows them to be closer to the experiences they want to tell, while other languages may lack such vocabularies for them to borrow. My favorite example is the Japanese word "積ん読" (*tsundoku*), which means the act of leaving a book unread after buying it—an expression that comforts me since the existence of such a word somehow proves that I am not the only one who is guilty for doing this. Although one could still describe this experience in other languages, the lack of a fixed expression makes this experience more ephemeral, fragile, and incomplete. This is perhaps why it is much easier for people who have shared linguistic trajectories to converse: the intimacy of languages harbors the intimacy of experiences.

However, Patel challenges this intimacy. He speaks Mandarin, but only to the extent that it sounds somehow synched to his face. In many ways, he is vulnerable to the language that he uses for "dubbing." In his performance, as Rau reveals his language scheme, the audience laughs. Patel continues repeating his words in Mandarin. Yet, the louder the laughter becomes, the more uncertain and frigid Patel behaves. Is he, we can ask, a fully *conscious* Mandarin speaker? When he seeks protection in a foreign language, wouldn't that language betray him in different ways? Later Patel recalls a scenario in which he learns a Mandarin phrase and asks a Chinese artist to hear it out. This is what happens to Patel:

> A few years ago I went to China for a few months, and I couldn't speak Chinese, and this frustrated me, so I wrote about this and had it translated into Chinese, and then I learned this by heart, like music, I guess.
>
> This phrase is now etched into my mind clearer than the pin number to my bank card, so I can pretend I speak Chinese fluently. When I had learned this phrase, I had an artist over there hear me out to see how accurate it sounded.
>
> I spoke the phrase, and then he laughed and told me, "Oh yeah, that's great, only it kind of sounds like a woman."
>
> I said, "What?"
>
> He said, "Yeah, you learned from a woman?"
>
> I said, "Yes. So?"
>
> He then explained the tonal differences between male and female voices are very different and distinct, and that I had learned it very well, but in a woman's voice.

In his performance, Patel attempts to hide his non-native English look in another language; yet this time, it is his gendered body that appears non-native to his impersonating voice. Ironically, Patel is no less vulnerable in a foreign language—which he initially embraces as a mask and a shelter—than in his mother tongue, although these two languages act on him in completely different ways. With English, Patel is exposed to the hyper-awareness of the acoustic image associated with his face; whereas with Mandarin, Patel is easily taken as a clown, a queer, or a daredevil. In general, when speaking a foreign language, one may find it liberating in the sense that many social prescriptions fail him and do not immediately claim his attention. "Lacking the reins of the maternal language," Julia Kristeva observes, "the foreigner who learns a new language is capable of the most unforeseen audacities when using it—intellectual daring and obscenities as well" (31). Such is the privilege of being a foreigner: she does not know exactly what she is saying. Yet at the same time, with no maps at hand that mark out social taboos, the speaker of a foreign language can become a landmine detector. Each time she treads on the bomb and hears its explosion (laughter, teasing, sneer, irresponsive and annoyed look, etc.), she makes a mental note to avoid that danger zone. She draws the map herself by suspending her social life once and again. The same goes for Patel: unintended, he transgresses the social norms that prescribe the nuanced layering of speech, gender, and voice.

The transgression is twofold: on the one hand, it happens between Patel as a speaker and the foreign language he is trying to synch to his mouth; on the other hand, it points to the breach of the "contract" between language and voice. In the first case, it is the gendered body of Patel that stands out; in the second, the uncanny presence of voice. In his book *A Voice and Nothing More* (2006), the film critic and cultural theorist Mladen Dolar has elaborated on the relation between language and voice. For Dolar, voice raises the expectation of meaning while, in most cases, giving rise to the utterance without intruding on the scene of communication. Unlike other kinds of sounds whose relation to meaning is loose, Dolar observes, "the voice has an intimate connection with meaning, it is a sound which appears to be endowed in itself with the will to 'say something,' with an inner intentionality" (14). At the same time, voice is what makes speech possible by having itself dissolved into the emergence of meaning. "The voice itself is like the Wittgensteinian ladder to be discarded when we have successfully climbed to the top—that is, when we have made our ascent to the peak of meaning" (15), writes Dolar.

While the voice appears closely intertwined with meaning and intentionality, it is nonetheless recalcitrant to meaning. The accent, as Dolar mentions, is one of the three modes—the other two being the intonation and the timbre—that index the traces of the voice in language:

> We can have some inkling of the voice if we listen to someone with an accent. Accent—*ad cantum*—is something which brings the voice into the vicinity of singing, and a heavy accent suddenly makes us aware of the material support of the voice which we tend immediately to discard. It appears as a distraction, or even an obstacle, to the smooth flow of signifiers and to the hermeneutics of understanding. After all, it is a norm which differs from the ruling norm—this is what makes it an accent,

and this is what makes it obtrusive, what makes it sing—and it can be described in the same way as the ruling norm. The ruling norm is but an accent which has been declared a non-accent in a gesture which always carries heavy social and political connotations. (20)

In a way, if the accent dramatizes the encounter of language and body, it is the voice that often leads the role. The accent makes audible a vocal body that sings out language like music notes. The lyrics of the language are transported from ear to ear, while the distinct and embodied melody of the accent lingers and makes the air rustle. The accent arrests the voice from its sly trick of disappearance. It *arrests* because the kind of voice that the accent takes hold of is usually a deviant one, one that is off the key of the norm and that showcases how language can go astray in the flesh.

Hoffman, for example, notices that her voice has undergone drastic changes when she tries to speak English. It is as if her voice and body are taken hostage by the accent:

> My voice is doing funny things. It does not seem to emerge from the same parts of my body as before. It comes out from somewhere in my throat, tight, thin, and mat—a voice without the modulations, dips, and rises that it had before, when it went from my stomach all the way through my head. There is, of course, the constraint and the self-consciousness of an accent that I hear but cannot control. Some of my high school peers accuse me of putting it on in order to appear more "interesting." In fact, I'd do anything to get rid of it, and when I'm alone, I practice sounds for which my speech organs have no intuitions, such as "th" (I do this by putting my tongue between my teeth) and "a," which is longer and more open in Polish (by shaping my mouth into a sort of arrested grin). (121–22)

Here Hoffman suggests that speaking in a foreign language unsettles the original configuration of body and voice embedded in her mother tongue. It was once a voluptuous voice that modulated, dipped, and rose, meandering all the way from stomach to head. For Hoffman, the voice of the mother tongue is both concrete and abstract, corporeal and ideational. Most importantly, her *maternal* voice seems to be journeying toward a clear destination: it departs from the organ of digestion—where the voice seems inseparable from the most trivial, mundane, consumable chunks of food—and ends up in the most specialized compartment of the body where impalpable thoughts and intricate feelings are formed and processed. The route of the *maternal* voice, in a way, permits symbolic transcendence: because such a voice seems immanent to meaning and expression, through it, the speaker is able to digress from the concreteness of her being, existing purely as an idea, a concept, a string of utterances that resides in nowhere and anywhere.

In contrast, for Hoffman, the *foreign* voice does not travel; nor does it transport the speaker. It is *stuck* in the throat, "thin and mat," ready to die out at any moment. Whereas the *maternal* voice acts out the existence of the body as a spatio-temporal unfolding, the *foreign* voice cries out an instant seizure and suspension of time and space. Bare, drifting, and uprooted, the foreign voice bears no quality of sharpness or weight of significance that can (re)inscribe the speaking body in the time-space continuum through a *cut*. The foreignness of the voice is thus the foreignness of time and space. As Kristeva comments, "Your speech has no past and will have no power over the future of the group: why should one listen to it? You do not have enough status—'no social standing'—to make your speech useful. It may be desirable, to be sure, surprising, too, bizarre or attractive, if you wish. But such lures are of little consequence when set against the interest—which is precisely lacking—of those you are speaking to" (20).

Often people perceive the accented and "broken" speech as an interruption of the smooth passage of time and space. However, I want to suggest the possibility of another reading: the "brokenness" of the foreign voice lies in the fact that it fails to offer such a breach, through which the speaking body can insert herself into the otherwise enclosed and indifferent flow of time and space. The speaker should be someone who *punctuates* the continuous flow of language and discourse, making it readable and inhabitable. To offer as an example, the novelist Theresa Hak Kyung Cha's book *Dictee* (2009) touches on this aspect. Cha writes about the painful experience of searching for the voice in French. In a tone laden with despair, Cha writes, "She would take on their punctuation. She waits to service this. Theirs. Punctuation. She would become, herself, demarcations. Absorb it. Spill it. Seize upon the punctuation. Last air. Give her. Her. The relay. Voice. Assign. Hand it. Deliver it. Deliver" (4). Here, the anxiety of speaking a foreign language is transformed into an anxiety over punctuation: where to punctuate, how to take on other people's punctuation, to whom the punctuation belongs.

In fact, the entire book of *Dictee* is haunted by a concern with punctuation. The text demonstrates a graphic rebellion of the rules of punctuation: large and irregular scales of blankness appear unexpectedly between lines and paragraphs. Fragmented words and sentences are given unexpected full stops. For instance, Cha writes, "Of her. Own. Unbegotten. Name. Name only. Name without substance. The everlasting, Forever. Without end" (88). Sentences like this give the impression that the language becomes a trauma for the narrator: either her memory stammers and forbids her a lucid narration, or she is incapable of inhaling and exhaling properly throughout her narration. Sometimes in the text, the punctuation marks are completely missing: "The voices ring shout one voice then many voices they are waves they echo I am moving in the direction the only one direction with the voices the only direction" (81). Sometimes the punctuation marks are replaced by their proper names or by the extra spaces in between of words and phrases: "Open paragraph   It was the first day   period   She had come from a far   period   tonight at dinner   comma   the families would ask   comma   open   quotation marks   How was the first day interrogation mark   close quotation marks" (1).

Either in shortage or in excess, the punctuation in Cha's book seldom composes the narration into an anticipated and readable form. The narrator, therefore, always appears at odds with the rules, norms, and the syntaxes to which she seems to entrust herself. Occasionally this misfit is conveyed through grammar mistakes. Cha writes, "She call   she believe   she calling to   she has calling because there no response   she believe   she calling and the other end must hear" (15). While the grammar mistakes indicate the impossibility of the narrator to trust the language she is using and to be trusted as a reliable writer, the oddity of the punctuation embodies an odd *voice* that sometimes becomes gagged in silence, and sometimes outpours without restraint. This voice, in Cha's book, is curiously intertwined with miscellaneous historical and biographical sources—uncaptioned photographs, handwritten letters, anatomical charts, excerpts from language textbooks—whose relation to the voice is not always obvious. These sources add another layer to the oddity of the voice, which crafts a stylized narrative but is unable to claim ownership of it. Such voice is odd because it is outside the rhythm of history, the formalized time-space composition that gives a voice its grain.

What happens to the voice without the grain? Could the accented voice be audible at all? Is the voice outside time and space still a voice per se? The linguistic dilemma of the foreigner, I suggest, is about being stuck in a long-run state of *voicing*. For Dolar, the voice denotes an interstice between a mere sound and a determined field of meaning. Unlike other sounds, the voice "implies a subjectivity which 'expresses itself' and itself inhabits the means of expression" (15). Unlike speech, the voice operates inside and outside language and therefore does not hand itself over to the totalizing gesture of signification. In a way, the foreigner does not speak but simply lends her *voice* to language. Let me explain this with a fragment of Cha's writing:

She mimics the speaking. That might resemble speech. (Anything at all.) Bared noise, groan, bits torn from words. Since she hesitates to measure the accuracy, she resorts to mimicking gestures with the mouth. The entire lower lip would lift upwards then sink back to its original place. She would then gather both lips and protrude them in a pout taking in the breath that might utter some thing. (One thing. Just one.) But the breath falls away. With a slight tilting of her head backwards, she would gather the strength in her shoulders and remain in this position.

It murmurs inside. It murmurs. Inside is the pain of speech the pain to say. Larger still. Greater than is the pain not to say. To not say. Says nothing against the pain to speak. It festers inside. The wound, liquid, dust. Must break. Must void.

From the back of neck she releases her shoulders free. She swallows once more. (Once more. One more time would do.) In preparation. It augments. To such a pitch. Endless drone, refueling itself. Autonomous. Self-generating. Swallows with last efforts last wills against the pain that wishes it to speak. (3)

Noise, groan, bits of fragmented sounds: as the speaker struggles to produce sounds, the speech is relegated to a *resemblance* of speech, whereas the act of speaking is stripped down to the physical labor of moving the mouth, lifting and gathering lips, tilting the head, releasing shoulders. Even though the speaker has clearly demonstrated a will to speak, she has to surpass the physical pain of vocalization. Dangling between the primitive state of sound and noise and the more or less formal event of speech, she who tries to tease out meaning from a deliberate configuration of mouth and lips becomes the embodiment of the transient but prolonged happening of voicing.

To come back to Patel's performance, it is not only the gendered body that becomes audible through his linguistic impersonation. The problem of being heard speaking Mandarin in a woman's voice also has to do with the unsolicited audibility of the voice itself, which usually remains behind the scenes. On the one hand, there is a voice that seems immanent to meaning, a voice that is born out of, and thus inalienable from, the mother tongue. On the other hand, we see a kind of voice that seems *dubbed, rented, superimposed*. Patel's voice in Mandarin belongs to the latter. Such voice does not speak; it makes meaning delayed and uncertain, hanging it off the cliff of voicing. The emergence of meaning, in such cases, occasions voice by coincidence. For Patel, those Mandarin phrases happen to mean something, not because he understands what he is saying but because he happens to copy the movements of the native speaker's mouth accurately enough.

In the beginning of his performance, Patel manipulates his face-and-speech configuration after the fashion of exoticism to transform his presence into an audiovisual spectacle. Later the anecdote of him trying to pass as a Mandarin speaker at once intensifies and undoes the *spectacular* impression. When they perform the story, Patel stands in front of the stage—face toward the audience, lips moving but without sound, whereas Rau hides behind him, telling the story in her accented voice, and gesturing with her hands and arms, which stick out from under Patel's armpits. At this point, we see a man's face; we hear a woman's voice. Yet the spectacle of the audiovisual dissonance results neither in fetishization nor in disfigurement of the speaking body. We know the spectacle is to be dismantled and the peculiar combination of a man's face and a woman's voice in one body is no less banal than a two-man comic show. Whereas Patel's face lingers on the stage as the residue of a spectacular vision and of over-played foreignness, Rau's high-pitched, accented voice, as a counterpart of Patel's voice in Mandarin, makes his moving lips a melodrama of voicing and a physical labor to account for the otherly everydayness. If Guattari relates everydayness to a sort of normality and nativeness, Patel demonstrates that the idea of the "perfect" native and the "perfect" *face-type* is impossible: one is inevitably and often unknowingly foreign in one way or another.

3. From the Buccal Tribunal to the Buccal Theater

Investigations of a Murder Case of Language

Abstract: Drawing on Peter Schwenger's work, I explore how language is often conceptualized as a site of "death" or "murder." This chapter, however, shifts from viewing the mouth as a tribunal of linguistic violence to understanding it as a "buccal theatre" of exploration. To deepen this analysis, I turn to Samuel Beckett's plays *Not I* and *A Piece of Monologue*, where the act of speaking is reduced to the performative presence of the mouth. I then introduce the concept of "buccal theatre," borrowed from Kleinian psychoanalyst Donald Meltzer, to reinterpret this stage of linguistic exploration, where one's relationship to words and the world is performed through the preverbal act of mouthing, suggesting a process of linguistic experimentation rather than destruction.

Keywords: exploratory mouthing; words and things; Samuel Beckett; Vladimir Nabokov

Second Amended Complaint for Personal Injury and Wrongful Death

> The English Language,
>   Plaintiff
> vs.
> Timofey Pavlovich Pnin,
>   Defendant

Statement of the Case
During the years that the defendant, a Russian-born assistant professor, lived in the United States, the defendant had been witnessed and accused

---

Hui, Tingting. *Accented Speech in Literature, Art, and Theory: Melodramas of the Foreign Tongue.* Amsterdam: Amsterdam University Press, 2025.
DOI: 10.5117/9789048569007_CH03

of inflicting severe damage and wrongful death on the plaintiff. Relevant clinical manifestations of the damage include but are not limited to mispronunciation, murderous accent, and illegitimate mixture of linguistic codes. The plaintiff seeks compensatory and punitive damages and an injunction.

Plaintiff
"If his Russian was music, his English was murder. He had enormous difficulty ('dzeefeecooltsee' in Pninian English) with depalatization, never managing to remove the extra Russian moisture from *t*'s and *d*'s before the vowels he so quaintly softened. His explosive 'hat' ('I never go in a hat even in winter') differed from the common American pronunciation of 'hot' (typical of Waindell townspeople, for example) only by its briefer duration, and thus sounded very much like the German verb *hat* (has). Long *o*'s with him inevitably became short ones: his 'no' sounded positively Italian, and this was accentuated by his trick of triplicating the simple negative ('May I give a lift, Mr. Pnin?' 'No-no-no, I have only two paces from here.'). He did not possess (nor was he aware of this lack) any long *oo*: all he could muster when called upon to utter 'noon' was the lax vowel of the German '*nun*' ('I have no classes in after*nun* on Tuesday. Today is Tuesday.')" (*Pnin* 56).

Defendant
"The consequence of this is that we might think that Pnin cannot be reached/damaged/hurt through language (((only the Pnin inside is vulnerable))), but the bad accent tells us that he can be hurt; his language can be broken like his physical body. His halting accent and broken language reveal his vulnerability and catalyze our vision of him as human. Language becomes inextricable from the formation of an interior; we see that to injure one part of Pnin's language is to injure his linguistic existence as a whole" (Ch'ien 67).

First Investigation Report: The Metaphor of Death

We are presented with a murder case. The plaintiff attorney is Vladimir Nabokov, who has compiled his charges and statements into a book called *Pnin*, which is named after the defendant. A Russian-born professor who taught Russian at a college in the United States, Pnin became dangerously close to English and exhibited, as many witnesses came to testify, destructive and murderous behaviors toward the English language. "Cata-stroph," "nofing," "okh-okh-okh" are some of the examples that Nabokov mentions. The defendant attorney is Evelyn Nien-Ming Ch'ien. Her defense, which is included in her book *Weird English* (2004), though appearing much later than Nabokov's, gives the case a twist by arguing that whatever damage Pnin inflicted on English is motivated and justified by the right of self-defense. The shattering of his words is precisely the shattering of his body. Therefore, the question of how severely damaged those English words are should not make one concerned—since the continuation and vitality of the English language depends not on Pnin alone but rather on the whole community of English speakers. It seems more relevant to ask, as Ch'ien implies, whether and how Pnin is to survive the repeated threats posed by this hostile tongue.

On one hand, this indictment is rather curious. Wise folks, very often, deal with language in the same manner as a craftsman hammers a nail or as a fisher casts his net; once the nail is pounded in the wall and the fish flops into the net, both the hammer and the net are abandoned and forgotten. Only very few people—among whom are lunatics, poets, witches and sorcerers, suffers of dysphasia, and avant-gardes—risk, willingly or helplessly, a relation with language that goes beyond a means to an end. The case concerning Pnin clearly demonstrates how threatening and punishable it is to have a relation to language other than the one defined by utilitarian and instrumental terms. Language is the invisible vessel that carries its speaker from the shore of objects to that of symbols. When one starts to drill holes instead of rowing, one should not be surprised to find the ground become shaky and the river of meaning bleak and deep.

On the other hand, the accusation of murder should not surprise us as unprecedented. Western philosophers, in particular, frequently draw upon the metaphor of replacement, substitution, death, and murder to frame and interpret the mechanism of representation. Roland Barthes, for example, arguing that photographs invoke an image of death-in-life, aims to inquire into "the anthropological place of Death and of the new image" (92) in his seminal book *Camera Lucida* (2010). "All those young photographers who are at work in the world, determined upon the capture of actuality, do not know that they are agents of Death," writes Barthes. The melancholic tone that permeates through Barthes's discussion of photography, which makes Death aesthetically appealing and even desirable, continues to haunt the theory of photography. Another French philosopher, Jean Baudrillard, who appears more anguished than melancholic in his writing about the simulacra, proclaims that it is the fate of the modern man to be absorbed into a flat hyperreal world where signs and images take the places of reality. Baudrillard makes the smell of death and murder unmistakably felt: "Thus perhaps at stake has always been the murderous capacity of images, murderers of the real, murderers of their own model as the Byzantine icons could murder the divine identity" (1735). The modern man has lost good faith in representation. A disenchanted world filled with the violence of killing and such metaphors is all what we have. As if in competition, one after another, Friedrich Nietzsche announced the death of God, Barthes declared the death of author, and Michel Foucault prophesied the death of man...

The metaphor of death is ubiquitous not only in the discussions about images and visual representations but also in terms of how some philosophers conceptualize the relation between words and the things they refer to. The temptation of the metaphor of annihilation and killing seems to lie in its inherent narrative and dramatic tension, which, if it cannot be attributed to a philosopher's conscious attempt of spicing up a philosophical proposition with the art of storytelling, at least makes it easier for philosophy to be read *as if* it were a well-told story.

To begin with, Nietzsche's story is a mild one. In "On Truth and Lies in a Nonmoral Sense," Nietzsche perceives the entanglement between words and things in terms of "an allusive transference, a stammering translation" (880). "We believe that when we speak of trees, colours, snow, and flowers, we have knowledge of the things themselves, and yet we possess only metaphors of things which in no way correspond to the original entities" (877). Nietzsche considers words to be neither valid tokens nor adequate expressions of things. Words are metaphorical transferences of things in the sense that they carry over the stimulation of a nerve into an image and then into an articulated sound.

What is truth then? Nietzsche explains in a cynical tone, "A mobile army of metaphors, metonymies, anthropomorphisms [...] truths are illusions of which we have forgotten that they are illusions, metaphors which have become worn by frequent use and have lost all sensuous vigour" (878). The metaphorical transference of language, in Nietzsche's reading, is a reductive process. On one hand, what metaphors serve to bridge in terms of language and the phenomenal world are very different spheres, ranging from the empirical to the perceptive and the vocal. A metaphor can "tame" the differences yet is unable to close the gaps. Although it can sometimes express "a sensuous perception" (878) that escapes classification, a metaphor, when hardened into a concept, often trims down "the unique, utterly individualized, primary experience to which it owes its existence." On the other hand, the process of *metamorphosis* is a monkey business of sneaky concealment and substitution that manipulates the forgetfulness of human nature and the mechanism of anthropomorphism. What language is able to metaphorize is nothing but man's relation to things, or to use Nietzsche's words, "the metamorphosis of the world in human beings" (879).

The protagonist in Nietzsche's story, the one who "hides something behind a bush, looks for it in the same place and then finds it there" (879), is either a narcissist or a simpleton, but not a murderer. However, the shadow of death has never ceased to loom over the philosophy of language, encircling it with an uncanny aura of excitement and danger that is known to detective stories. Philosophers thus busy themselves with a detective's concern: *who kills whom, under what circumstances, and with what intention and motivation.* Peter Schwenger, the Conan Doyle in academia, in his text "Words and the Murder of Things," undertakes the investigation of a murder case that Hegel filed in *First Philosophy of Spirit*. Hegel suggests that "[t]he first act, by which Adam established his lordship over the animals, is this, that he gave them a name, i.e., he nullified them as beings on their own account, and made them into ideal [entities]" (221–22). For Hegel, the consequence of being named is that from that moment on, the phenomenal world of things and animals is gobbled up, whose faint surviving breath can only be felt through the opening and closing of the human mouth. The naming scene that Adam performed brings forth the first omen of death. Since then, the soil that nourishes existence has to be sought in the conceptual domain of language, where the absence of stones, lions, and trolley cars is glossed over by signs and symbols, which serve to invoke the idea of continued, metaphorical presence.

What about, as Jonathan Swift suggests in *Gulliver's Travels*, banning words altogether and asking men to carry about things that are necessary for them to "converse" about a particular subject? The hassle is too obvious for anyone to believe that Swift really means what he says. Schwenger argues that words and things "may be fated, indeed, to an actual fatality. For in the space of that difference hovers death—or so it is asserted in a recurrent metaphor" (100). The metaphor of death is what brings us face-to-face with the abyss of meaning, which drowns the dream of a perfect correspondence between words and things. It is the way for philosophy to acknowledge, although negatively, that there is a limit to what we can know and achieve through words.

But, then, what is the motivation of this murder? Ruthless as it may sound, "we murder *to create* [...] The death of the thing, then, is the price we pay for the word" (100). According to Schwenger, humans connive with language to accomplish the death of things. Trimming down the strangeness of things that eludes human perception and knowledge, words transform things into objects, whose mode of existence is dependent on a corresponding notion of subject. Schwenger explains, "When such a being is named, then, it is also changed. It is assimilated into the terms of the human subject at the same time that it is opposed to it as object, an opposition that is indeed necessary for the subject's separation and definition" (101). Language implies, again, as it is in Nietzsche, a field of anthropomorphism. The metaphorical act of murder has to be performed over and over again, till it is ritualized into a collective unconscious, so that the image of a speaking subject can rise above the ruin of objects, recreating him/herself as a name-giving agent who is protected from representation.

Second Investigation Report: The Buccal Tribunal

What Schwenger's report shows is that, if the difference between words and things is doomed to be fatal, no singular and identifiable culprit is to be brought to court. Schwenger is not so much concerned about *who does it* as about *how to facilitate the return of (the ghost of) the thing*. It is from Maurice Blanchot that Schwenger initially draws inspiration for remedies against the death of the thing: "My hope lies in the materiality of language, in the fact that words are things, too, are a kind of nature" (Blanchot 327). Words await growing into a solid mass, which is to be twisted, hurled, and broken into pieces. When the boundary set by sense becomes fragile and pervious, the quality of strangeness is no longer what separates things from words but what brings them together. Hence Gertrude Stein, hence Francis Ponge: these are Schwenger's heroine and hero, who shatter the conventional language to allow words and things to cast strange and curious glances upon each other across the threatening gap of meaning.

"If there is a murder of the thing by the word, then," concludes Schwenger, "this does not definitively annihilate that thing; it only transposes it to the scene of an interminable haunting of language" (113). Schwenger, by the end of his report, tempers his initial charge of murder, arguing that the murderous act does not necessarily result in the fatal death of things. Sharp and insightful as he is, Schwenger fails to see that what seems to be a singular criminal case might unwittingly implicate a series of interconnected murder cases—for there is not only a lack of correspondence between words and things but also a threatening discordance between humans and languages. As the role of the victim and that of the perpetrator seem to be constantly in exchange—all depends on whose perspective we are taking—what are we going to make of the charge of murder filed by Nabokov in the opening of this chapter?

Let me first return to the claim of Hegel and begin with Adam's murderous naming, which, I believe, should be investigated in the context of the fall of the Babel, after which humans lost the power of designating an exclusively one-to-one relation between words and things. If Adam kills things by naming them, the destruction of the Tower of Babel proves that the tool of murder can turn against him and his descendants, making them lost and isolated in the confusion of tongues. Whereas the faculty of speaking often creates the illusion of the speaking body as a ready-made vessel for language and of language as an exclusive property of man, the aftermath of the fall of Babel manifests its force not only through the necessity of translation but also on occasions where a speaking body strains his or her tongue to aim for the correct sounds and meanings.

Just taking as an example the quotidian scene of meeting a foreigner, the exchange of names can be quite tricky, triggering sometimes the suspicion that some words and names exist so as to embarrass us. Even after pleading—"Say it again? Is it 'Chou' or 'Ciao'?" "Do you mind repeating it?"—the obscure syllables may still refuse to make an impression on us. We may even venture a syllable or two. They are not completely illegible, but they are not quite right. Fortunately, the foreigner is ready to give in. She says "That's it" without meaning it. When a name is caught between tongues, the speaker is lured to give away sovereignty and to conform to a new linguistic reality. One can no longer dismiss the fact that language is not at all a singular contract signed with God, which bequeaths man alone a majestic naming power. The name-giver is not a blind spot of language: she is no less subject to the act of being named and represented in language. With the fall of Babel, it is not only the naming power of man that gets lost but also the prescriptive impulse of language that becomes diluted upon foreign lips and tied tongues. Language grows into a myriad of scattered tiles with jagged edges that could hurt those careless and unskilled practitioners. The situation seems irreconcilable: either the speaker is wounded, or the language is debilitated.

If there is an unresolved war going on between speakers and languages, no other battlefield is more visible and determined than in the writings of bilingual writers, among whom Nabokov is a prominent one. Decided to wrestle with English after the success of his Russian novels, Nabokov makes his works a stage for "tongue-tied" characters, whose intricate linguistic backgrounds lead them to daily dramas of tongues. Nabokov's first English novel *The Real Life of Sebastian Knight* (1959) preludes this persistent struggle of his polyglot characters trapped in tongues. The novel resembles a literary detective story in which the narrator investigates and composes the life of his recently deceased half-brother Sebastian Knight, a distinguished Russian-born English novelist. It is difficult to say whether the enigma of

Sebastian Knight is essentially of a linguistic kind; nor are there any clues indicating that the detective impulse of the narrator relies on an instinctual association of the mysterious death of his half-brother with his languages. Yet, it is clear that some critics, whose opinions the narrator obviously opposes, try to use Sebastian Knight's long-time combat with Russian and English to make a sorry epitaph to his career as an English writer. The first type of critique goes as follows:

> There is no libel in asserting that alone the impetus of a clicking typewriter could enable Mr. Goodman to remark that "a Russian education was forced upon a small boy always conscious of the rich English strain in his blood." This foreign influence, Mr. Goodman goes on, "brought acute suffering to the child, so that in his riper years it was with a shudder that he recalled the bearded moujiks, the ikons, the drone of balalaikas, all of which displaced a healthy English upbringing." (15)

To the literary critic Mr. Goodman, who is a fictional character in the novel, the life of Sebastian Knight is an eroded venue where languages clash. Whereas Mr. Goodman seems positive about Sebastian Knight's English writings, the price for this enthusiasm is the stigmatization of his Russian background as a false origin. The Russian words and the images they bring forth are perceived to be curiously at odds with Sebastian Knight's sense of self. The occasional flashback of his early memories gives him shudders since they all appear foreign to the ideal of "a healthy English upbringing." Therefore, Sebastian Knight does not win English over by simply suppressing the Russian in him; Russian is by nature a hostile host that obstructs his destined alliance with English.

The other type of critique gestures toward a similar kind of linguistic battle, yet the focus is shifted to Sebastian Knight's English writings. "Poor knight! he really had two periods, the first—a dull man writing broken English, the second—a broken man writing dull English," says a celebrated critic at a literary lunch gathering (7). Dull and broken, neither the deceased writer Sebastian Knight nor his English seems to gain vitality or benefit from this lifelong grapple. These two periods of struggle, which yield to nothing but a state of weariness and a loss of dignity, hint at the unprofitable nature of such a battle. A decent writer, as the critic implies, should not have bothered himself in the first place with an adoptive tongue.

While Sebastian Knight's wrestle with Russian and English is devastating but not yet criminal, it is in *Pnin* that the wrestle reaches its crescendo, amounting to an accusation of murder:

> The organs concerned in the pronunciation of English speech sounds are the larynx, the velum, the lips, the tongue (that punchinello in the troupe), and, last but not least, the lower jaw; mainly upon its over-energetic and somewhat ruminant motion did Pnin rely when translating in class passages in the Russian grammar or some poem by Pushkin. If his Russian was music, his English was murder. (56)

Ironically, both Sebastian Knight and Pnin—one a writer and the other a literary scholar—work in the field of literature, which is traditionally (and maybe still) associated with the guardian and promoter of an elite and refined form of language. However, unlike Sebastian Knight whose glory and failure belong to the battlefield of inked words, Pnin's struggle with English takes place on a different plane. Since it is primarily English as a spoken language that concerns Pnin, the crime scene is univocally identified and localized in the mouth. It is from and in the buccal area—the larynx, the velum, the lips, the tongue, and the lower jaw—that the triumphant music of Russian is overheard while English words are being crushed and executed.

"[H]is English was murder," states the narrator. Yet, murder of what and/or whom?

The narrator associates Pnin's English with the power of extreme violence. The charge that follows, however, seems to contradict this blunt statement, in the sense that it identifies Pnin's English as a *victim* rather than a perpetrator:

> He had enormous difficulty ("dzeefeecooltsee" in Pninian English) with depalatization, never managing to remove the extra Russian moisture from *t*'s and *d*'s before the vowels he so quaintly softened. His explosive "hat" ("I never go in a hat even in winter") differed from the common American pronunciation of "hot" (typical of Waindell townspeople, for example) only by its briefer duration, and thus sounded very much like the German verb *hat* (has). Long *o*'s with him inevitably became short ones: his "no" sounded positively Italian, and this was accentuated by his trick of triplicating the simple negative ("May I give a lift, Mr. Pnin?" "No-no-no, I have only two paces from here."). He did not possess (nor was he aware of this lack) any long *oo*: all he could muster when called upon to utter "noon" was the lax vowel of the German "*nun*" ("I have no classes in after*nun* on Tuesday. Today is Tuesday."). (56)

The murderous act on English is disentangled into three components. Firstly, a stroke by the Russian tongue: the English consonants are backed into the corner of the palate, whose humidity, duration, and stress have suffered a heavy blow. Secondly, a slay of certain compound vowels: long "oo" becomes blindly eradicated. Finally, an illegitimate practice of "denaturalization": the nationality of English words is unjustly bereft; a German identity is wrongly imposed on the word "hat," while the word "no" suddenly acquires an Italian origin.

The question is: Are these evidences solid and sufficient enough for Pnin to take full responsibility for the wrongfully wounded and dead English words? The ironic tone of the novel seems to suggest so. Yet our devotion to justice should prevent us from rushing to any conclusion before taking into consideration that Pnin's murderous pronunciation is more or less suicidal. The case at hand proves to be more vexed than we thought.

On the one hand, nurtured and raised up by his Russian mother tongue, the mouth of Pnin seems to have obtained a limited articulating scope that makes English words fall apart on his tongue and lips. "His life was a constant war," says the narrator, "with insensate objects that fell apart, or attacked him, or refused to function, or viciously got themselves lost as soon as they entered the sphere of his existence" (13). When words fail to conform to the articulatory potential of the mouth, the sensuality of the mouth—how it used to smack, burp, and hold the shape of Russian syllables—will start to haunt English words like a piece of repressed memory. On the other hand, Pnin's lack of command in English constantly turns his mouth against itself, resulting in a repeated misfiring of the tongue. The pain is fully embodied in the scene where Pnin has all his teeth pulled out:

> A warm flow of pain was gradually replacing the ice and wood of the anesthetic in his thawing, still half-dead, abominably martyred mouth. After that, during a few days he was in mourning for an intimate part of himself. It surprised him to realize how fond he had been of his teeth. His tongue, a fat sleek seal, used to flop and slide so happily among the familiar rocks, checking the contours of a battered but still secure kingdom, plunging from cave to cove, climbing this jag, nuzzling that notch, finding a shred of sweet seaweed in the same old cleft; but now not a landmark remained, and all there existed was a great dark wound, a terra incognita of gums which dread and disgust forbade one to investigate. And when the plates were thrust in, it was like a poor fossil skull being fitted with the grinning jaws of a perfect stranger. (32)

Nabokov does not go to great lengths to explain why Pnin decides to replace his teeth with dentures, except that after the tooth extraction, Pnin's headaches are gone. The moment that one realizes some change has been done to his mouth is where Pnin comes back alone, toothless, with the sensation of pain turned loose gradually. When read in light of the language leitmotif of the novel, this event has its symbolic significance: it stands for the painful and transformative experience of uprooting the mother tongue to implant a new, "artificial" language. To some extent, Pnin's linguistic transformation from Russian to English is comparable to and no less violent and bloody than an operation in the mouth. The mouth, being the location of the accused crime of murder, at this point, does stink of blood. Here, however, it stages a different scene of violence than the explicit charge of murder pronounced by Nabokov: the victim of the murder is no longer the English language but Pnin himself and his mother tongue. The dental operation, first and foremost, transforms the mouth into a martyr, a dark wound, and a perfect stranger. The lingering taste of Russian reminds one of Pnin's original teeth—aching once but gone now, used to be an organic and intimate part of him but has become eroded and troublesome in the end. Moreover, Pnin relates to English in the same way that he does with the new dental plate, which first appears to him like "a poor fossil skull" smelling of death, and then like a "new gadget" and "a firm mouthful of efficient, alabastrine, humane America" (32–33). Pnin enjoys his triumph *spectacularly*, "with headaches gone, and this new amphitheatre of translucid plastics implying, as it were, a stage and a performance" (33).

The mouth is the place where the speaking body is bent and molded, year after year, without noticing, according to demands of the mother tongue. Conflicts arise when the same mouth is subject to two wills, with one commanding it to stay loyal to the original and the other luring it to strain for transformation. The invasion of foreign words triggers, almost inevitably, the resistance from the vocal organs. Besides being the location of a crime scene, the mouth seems to constitute a tribunal of its own, with consciousness and desire being at its trial jury. A tribunal is literally a court or forum of justice where a case is heard and judged, where words and deeds are put under scrutiny, and where collective consciousness is tested and restored. With the *buccal* tribunal, I mean to say that the act of speaking may unwittingly present the mouth as a site charged with prescriptive rigor and punitive zest. Is the speaker aware of his or her mistakes in pronunciation? Is it not too vulgar to say "crap" in front of your parents? Why do you want to learn English from a Singaporean when American or British accents clearly do a better job to get you further in life? The mouth, while being the crime scene that gives rise to questions related to loyalty, capital, and appropriateness, is also the tribunal where such judgments are passed to inspire the self-consciousness of shame and guilt, and to provoke the desire of restoring dignity and decency.

To use an example, Chang-Rae Lee's debut novel *Native Speaker* showcases the mouth as a locus of discourse whose function oscillates between a crime scene and a buccal tribunal, subjecting the speaking body to a split consciousness and a desire for perfect sounds. The novel examines the life of a Korean American spy named Henry Park, who had a traditional and strict Korean upbringing and later marries a white American speech therapist called Lelia. As suggested in the title of the book, Henry longs to become a real American native speaker. His fascination with language, in some ways both delightful and nightmarish, as Henry narrates, can be traced back to his childhood spent in kindergarten, where he had to interact with other kids in English. Henry says, "I didn't know what a difference in language meant then. Or how my tongue would tie in the initial attempts, stiffen so, struggle like an animal booby-trapped and dying inside my head" (234). Henry describes his tongue as a desperate and short-breathed animal invaded and besieged by English, a language that distinguishes sounds which, in the beginning, register no difference in his ears: "There is no B and V for us, no P and F. I always thought someone must have invented certain words to torture us. *Frivolous. Barbarian.*" Alien and rough-edged words stuff his mouth, making it open as if to release a caged and roaring animal.

To Henry, the drama of speaking is embodied in the tension between his tongue and different alphabets. If the shaping force of the mother tongue on the vocal organs usually acts out in a less visible manner, Korean is a fascinating case because it makes the process perceivable via written signs. The Korean alphabet, Hangeul, was invented in 1443 by King Sejong the Great to instruct people for correct sounds (Lee 202). It is a featural writing system that makes sounds visible by drawing inspiration from the positional shape of the mouth, lips, and teeth. Especially in terms of consonants, the shapes of those letters are graphical representations of the speech organs involved in articulating the respective sound (203). For instance, ㄴ, which resembles the coronal consonant "n," is a side view of the tip of the tongue raised against the gum ridge. In this way, written signs are aligned with vocal sounds to instruct and discipline speech organs. Inflicting opposing impulses on the Korean tongue, here the words "frivolous" and "barbarian" are not simply visual forms of speech that can be transcribed univocally. Among the evenly distributed letters, a stammering tongue taken hostage by the uncanny grouping of L/R and B/V is inserted. In a sense, the phonetic difference of these consonants is rather a physical one. The subtle distinction of these English consonants traps the Korean tongue in a contradictory manner: on the one hand, the tongue is overexposed as if it were a battlefield of languages; on the other hand, the tongue invokes the image of an inert and inapt form of life, hiding and withdrawing itself from both the speaker and the listener.

"In kindergarten," says Henry, "kids would call me 'Marble Mouth' because I spoke in a garbled voice, my bound tongue wrenching itself to move in the right ways" (234). His classmates sneered at him for not being able to speak "intelligibly" and he was sent to a class of Remedial Speech. "We were the school retards, the mentals, the losers who stuttered or could explode in rage or wet their pants or who just couldn't say the words." Instead of speaking out, the tongue pulls in and bends itself toward the gravity of internal organs. The shame of the tongue is the shame of exposure. If internal organs are shunned from visibility so as to preserve a sense of decency, the moment of being laughed at has seized the tongue in isolation, making what is supposed to be unseen visible.

Just as Henry discovers an erroneous body that appears incongruous to sounds of the English language, his fantasy of the union between language and body is mediated through his detailed account of the perfect verbal performance of his classmate back then. Henry recalls, "'Thus flies foul our fearless night owl,' she might say, the words forming so punctiliously on her lips, her head raised and neck straight and her eyes fixed on our teacher. Alice Eckles." The native body, it seems, is naturally engaged with an upward movement. His classmate Alice Eckles's lips stretch so that words can descend upon it precisely, her neck straightens in a proud manner, and her eyes settle upon the teacher with ease and confidence. His desire for perfect sounds is translated into the envy for the native, female body that "possesses" and emits such sounds. Indeed, how is one supposed to make sounds become flesh, if not through the mimetic relay of bodies? The discrepancy between a certain language and a speaking body is rendered into a problem of the mouth that fails to ventriloquize the voice of an idealized native body.

The same vocal and bodily fascination is vividly spelled out in Henry's relationship and marriage with Lelia. When they met for the first time, Henry was impressed by Lelia's verbal charm:

> I was immediately drawn to her. I liked the way she moved. I know how men will say this, to describe that womanly affect they find ineffable. I am as guilty as them all. There is a hurt that pinches your throat or chest when you look. But even before I took measure of her face and her manner, the shape of her body, her indefinite scent, all of which occurred

so instantly anyway, I noticed how closely I was listening to her. What I found was this: that she could really speak. At first I took her as being exceedingly proper, but I soon realized that she was simply executing the language. She went word by word. Every letter had a border. I watched her wide full mouth sweep through her sentences like a figure touring a dark house, flipping on spots and banks of perfectly drawn light.

The sensuality, in certain rigor. (10–11)

Henry listens to her closely. He listens not only to what she says but also how she says it. He has ears for the sensual touch that words place upon her tongue. Henry relates to her language in a way as if it had the power to bare and illuminate a body. Taking measure of the pace and manner in which Lelia "executes" her speech, the body of Henry becomes porously susceptible to sounds. The well-defined border of each letter singles out a sensual experience of words, which fill up the mouth "wide full" and make it glow with the rigor of light.

The shared craft of cautious speech and attentive listening is their initial bond with each other. Once and again, we witness that the desire to replicate the sounds of a foreign language corresponds to a logic of metonymy, which associates the tongue that produces sounds with the tongue that represents a sensuous body. In a conversation, Lelia commented that she could tell that Henry might think about still having an accent.

"You mean it's my face."
"No, it's not that," she answered. She reached over as if to touch my cheek but rested her arm instead on the bench back, grazing my neck. "Your face is part of the equation, but not in the way you're thinking. You look like someone listening to himself. You pay attention to what you're doing. If I had to guess, you're not a native speaker. Say something." (12)

Other than the common practice of attributing certain facial features to an ethnic revelation of the accent, the cited dialogue suggests an alternative and subtle way of accentuating one's foreignness. Lelia interprets Henry's steadfast and vigilant attention to his mouth and speech as a symptom that evidences that he is not at home in his language. His accent manifests precisely through his careful and successful efforts of undoing it. Though being equally articulate, Henry and Lelia relate to this consciously careful way of speaking in different manners: Henry's is owing to the fact that he is not born into that language and retains certain degree of uneasiness with his speech, whereas Lelia's results from her profession as a speech therapist and her social status as a native speaker. The former means to measure up to the norms by executing each syllable with precision, while the latter acts out the expected role as what Lelia calls "the standard-bearer."

The Final Report: The Buccal Theater

The murder case has brought us to a reevaluation of death and murder at different levels: the annihilation and replacement of the named things, according to Nietzsche, Hegel, and Schwenger; the murder of words, according to Nabokov; and, lastly, the suffering and shattering of the speaking body, as Nabokov implies and Ch'ien explicitly argues. We have thus reached a point where my investigation leaves no better advice than dropping the charge. Insofar as the alleged crime subjects the speaking body to an irreconcilable and oscillating narrative of being a victim and a perpetrator, it is futile to hope for closing the case by singling out a particular culprit. So, instead, I suggest that it is the logic of negativity that underlines the formulation of the mouth as a buccal tribunal that has to be worked through. The key to resolving a case like this is to move beyond the narrative of murder and death, reconceptualizing the mouth in terms that undo the juridical metaphor, while reviving alternative modes of relationality between languages and speakers.

With this in mind, I propose to have a look at Samuel Beckett's short plays *Not I* (1972) and *A Piece of Monologue* (1979), which concentrate on the act of speaking by reducing the theatrical stage to a minimalist expression of a speaking body or a disembodied mouth in darkness. In both plays, the narrators, identified simply as Mouth in *Not I* and Speaker in *A Piece of Monologue*, have difficulty employing the first-person pronoun to tell their stories. Mouthing their monologues and confessions in a style of third-person narrative, they alienate the "I" from the act of speaking, making the mouth a theatrical stage that is transformed by the performance of words. Whereas Beckett's plays stage literally the conflation of theater and mouth, I will turn to the Kleinian psychoanalyst Donald Meltzer, who employs the concept of "the buccal theater" to analyze the preverbal stage of child development, in which one's relationship to words and the world is informed and performed out through the act of mouthing.

Beckett's *Not I* is an unsettling play. Imagine being in an enclosed space where darkness is dense and smothering. In front is a disembodied mouth throbbing. A mouth without a face. All you can make out is thin red lips moving, white teeth clenching, and tongue thrusting in and out nervously.

The mouth is pouring out words, spasmodic and hysterical words. Such is the minimalist setting of Beckett's play. As the stage is given in to a mouth that is cracked open by the explosive force of words, the audience may experience an uneasy sensation of being sucked in. Words bend and uncurl the tongue, weighing heavily on the lips, then fleeting into darkness as if terrified of their power:

> ...words were coming... Imagine!... words were coming... a voice she did not recognize... at first... so long since it had sounded... then finally had to admit... could be none other... than her own... certain vowel sounds... she had never heard... after long efforts... when suddenly she felt... gradually she felt... her lips moving... imagine!... her lips moving... as of course till then she had not... and not alone the lips... the cheeks... the jaws...the whole face... all those—... what?... the tongue?... yes... the tongue in the mouth... all those contortions without which... no speech possible... and yet in the ordinary way... not felt at all...

The mouth that is now shooting bullets of words once waited for words to come. Beckett's theater of the mouth visualizes the uneasy passage of words. The difficulty in telling and making sense of what happened to her is embodied in and translated into the physical obstruction of movements in the buccal area. The nervous opening and closing of the mouth, on the one hand, is a celebration of the birth and rebirth of words and, on the other hand, dreads the story that is taking shape and has to survive it by shattering words.

Whereas *Not I* literally transforms the theater into a disembodied mouth that takes pains in giving birth to words, it is in Beckett's short play *A Piece of Monologue* that the unsettling birth of words relies on the mouth to partake in the unity of sense and meaning. "Faint diffuse light [...]. Lamp out. Silence. Speaker, globe, foot of pallet, barely visible in diffuse light" (1). "Nothing to be heard anywhere. Room once full of sounds. Faint sounds. Whence unknown" (3). "Fade. Gone. Cry. Snuffed with breath of nostrils. Again and Again. Again and again gone. Till whose grave?" (4). Beckett's stage, vague and viscous, melts into a state of vortex, awaiting the birth of first word. Vast blackness, with lamplight piercing through and diming down, enwraps Speaker, so that he could merge into his surroundings at any moment. "From funeral to funeral [...]. Funerals of [...] loved ones," Speaker makes birth "the death of him" (1); and death punctuates life as punctuation separates words. Nothing is steady; everything is muddy.

First word is born of "the black ditch beneath" (3), overheard and half-heard at the graveside. "Stands staring beyond half hearing what he's saying.

He? The words falling from his mouth. Making do with his mouth [...]. Waits for first word always the same. It gathers in his mouth. Parts lips and thrusts tongue forward. Birth. Parts the dark" (3). Words gather and grow, sprout and overtake. They become heavy, bulky, glutinous, dribbling and trickling out of the mouth and across the chin. Words gain a material intensity, which opposes to the features (lightness and invisibility) that define their acoustic quality. Words move the mouth, whereas the mouth makes words flesh. Intrigued by the bodily birth of words suggested in the sentence "parts lips and thrusts tongue forward," the Polish translator Antoni Libera comments,

> Parting the lips is both a condition for and a result of pronouncing the plosive consonant "b"; thrusting the tongue forward, more precisely, pushing it out through the parted lips and teeth, describes in turn the action involved in pronouncing the sound "th"... This connection links the parting of lips and thrusting forward of the tongue, necessary for the articulation of the word "birth," with the actual act of birth. In other words, the pronunciation of this word is simultaneously the image or symbol of that which it signifies. ("A Piece of Monologue")

As the word "birth" is brought forth by the intimate and powerful contact of lips and tongue, the world of things and events collides with that of words and speech. The point is not to read lips and tongue as a metaphor or imitation of sexualized organs (although such reading is not completely unfounded). Rather, the birth of words, in Beckett's play, retains its rawness and roughness; it is physical and concrete, whose effect can only be maximized through a literal reading. This vocal birth is no less powerful and exciting than the actual birth, because at the moment of speaking, the sensory reality and the sensation of it strike repercussions. The brief, fleeting contact of lips temporarily inhibits air in the mouth, breeding a momentum of explosion; and the following thrust of the tongue prolongs this momentum, breathing air into life and making words flesh. The mouth, in Beckett's play, is versatile: it is the womb, the language machine, the house of being. The mouth is no trifle matter. It conceives words that are blossomed from things themselves. It gives birth to words that are going to outlive and defy the mouth. Words and things unite upon the lips as carriers of sensations. The contact of lips and the gliding of the tongue materializes sounds, making them resonate performatively with the designated things and events.

Donald Meltzer, a Kleinian psychoanalyst who combined the mother-baby model of early learning processes with aesthetic experience and creativity, sees the mouth not as a juncture between words and things, but a passageway that stretches all the way from internal thought to external play. In his paper "Concerning the Perception of One's Own Attributes and Its Relation to Language Development," Meltzer writes,

> Lalling is to be seen as the vocal aspect of a more general phase in cognitive development in which the physical space of the oral cavity is utilised as the theatre of phantasy and play, a mid-point between external play and internal thought (dream-thought or phantasy) [...]. In this theatre of phantasy the sounds can be manipulated as concrete objects devoid of fixed or determined meaning but rather deriving their meaning from the immediate juxtaposition with other sounds and buccal objects. When the child moves on to accept the conventional meaning of the words in the discourse that he achieves through various forms of identification, this buccal theatre is moved outside the body because manual dexterity improves and play becomes less frustrating. But the tendency to employ the buccal theatre continues in the form of play with words based on homonymity, splitting and recombination of syllables, spoonerisms, puns, alliteration, ambiguity—in short all the devices of poetic diction. (179)

Meltzer suggests that words, journeying through the mouth, have the ability to reach both ends; they can be as invisible and elusive as dream-thoughts and as concrete as buccal objects. Although this duality of language and speech seems to manifest itself primarily in an early infantile stage of language learning where speech borders on lolling, Meltzer emphasizes that the impulse for pleasure associated with the dual play of words in what he calls "the buccal theater" does not totally fade into obscurity after the child learns to conform to the conventional meaning of words; on the contrary, it comes back every now and then in a form of phonetical and grammatical variance that diverges from the everyday use of language and the overarching functionality of communication.

Noticeably, the examples given by Meltzer, be it spoonerism or puns, homonymity or alliteration, more or less possess a poetic implication and thus run the risk of suggesting that the duality of language appeals only to aesthetic experience and poetic diction. It is through Maria Rhode's reading of Meltzer, especially with the two articles "The Physicality of Words: Some Implications of Donald Meltzer's Writings on Language" and "Sensory Aspects of Language Development in Relation to Primitive Anxieties," that the "non-communicative use of vocalisation" and "the interplay between sound and meaning" is closely analyzed in combination with infant observations and clinical cases. The aesthetic experience of language gains its foundation in the lived experiences of preverbal and autistic children.

Rhode aims to develop Meltzer's concept of the infantile "exploratory mouthing" (Meltzer 175), shedding light on what Meltzer calls the "song and dance level" of language. Inspired by Meltzer and Susanne Langer's distinction between the semantic component and the musical component of language, Rhode emphasizes that there are two aspects of language: one has to do with meaning, sense, and communication, whereas the other deals with words as "sensory constructs with rhythmical and musical properties" ("Sensory Aspect" 12). Children with autism grant us access to the sensory and material aspect of language in a fashion of disjunction between sense and sound, as they "often focus on the sensory level at the expense of meaning" (271).

One illustrative case concerns Patrick, a four-year-old boy with autism. Rhode observed that Patrick obsessively repeated "Whhzzt ... whhzzt" while being tripped by or falling off his chair. She had been unable to make sense of Patrick's idiosyncratic repetition of "whhzzt," until later in an occasion Patrick asked her "What's that?". "With something of a shock," Rhode wrote, "I realised that 'What's that?' was an expansion of his original 'Whhzzt?'" Rhode explained further,

> I think that he was attempting to control the threatening aspects of reality by magical means. If he equates the space in his mouth with the space of the room, then collapsing the vowel-spaces of his words could be a way of trying to manage his frightening experience of space and the associated threat of falling. [...] Conversely, children who omit consonants when they begin to speak—what French workers call a 'démutisation en voyelles'—seem to be denying the presence of boundaries. ("The Physicality of Words" 276)

In the case of Patrick, language relates to body and space not only in terms of referentiality and addressability, but it interacts with both through the act of performative imitation. According to Rhode, primitive and bodily anxieties lead Patrick to an interiorization of the physical space of the room; through omitting vowels in the sentence, Patrick verbally removes the obstacles that threaten him physically. However, Patrick does not completely invent his own speech codes; although being barely intelligible, "whhzzt" still resembles its conventional and communicative double, "What's that." This resemblance becomes identifiable for Rhode after hearing Patrick switch back to the more conventional way of expression that involves Rhode as a potential participant and generator of meanings. As Patrick deploys the mouth to navigate himself in the space, he modifies sounds in a way that it makes his act of speaking a sensory experience of space and a means to overcome his bodily anxiety about boundaries.

Rhode's analysis gives a glimpse of Meltzer's conceptualization of the mouth "as the site where, during babyhood and early toddlerhood, exploratory mouthing involves both the manipulation of objects and the generation of meaning" (Meltzer 175). Here the "exploratory mouthing" and the play of sound and meaning is significant, since the verbal imitation points not to the desire of communication with other humans but to a bodily navigation among and toward physical things. This tendency, as Rhode explains, is also common among non-autistic children. She gives the example of a little boy of eighteen months, who, after being introduced to a pregnant woman whose name was Meg, pointed to her breast and said, "Mummy Egg!" Rhode observed that "for him, the name Meg was neither abstract nor arbitrary: he construed it as a combination of two familiar words that conveyed important information about her condition" (275). Unconsciously imitating the physical state of the pregnant woman through reconfiguring words in his mouth, the boy speaks so as to make sense of the happening ("Egg") and, at the same time, to measure the force that may take hold of an intimate part of him ("Mummy").

Instead of murdering languages and things via the act of speaking or putting the speaking bodies on trial, the theater of the mouth, as it is depicted by Beckett and Meltzer, is intimately involved in the linguistic emergence and transformation of the world through translating the condition of the speaking body and the physicality of the language into a sensory encounter with designated things. In Beckett's plays, the opening of the mouth is driven by the gathering of words. Whereas words force their weight and volume upon the lips and tongue, the mouth opens itself up to the acoustic and expressive quality of things. While being in line with Beckett's theatrical staging of the mouth as the locus for the problematic birth of words, Meltzer's conceptualization of the mouth being the buccal theater and Rhode's clinical analysis and application of it fully explore the implications of the performative imitation between words and things in and through the mouth. For Meltzer and Rhode, speech emerges through a vocal transference of things to the sensory and perceptive scope of the body. Before words are released from the gloomy underground of the belly, the body breathes things, images, and ideas in and out, having them rub the vocal cords and vibrate in the chamber of the mouth. The moment of speaking, with voice running after the roaming words, pronounces the actual birth of a possible relation between words and things.

However, the vocal transference does not lead to what Nietzsche conceives to be "the metamorphosis of the world in human beings" (879). The performative imitation of the mouth is twofold. On the one hand, it happens between words and objects. As the inventive phrase of "Mummy Egg" shows, the child may identify the structure of the word with the physical shape of the object it denotes (280). On the other hand, it implies the bodily and vocal orientation that caters to the ambience of the designated thing. For instance, Rhode observes that Patrick seems to "equate the space in his mouth with the space of the room" (276), and the collapse of the vowel-space suggests an attempt to deterritorialize the external space. In either case, the vocal imitation does not point directly to the representation of the named thing in question but rather to the attempt of attributing meaning to the thing and of negotiating its relation to the body. Meltzer and Rhode, therefore, shift the discussion of the relation between language and the speaker from Nietzsche's conception of an anthropocentric metamorphosis to the multi-adaptation of things, languages, and bodies upon their encounter in the mouth.

A few final words to persuade the prosecutor to drop the charge of murder: there is always birth and death in the act of speaking. Affection may wither (with a dry and cold voice), just as hope may revive (so that we may release the cat or frog in the throat). Insofar as the mouth offers a stage for words to (re)invent themselves, new possible sets of relations come into being and acquire new meanings. A foreigner's rebirth happens when the mouth is transformed from a tribunal to a theater, where speaking is no longer associated with a debt to be repaid or a misdeed to be atoned for, but with a virtual and sensual form of life that is taking shape at the tip of the tongue. Language is more than a tool, and the mouth more than a tribunal. Moreover, I propose that literary theorization, likewise, should be disengaged from the metaphor of killing and murdering. Eve Kosofsky Sedgwick argues that critical inquiry has been increasingly and exclusively equated to a mode of what she calls "*paranoid* reading," which places faith in hermeneutics of suspicion and exposure (123). Instead, she calls for the integration of "*reparative* reading" into literary and cultural criticism. Indeed, a reparative approach to the mouth, the speaker, and to language and literature—this is what this chapter is aiming for. To theorize is to translate the murmur of literary texts into the language of a touching hand, to stay attentively close to the sensuous, and, at the same time, to sense the sense of sensation.

4. Onomatopoeic Translation

On Speaking as Such and on Speaking a Foreign Tongue

Abstract: This chapter explores the practice of imitating the sounds of a foreign language, framing it as a form of onomatopoeic translation, emphasizing the uneven transfer of the speaking body from one language to another through imitation. Drawing on Walter Benjamin's idea of translation as essential to language and as a mimetic, non-sensuous process, I analyze Eva Hoffman's *Lost in Translation* to describe how foreign sounds, particularly names, are imitated and how this shapes one's perception of words and bodies. I argue that onomatopoeia and translation function as strategies to tame foreign sounds while also challenging our understanding of linguistic and bodily legitimacy.

Keywords: onomatopoeia; mimesis; naming; Walter Benjamin; Eva Hoffman

Travelogue

How does a cat purr?

American English says "meow," and British "miaow." Apparently, our American cats have adopted a different way of speaking than British ones. It is not a problem for us to communicate, though. Our ways of speaking are similar enough to make fun of one another's language as a vulgar dialect. (Who says we don't have the problem of communication!)

I have always been a big fan of traveling, but the world I'm discovering along the journey becomes less and less recognizable. How am I going to survive the disastrous flooding of computers and inedible mice? I've witnessed—yes, I am no longer a kitty still wet behind the ears—a growing number of Japanese cats, most of whom are immigrants, expats, and students, landing on the sacred territory of our country. Just imagine it: How come, after many years of living here, Japanese cats are still bowing while mumbling "*nyā nyā nyā*," instead of looking into the other's eyes and saying "meow meow meow"!

Is it true that to Japanese ears cats do naturally purr this way? Or does it have to do with Japanese mouths, which are attuned to the Japanese script notoriously known for its limited range of phonetic sounds? These questions keep my mind so occupied that I finally decided to travel to Tokyo. I've learned that Japanese syllables generally consist of vowels and consonant-vowel compounds. English words that end with consonants, such as "email" and "food," often stop too abruptly and harshly to fully reach Japanese ears. A certain Japanese cat told me last night—we met at a mice-hunting club, if I remember correctly—that these words made him sick. They reminded him of mice feasting on exotic olives: without noticing the pits inside, they all ended up having the pits clogged in their throats and being choked to death. He swore that he had seen it with his own eyes. "A horrible scene! Disgusting! But, well," he shrugged his shoulders and continued, "at least it spared me the trouble of killing them..." To prevent Japanese cats from neurosis, and to assist the "crippling" English words, he told me, Japanese cats generously lend each lonely English consonant the clutch of a vowel. "English with a vowel clutch: we call it Katakana English," he winked at me curiously.

And he is right. The clutch is a magic wand! *Kizzu* (kids), *biiru* (beer), *beddo* (bed), *bicchi* (beach)... My hurl and fling of English words used to knock myself into a Japanese face shrouded by sheer blankness. But now, with the assistance of the vowel clutch, the stony face is restored to its humanity—oh no, wait, *cat*-ity, as I try to undo anthropocentric metaphors—and transfigured instead into an empathetic and readable mask. (Life Tip: next time, try *basu* instead of "bus," unless you do not mind the everyday bus-catch drama of almost-make-it.) This is a survivor's tale: in order to make myself understood, I have to trust and imitate the uncanny sounds, to let my language cripple and suffer, and to accept the inadequacy of my cat language. So, lips are parted and vowels crash in: *Hurrah!* What a cute, fresh, newborn—but wait, a newborn *bastard*—thing?

Yes, a bastardized language, a word salad of exotic taste, the most pathetic form of life. What am I supposed to do with a language that bends too easily to the will of the tongue? Or, perhaps, I should never have had trusted a faithless cat tongue which possesses no ears and hands to feel the lustrous body of sounds? Ach, can you imagine, by the end of this trip, I became very much tired of traveling from one tongue to another. Onomatopoeia: this is the cursed state that marks the fall of Babel in the cat world.

The Accent: An Onomatopoeic Tongue in Translation

Suppose that a cat could talk, would the differences of cat tongues bother her in the same way that accents and speech variations come to annoy us? The curious but exhausted cat traveler, who kept a journal to record her language adventures, went all the way to Tokyo to figure out what has made the Japanese cats in the United States unable to speak and behave like American cats. However, upon arriving in Japan, with her tongue orphaned and exiled from the maternal protection, the traveler realized, to her disappointment, that her relation to her native language degenerated into a state of approximation, compromise, and mutilation. The clutch of the vowel, necessitated by the speaking habits of Japanese cats, was the token of triumph and humiliation. The price she had to pay for mutual understanding was to tolerate the minor linguistic practice of putting on an off-center accent and to have her mother tongue be influenced and transformed by the Japanese script. It horrified her, in the end, to adopt a hybrid and imprecise tongue, disloyal to both Japanese and English.

The trip did not seem to be an easy one. Yet, to some extent, didn't the traveler get what she was looking for? Her experience in Tokyo resembled that of the Japanese cats in the United States, whose tongues were stuck in between languages. They had to be parted from the ease of the mother tongue. The seemingly natural and unmediated relation to words and sounds was replaced by a new self-conscious way of listening and speaking. The process went as follows: "meow" ... "*nyā*" ... "meow-*ā*?" Here, the Japanese way of purring and speaking served as a middle ground, which brought the Japanese cat tongue closer to English while preventing them from becoming assimilated and identical.

By the end of her trip, the cat traveler was afraid that onomatopoeia was the unwanted but authentic term that defined her migration from one tongue to another. Think about it: the way that a speaker relates to a foreign tongue is often onomatopoeic. To purr like a cat, one cannot escape the phonetic rule of the language in question, which transcribes the purr as "meow," "miaow," or "*nyā*." Language gives orders and the mouth disciplines itself accordingly. Likewise, when learning to speak a foreign language, one has to listen to the native speaker attentively, with the hope to reproduce each sound—be it the rolling /r/, the lulling /l/, the burping /sch/, or the varying tones—down to the last detail. It is not so much that the body speaks a language as that the language speaks the body, making it a delimiting mouthpiece of its overall constellation. The tongue has to reinvent itself without betraying the original. However, considering the fact that onomatopoeia often brings together entities of a heterogeneous nature and quality—for instance, between animal and human, sound and language—it is difficult, if not impossible, to make them fully resemble one another. The accuracy of the vocal imitation and the desire to become a total instrument of the foreign language is inevitably conditioned by the linguistic codes of the mother tongue and the specificities of the speaking body (in terms of its biological makeup, past, experience, etc.). The ears start to listen wishfully, and the mouth is inclined to producing the sound dogmatically.

A cat will not protest: "Who says I purr with the sound of 'meow' or '*nyā*'?" Even if it does, human ears are not delicate enough to crack the code of a cat's language. Yet, a person will surely be unhappy if someone describes his or her speech "barbarous." The Greek word βάρβαρος is an onomatopoeic word, deriving from the βαρ-βαρ (bar-bar) sounds that the ancient Greeks used to imitate and belittle the foreign tongue incomprehensible to them.[1] Here, onomatopoeia, as a rhetoric, is deployed to illustrate the reductiveness and alienness of a foreign tongue. At the same time, the practice of imitating the sounds of a foreign language is sometimes framed as onomatopoeic, which is equally meant to evoke the image of an incompetent and inadequate tongue. The lyric of John Prine's song "Onomatopoeia" goes: "Bang! went the pistol. Crash! went the window. Ouch! went the son of a gun. Onomatopoeia: I don't want to see ya speaking in a foreign tongue."

In the great adventure of the migrating tongue, some acoustic traits of the mother tongue are assimilated and smoothed out, whereas some persist and stand out as the untranslatable chunks of foreignness. The onomatopoeic imitation of the speaking body thus can produce a vocal trace and an acoustic remnant—the accent. Roman Jakobson, a Russian linguist and literary theorist who spoke many languages "with a recognizable Russian accent," was jokingly said to "speak Russian in seven different languages" (Pearson 100). The accent testifies the omnipresence of the mother tongue, which, in Jakobson's case, seems to make all languages nothing but Russian in disguise. Another hilarious example can be found in the English textbook of a first-year Chinese student. Reflecting on the Chinese students' imitation

---

[1] One of the conceptual potentials of onomatopoeia lies in its ability to trigger a crisis of the distinction between resemblance and alienness, between inside and outside. It is similar to how the figure of the barbarian has been constructed and used to reinforce the idea of a civilized us versus a barbarian other. In this way, the outside is not a static outside which can exist independently; it is constitutive to the production of the civilized, superior us. The inside and outside enter into a relation of constant production, and the boundary is being produced and defined repeatedly. See *Barbarism Revisited: New Perspectives on an Old Concept*, edited by Maria Boletsi and Christian Moser.

and acquisition of the English pronunciation, an English teacher explains in a journal article,

> In order to get a direct sense of pronunciation many English beginners write Chinese words under the English words to indicate the English pronunciation. "Good morning" for example, they write "狗得猫娘" prononnced [sic] "go de mau niang" which the English meaning is like 'the dog gets cat's mother'. The word "bag" they write "白鸽" under the English word which is pronounced "bai ge". It's [sic] English meaning is like 'white pigeon'. Some even write Chinese words under the English words of a whole English text. Learning English like this they got poor pronunciation. When they read the English text, you may properbly [sic] think they read Chinese. They can't get rid of the Chinese dialect when speak [sic] English. (Dong 55)

Scribbled with Chinese characters floundering to instruct the English pronunciation, the textbook becomes shot through with spelled-out accents. The Chinese characters "狗得猫娘" and "白鸽," written under English words, may be mistaken, at first glance, as translations of the sentences. However, the linguistic equivalence, in this scenario, has to do with sounds instead of meanings. The senses of Chinese characters are disregarded so as to be deployed as devices for sound imitation. The contrived association of the phrase "the dog gets cat's mother" with "good morning" becomes imposed on the tongue because of the onomatopoeic potentiality of those Chinese characters. Or, strictly speaking, the senses, although having nothing to do with the "original," are not exactly disregarded but rather evoked and manipulated in such a way to build up a dramatic effect and to enhance the memorization of the pronunciation. In this way, the pure sensational rendering of sounds becomes mediated through and supplemented by the semantic quality of Chinese characters. The hassle is, however, that the distinguished tone of each Chinese character lingers and becomes an integral part of the English pronunciation. This is how we arrive at a "tonalized" English. The odd sensation of hearing words with tones is not unlike seeing two sets of jigsaw puzzles mixed up by mistake, with the pieces being too detailed and myriad to be disentangled to give a complete picture of either set. The accent, as the token of the phonetic non-equivalence between two languages, makes the practice of learning to speak a new language a laboratory for experimenting with the (un)translatability and (in)compatibility of languages at the sound level.

Therefore, to speak with a foreign accent often unwittingly stages the process of translating the mother tongue—with the tongue both as a language and a speech organ—into another language. The speaker may draw upon the mother tongue, with its entire repertoire of sounds, shapes, and senses, to tone down the alienness of the foreign language, translating unfavorable chunks into familiar terms. On the other hand, the mother tongue, which comes first in harnessing and shaping the speaking body, seems to ascend to the state of the original, which forbids the tongue to become fully assimilated into other languages. Because of the sustenance and interference of the mother tongue, the speaking body relates to a foreign language in a *translational* and *onomatopoeic* fashion—in the sense that the vocal imitation of the foreign tongue is underlined with a conflicting tendency of approximation and imprecision and a double articulation of junction and disjunction.

I propose the initiation of the tongue into a foreign language be framed as a practice of onomatopoeic translation, which foregrounds the uneven transference of the speaking body from one language to another under the regime of imitation. The adjective "onomatopoeic" is meant to emphasize that, firstly, the drama of a translated tongue is carried out at the sound level; and, secondly, the tension between faithfulness and betrayal—concepts that are often invoked in the discussion on translation—comes into play as well at the sound level. The questions are, however: Is the translated tongue an exceptional state of being? Is there a mode of speaking that is not a translation by definition?

Walter Benjamin, in his essay "On Language as Such and on the Language of Man," written in 1916 but published posthumously, proposes a different way of defining language that liberates the definition of translation from the conventional focus on the linguistic realm. Benjamin argues that language is not an exclusive phenomenon of the human world; we can talk about language that issues from matter—for example, the language of sculptures, lamps, or music. Language, in this case, is the medium through which an entity expresses its mental and linguistic being. "The language of this lamp, for example," writes Benjamin, "communicates not the lamp (for the mental being of the lamp, insofar as it is communicable, is by no means the lamp itself) but the language-lamp, the lamp in communication, the lamp in expression" (63). Benjamin further makes a distinction between the thing-language—with the language of the lamp being one example—and the name language of man. The language of sculptures and paintings, argues Benjamin, is a translation of thing-languages, whereas poetry finds its expression in and through the name language. Benjamin proposes that translation is not a consequence of the communication among languages but is essential to what language is: "It is necessary to found the concept of translation at the deepest level of linguistic theory, for it is much too far-reaching and powerful to be treated in any way as an afterthought, as has happened occasionally" (69). Benjamin defines translation rather broadly: it refers not only to the transmission of meaning from one language to another but also to a transference of expressible contents among entities of various sorts and a negotiation of compatibility, singularity, and otherness.

    I would argue that a translated tongue, to read along the lines of Benjamin's understanding of translation, is all that we have. Language filters out the unrepresentable layers of the infinite that each thing and experience potentially points to, giving it a relatively traceable and steady quality to which the psyche can be anchored. The uniqueness of each experience has to be flattened to a certain degree so as to make it communicable and exchangeable. Similarly, language recognizes the singularity of a thing or a phenomenon only to the extent that it leaves room for each emergence to grow under its linguistic skin. The readability and representability of each thing and event relies on its translatability into something less and other than itself. To speak is to translate: vocal sounds take shape by translating things into a sensory encounter with the tongue. The act of speaking and translating not only orients itself toward the referent as its original but also stays attuned to the specificity of the speaking body.

    Onomatopoeia, in a way, exemplifies the process of translation among words, things, and bodies at the level of speech. It reveals how they relate to one another via acoustic and vocal imitation, how such relation is limited and modified by rules and conventions, and how they inevitably bear traces of otherness. However, even though the concept of onomatopoeic translation is applicable to the act of speaking as such, depending on which language we are dealing with, its significance varies. With the mother tongue, we expect words and things to be intimate with each other, sharing an undistinguished existence. The mechanism of translation remains a blind spot, which guarantees the consistency of reality in representation and experience. Yet, when a foreign language is concerned, we are forced to realize and forsake this expectation, which often results in a heightened awareness of translation as an existential condition. The foreign accent, in particular, as mentioned, stands as a reminder for the tongue's onomatopoeic and translational relation to the foreign language and to the world it aims to name and describe. In the remainder of this chapter, I will expand the conceptualization of onomatopoeic translation from *an imitative apparatus* that captures and reveals a tongue in migration, as the case of the foreign accent illuminates, to *a linguistic and cultural practice* that characterizes how we tend to deal with sounds and bodies that are deemed foreign to a certain linguistic system. The concept of onomatopoeic translation derives from Benjamin's understanding of translation as integral to what language is and as a mimetic process in a non-sensuous manner. I will expand it to describe and encapsulate the experience of relating to foreign sounds—especially in terms of the name—as an imitation at the sound level, which in turn influences how one perceives the "aura" of words and the image of one's body. I single out two moments: the onomatopoeic translation of natural sounds into language and that of foreign names into the native tongue. On the one hand, onomatopoeia and translation can both function as strategies or devices for domesticating and taming sounds and noises; and on the other hand, they can lead to a crisis of exemplarity and legitimacy, which challenges our understanding of language and body.

Onomatopoeia: When Language Sounds Barbarous

Onomatopoeia refers to the formation of a word based on the imitation of a sound made by or associated with the thing or action it names. The English language, for instance, borrows a wide range of sounds from the chit-chat of animals and things: *tick tock* walks the clock; *chirp chirp* sings the bird; *oink oink* grunts the pig. The imitative relation between a word and its referent makes language a sensuous experience. As if a coil spring or the beak were placed into the mouth, the onomatopoeic words bring one closer to a melodic and turbulent world populated by sounds.

There is something archaic in the pleasure one feels upon hearing these words. The *peekaboo* effect, as I call it: the acoustic resemblance of the word to its referent seems able to deliver the immediate presence of the lost object, assuring one that he or she is not alone and that the caretaker is about to restore the peace and order following the magic sound. Onomatopoeia is the cure for the primal anxiety over absence and loss. For children, onomatopoeic words can often be understood with the least efforts and can be enjoyed alongside their rattle balls and bath squeeze toys. Intermingled with sounds emitted from the "voicing" objects other than the human mouth, words inspired by the polyphony of the world form a middle ground on which children are trained to reach further to words that appear less natural and straightforward. No wonder comics, primers, and children's literature are the territory where it reigns with rigor and legitimacy. In *We're Going on a Bear Hunt* (1989), the family adventure of wild animal hunting turns out to be a hunt for onomatopoeic words. The natural obstacles (grass, rive, mud, forest, snowstorm, cave) that make the family cry out in despair—"We can't go over it. We can't under it. Oh no! We've got to go through it"—all end up being removed through the conquering sounds of "swishy swashy," "splash splosh," "squelch squerch," "stumble trip," "hoooo woooo," and "tiptoe" without exception. The mouthful of explosive and articulate sounds seizes the attention of children immediately not only because it can be understood intuitively and without a rich base of knowledge, but also because it transforms the mouth into a theater that promises an immersive and sensuous experience of language as a sound object.

The earliest primers, which Walter Benjamin refers to as "voice books" in his essay "Children's Literature," "were based on onomatopoeia. The *O* rang out in the mouth of a drayman urging his horses on in the illustration; the *Sh* comes from a woman shooing the hens in another picture; the *R* is a dog growling; and the *S* is a hissing snake" (250–51). Whereas it is difficult to assert a univocal and straightforward connection between alphabetic letters and onomatopoeia, the onomatopoeic representation of letters helps to make language in its written form closer to speech for children who are at "the earliest stages, when each sign is a yoke under which hand and tongue have to humble themselves" (250). The imitative resemblance between the sound of a word and that of its referent is drawn upon so as to alleviate the alienness of written signs, smoothing the way for children to relate to language as a visual and spatial form.

The dramatic appeal of onomatopoeia, on the other hand, seems to lack finesse and sophistication, evoking a childish sort of pleasure and a primitive image of language. In "Speech Police and Polyglot Play," Yoko Tawada comments,

> In comics, *pst* or *hopp* ("quick") are placed in a dialogue bubble, whereas *zzz* or *bang* are placed in the air. They represent a form and manner of movement, but they can never become adverbs. Perhaps, because it is too obvious that they imitate noises. In general, language has to pretend that it has long ago abolished the gesture of imitation. Onomatopoeia in language is regarded as something primitive. (59)

According to Tawada, some onomatopoeic words are not readily integrated into language. Instead of making it more accessible and expressive, they threaten to downgrade language to the level of noise. Words such as "click," "tiptoe," and "flip" are formalized and conventionalized in English and thus can form a grammatical relation with other words. The sound imitation of sleep, *zzz*, or of hesitation, *ummm*, seems to challenge the linguistic codes of English, since it is relatively rare to have three consecutive consonants in English words. By failing to observe rules and conventions of a certain language, these alternatively coded representations of sounds risk the possibility of confusing language with noise and of mistaking bodily sounds for speech. They seem doomed to be expatriated, dismissed, and kept apart from the linguistic system, as if to prevent language from becoming less or other than itself.

So, who is afraid of onomatopoeia—the *buzz* and *boom*, the *smack slurp* and the *tinkle twang*? How does the tension between onomatopoeia and language manifest itself in theory? Ferdinand de Saussure, in *Course in General Linguistics* (1915), is rather quick to save his linguistic theory from the "contamination" of onomatopoeia. While foregrounding the arbitrariness of the linguistic sign as the first general principle, Saussure realizes that this formulation might invite two objections—one is from onomatopoeia, and the other is interjections. Because of the vocal association or resemblance between the word and its referent—which often results in the concurrence of sound and meaning—onomatopoeic formations can hardly be said to be completely unmotivated and arbitrary. Saussure responds to this objection by distinguishing what he considers to be "authentic onomatopoeic words" from fortuitous ones: Firstly, Saussure argues that the "authentic" onomatopoeia—under which category words such as *glug-glug* and *tick-cock* appear—is not only limited in number but also subject to conventions that evolve along history and vary from one language to another. Each language tends to render the rich sonorous quality of things and names into a limited set of potentiality based on its own phonetic possibilities. Secondly, the sonorous quality of words like the French *fouet* (whip) or *glas* (knell)—which derive respectively from *fagus* (beech-tree) and *classicum* (sound of a trumpet)—seems to come from an "impure" or "false" origin, being, to use Saussure's words, "a fortuitous result of phonetic evolution" (69). "Onomatopoeic formations and interjections are of secondary importance," thus concludes Saussure, "and their symbolic origin is in part open to dispute" (70).

This gesture of trivialization and rejection, which looks innocent and sensible at first glance, becomes suspected, dramatized, and rigorously questioned through Jacques Derrida's deconstructive reading in his book *Glas* (1986):

> But instead of concluding that there is then no authentically arbitrary element either, instead of taking an interest in the *contaminated* effects of onomatopoeia or of arbitrariness, in the drawing-along of the language

[*langue*] (with the *fouet* or *glas*), he runs ahead of the "danger" in order to save the thesis of the sign's arbitrariness. [...] What will remain of the internal system of the language [*langue*], of the "organic elements of a linguistic system," when it will have been purified, stripped of all those qualities, of those attributions, of that evolution? (93–94)

Even for a modern reader, well trained in theory and tolerant to Derrida's notorious obscurity, *Glas* would appear unreadable and challenging. Written in two parallel columns, it juxtaposes Derrida's reading of the Hegelian dialectic with that of the French novelist and playwright Jean Genet's literary works. The original French title of the book *Glas*, which the English translators decide to leave untranslated, evokes the image of the looking-glass or mirror. This association can barely be said to be fortuitous or uncalled-for—not only because the vocal and visual similarities between *glas* and "glass" is hard to miss, but also in the sense that the juxtaposed texts do imply the metaphor of showing as if with a mirror, inviting a gesture of looking alongside the habit of reading. The mechanism and sensation of mirroring, reflecting, and deflecting run back and forth among philosophy, literature, and the reading body.

On the other hand, the French word *glas* refers to the tolling of a death knell, which, according to Geoffrey H. Hartman, "is endlessly 'joyced' by the author, to suggest that voice has no monument except in the form of a rattle in the throat covered or sublimed by the passing bell. The sound reverberates in the labyrinth of writing and, in dying, lights it up" (765). The sound-word *glas* thus pronounces the unwavering influence of sound and voice on writing; and the death toll of logocentrism—whose dominance in Western philosophy was vigorously argued against in Derrida's earlier publication *Of Grammatology*—instead of performing a totalizing gesture of closure, unfolds a labyrinth of meaning where the specter of voice is invited to haunt the grand manner of the deconstructive rhetoric. Death finalizes or settles for nothing; it is meant to mark the impossibility of continuation, opening up a void of meaning and interpretation where one's relation to the reign of the old master—be it Hegel or Genet—becomes fictive and undecidable.

So, for whom does the French word *glas* toll? The word, as mentioned, appears in Saussure's argument as an example for fortuitous or "inauthentic" onomatopoeia. Derrida, by making the "suggestive sonority" (Saussure 69) resound here and there in his hypertext, brings forth a crisis of exemplarity, asking what Saussure has to preclude and render inessential so as to protect his linguistic system from contamination. A different set of questions that one needs to ask about the relation between onomatopoeia and language, as Derrida reframes it, are:

> what if *mimesis* no longer allowed itself to be arraigned, to be compelled to give accounts and reasons, to subject itself to a verification of identity within such a frame. And what if it operated according to ways [*voies*] and necessities whose laws are entangled and determined otherwise. (94)

If one allows laws and necessities to be measured and worked out by the untypical and the exceptional, as Derrida suggests, onomatopoeia, which implies an imitative and acoustic relation between a word and its referent, entails language be reexamined, firstly, in relation to voice and sound, and secondly, in terms of the linguistic principle of arbitrariness proposed by Saussure. The specter of voice returns to Derrida's writing in *Glas* in the form of a phonemic cluster *gl*, which comes to dissemble *glas* into a residue of voice and a bearer of otherness that is circulated and disseminated from one text to another: "*gl* remain(s) *gl* [...] for consonants without vowels, 'sounding' syllables, nonvocalizable letters, on some drive base of phonation, a voiceless voice stifling a sob [*sanglot*]" (119–20). Juliana De Nooy comments in her book *Derrida, Kristeva, and the Dividing Line* (1998) that "*gl* sticks close to the body that produces it, close to the voice (voice translates as *glas* in certain Slavic languages, 79) but even closer to the gluttonous mouth that gulps (glug-glug) and gurgles and gobbles with its globs of spittle around the glottis" (219). Therefore, what remains in *gl* is a noisy body *prior to* speech and language, whose instinctual investments in bodily sounds foretell an onomatopoeic relation to language mediated through the body.

This reading of onomatopoeia, in fact, is not all novel. It can be traced back to a traditional and mystical linguistic view that attributes meaning to sound while drawing upon the body to bridge the gap between a word and its referent. In *Cratylus*, which is one of the earliest records of men's inquiry into the nature of language, Plato writes that Socrates is consulted by two men, Cratylus and Hermogenes, about the appropriateness of names with regard to the things and people they signify and whether the relation between the two is intrinsic. Without objecting to Hermogenes' view on language as a matter of convention and agreement, Socrates nonetheless implies that correct names are those that genuinely imitate and embody the essential nature of things. According to Socrates, the name "is able to embody its form in the letters and syllables" (31), whose meaning is sensuously circulated along with the movements of the tongue. For instance, the letter "rho" (ρ, ρώ) expresses motion, as the words "strike" (κρούειν), "trembling" (τρόμος), and "current" (*ροή*) indicate. The reason for the name-giver to employ it for these words, Socrates proposes, is that "the tongue is least at rest and most agitated in pronouncing this letter" (145). In the same manner, Socrates postulates, "the compression and pressure of the tongue in the pronunciation of *delta* and *tau* was naturally fitted to imitate the notion of binding and rest" (147). For Socrates, the mouth is an audible and portable universe where the motion of the tongue reflects and justifies the particular meaning of a word or a syllable.

This view of language, without doubt, appears rather "naïve" and "primitive" to the modern man. It was marginalized after Saussure's semiotic approach to language gained popularity. However, it has never entirely perished. The avant-gardes, for instance, call for artists to search for inspiration and creativity in a universal language that unifies sound, image, and significance. The Italian futurist poet Filippo Tommaso Marinetti's sound poem "Zang Tumb Tumb" (1914) is exemplary in showing the avant-gardes' ambition of deploying the sound and shape of words to generate meaning of contingency and spontaneity. Marinetti moves the wartime battlefield to the domain of language: his impression on the Siege of Adrianople is directly translated into words-bombs dropped on the page, exploded in all directions and with various intensities. Sensations of all kinds—"weights thicknesses noises smells whirlwinds"—are marching on in the din of mechanized war: "**zang-tooomb-tooomb-zang-zang-tooomb tatatatatatatata picpacpam-pacpacpicpampampac** *ooooooooooooooooo*" (436). Through maximizing onomatopoeic and graphic possibilities of words, language becomes a war machine that destroys not only life but also syntax. The Russian Futurist Velimir Khlebnikov, on the other hand, approaches the alphabet as a universal revelation of space, with the body being the axis of orientation. Khlebnikov claims in his manifesto "To the Artists of the World": "P (*r*) means the division of a smooth hollow body as a trace of the movement of another body through it" (149). Words that begin with the same consonantal sound, according to Khlebnikov, express similar conceptualization of space. For example, the "l" sound in *lodka* (boat), *lapa* (paw), and *ladon'* (palm of the hand) suggests "the conversion of a body stretched along the axis of movement into a body stretched in two directions perpendicular to the axis of motion" (Khlebnikov, qtd. in Ram 146). For Khlebnikov, the sound images of words concern variations of primal and universal structures manifested in elementary components of words.

Admittedly, Khlebnikov's approach is idiosyncratic and counterintuitive, yet his understanding of vocal sounds as semantic units that carry meaning in themselves should not be as queer as it seems. Sound symbolism, or phonosemantics, is, in fact, a minor branch of linguistics that has never lost sympathy and support. Linguists and philosophers whose initials have more than one acute angle—such as "W" and "M" in the case of Mikhail Lomonosov, Wilhelm van Humboldt, Maurice Grammont, or Margret Magnus, just to name a few that may support my bold proposal—are more susceptible to the temptation of this theory.[2] (For the sake of consistency of my theory, I apologize to readers for my deliberate omission of Roman Jakobson, whose book *The Sound Shape of Language* (2011), co-authored with Linda R. Waugh, is much discussed in the phonosemantics literature.) Magnus's dissertation *What's in a Word? Studies in Phonosemantics* (2001) is the most recent and comprehensive work in this field, in which she looks into the possibility of there being some level of correlation between the form of a word and its meaning. The phonestheme /gl/, for example, as Magnus explains, often has something to do with reflected light (as in the case of glare, glim, glint, glow, glitter, gloaming); the major semantic class of /str/, meanwhile, is straining (stress, stretch, strangle) and that of /b/ are bulging (bag, belch, blimp) and brushy (bang, beard, brake). Probing the possible sound-meaning correlation of words, Magnus makes it clear that onomatopoeia is not of her concern because the type of correlation suggested by onomatopoeic words "is limited to a precise function and a very small semantic domain—to words which either refer to a sound or to something which makes a sound" (7). For Magnus, the acoustic and imitative faculty of onomatopoeic words is too literal and restrictive of her ambition of re-motivating the linguistic system in relation to reality through what she refers to as phonosemantic association, which "is a side-effect of a natural and productive tendency in human psychology to associate any form with a coherent referent" (1).

While Magnus suspects that onomatopoeia may limit the scope of her study, Walter Benjamin, in contrast, speculates in his essay "Doctrine of the Similar" (1933) that onomatopoeia is a manifest formation of language that exemplifies the mimetic impulse and faculty of humans. Similarity and mimicry, as Benjamin explains, plays a significant role in how humans understand and interact with the phenomenal world. It is present in various domains of human activities that range from children's play (in which children play at being an adult or an inanimate object) to the interpretation of fortune based on the star constellation. In fact, as Benjamin points out, "the cases in which people consciously perceive similarities in everyday life

---

[2] For a comprehensive overview of phonosemantics literature, please refer to Magnus' book *Gods in the Word: Archetypes in the Consonants* (2010).

are a minute segment of those countless cases unconsciously determined by similarity" (65). Thus, for Benjamin, insight into the mimetic faculty benefits less from demonstrating such similarities than inquiring into the process that leads to the production of similarities. The questions are: What makes a child, running in circles while shouting "du du," comparable to a choo-choo train? What can the patterns of coffee grounds say about our fortune and misery? What is so similar between the word "cat" and the animal cat that the sight or thought of either one, as if it were a reflex action, makes us exchange one for another?

The similarity between the imitator and the imitatee, for Benjamin, does not always derive from a conscious act of perception; neither does it imply a detailed and homogeneous resemblance. The correspondence may be described as, to use Benjamin's words, non-sensuous and magical. It is a flash of inspiration, a fleeting sensation, a stream of vaguely felt impression, whose defining feature of a *non-sensuous* similarity is perfectly archived in language:

> Language is the highest application of the mimetic faculty: a medium which the earlier perceptive capabilities for recognizing the similar entered without residue, so that it is now language which represents medium in which objects meet and enter into relationship with each other, no longer directly, as once in the mind of the augur or priest, but in essences, in their most volatile and delicate substances, even in their aromata. (68)

A word gives rise to meaning by weaving sound, image, and its referent into a web of associations. The spoken and the written word, together with what is meant, enter into a state of interdependence and undistinguished exchangeability, which brings on an unconscious but instantaneous perception of similarity. "The pupil reads his ABC book, and astrologer reads the future in the stars" (68), writes Benjamin. The difference between these two acts of reading is that, as Benjamin explains, the former performs the act of reading in two steps—that is, first seeing and pronouncing the words and letters and then trading them for what they refer to—while the latter merges the act of reading off the constellation of stars and that of interpreting it in relation to one's fate. This understanding of language as a canon that brings clarification to the mimetic faculty has great implication as well to Benjamin's view on translation. Words from different languages, when grouped together because they mean the same thing, entail the question of, as Benjamin proposes, "how these words, which often have not the slightest similarity to each other, are similar to that meaning in their center" (67). The practice of translation, therefore, concerns not only linguistic equivalence and similarity but also the possibility of bringing together words of dissimilar sounds and shapes, the sum of which contributes to a totality of meaning that, according to Benjamin, resembles what is meant to the greatest extent.

Unlike Saussure and Magnus, both of whom, despite their disparate linguistic views, consider onomatopoeia to be a marginal exception to the organization and operation of language, Benjamin proposes that onomatopoeia should underline the mimetic faculty structuring man's experience of language:

> Mimetic behavior was at least granted a place in the origin of language as the onomatopoeic element. But if, as is obvious to perceptive people, language is not an agreed-upon system of signs, then the attempt to approach language will always have to reach back to a consideration of how these signs are given in their crudest and most primitive form in the onomatopoeic mode of explication. The question is: how can this onomatopoeic mode of explication be elaborated, and how can it be adapted to clearer insights? (67)

As Benjamin points out, non-sensuous similarity is the key to understanding the origin of language as onomatopoeic. The qualifying adjective "non-sensuous," which is used to suggest the quality of resemblance as being not consciously and self-evidently engaging the senses, makes the discussion about the degree of precision and faithfulness regarding the onomatopoeic imitation irrelevant. The onomatopoeic or non-sensuous similarity refers less to an overlapping of critical acoustic properties than to a subconscious or unconscious act of perceiving loose and arbitrary associations in the light of necessity and motivation. Instead of emphasizing the sonorous resemblance of onomatopoeic words to the natural sounds, Benjamin approaches onomatopoeia as a "mode of explication" that gives rise to an understanding of language with reference to the psychological makeup of man. As if in a conversation across time and space, Benjamin's essay unwittingly responds to Derrida's critique of Saussure, exploring the implication of Derrida's question—"what if *mimesis* no longer allowed itself to be arraigned, to be compelled to give accounts and reasons, to subject itself to a verification of identity within such a frame" (94).

In his attempt to rethink onomatopoeia and language, Benjamin does not stand alone. Hugh Bredin, in his essay "Onomatopoeia as a Figure and a Linguistic Principle," explains in more detail how the universal human disposition to coordinate sounds with things intervenes in our perception of language:

> It is as if our consciousness of words includes an instinctive desire to fit sounds with things, to experience some sort of phonetic appropriateness in human speech. Even the most tenuous of connections between the acoustic structure of a sentence and the fact that it articulates is often transformed in our experience of it into a sense of fitness and rightness. It is arguable that onomatopoeia is not a trivial and incidental phenomenon of usage, but answers to a deep-seated need that lies at the heart of the linguistic consciousness. *We want language to be onomatopoeic.* (559–60; emphasis added)

Writing against the structuralist linguistic view on onomatopoeia as an inorganic part and an exceptional case, Bredin proposes that language as such answers for a deep-seated psychological need to attribute "a kind of onomatopoeic aura" (559) to words, to perceive them as if they were issued from things themselves, and to enact meaning through the articulation of sounds. Even though most linguistic signs do not have a straightforward and indexical relation to their referents, a speaker is tempted to make the association "organic." From the horizon of the linguistic landscape arises the expectation of an onomatopoeic encounter with the world, and to inhabit a language means to stitch the seam between words and objects. The realization of the arbitrary relation between words and objects, in contrast, often seems to be a retrospective and acquired knowledge.

Onomatopoeic (Re-)Naming: After Such Knowledge

As a vocal mode of coming into contact with the world, onomatopoeia exteriorizes the very potential of bringing together sound and meaning, the sensible and the virtual. It exemplifies the duality of language, which is being at once an agreed-upon system of signs and a living organism fed on the psychological specificity of the speaker. The perception and expectation of an imitative economy between words and things, however, can become difficult to be held on to when one is introduced into a foreign tongue. The non-sensuous correspondence between words and things becomes displaced by an awareness of other possible ways of expressing and naming. The question of originality and singularity haunts the foreign tongue, making it an embodiment of the problems of translation. However, for a speaker of a foreign language, the issue is not only about rendering words arbitrary to the things they refer to, but also about having their own lives rendered arbitrary and inconsequential. Especially when the name of the speaker is pronounced and translated onomatopoeically, it often triggers an anxiety over the consistency and authenticity of the speaking body.

So, what makes the name special?

Think about the initial moment of receiving the name from an intimate voice from above. Oh, look at this cute creature, fresh and pure, immune to the anxious inquiry about "I am like this; I am like that." *Emma. Hey Emma! Look here. Who's this?* She calls her Emma; her lips gently press against each other in pronouncing the syllable /m/. *Emma. Emma! Emma?* As if unsure of the name—*Is this what she is? Is this what she will become?*—she experiments with the sound of it in various tones, caressing the baby with attentive gazes and a murmuring voice. She calls her Emma, so she becomes Emma.

The naming of a newborn can hardly be said to be representational or imitative since the baby is not anything yet. It is at most a representation of an intention and a potentiality. The act of naming (a baby, a pet, a ship, etc.), for Austin, when performed properly, constitutes a typical instance of performative speech, in which the utterance initiates and coincides with the installment of a new state of being (32). However, unlike other instances of performative speech—for example, promising, betting, declaring, etc.—the act of naming a newborn leads to a fantasy of an unbreachable tie and an imitative exchange between the name and the person being named. Proper names are meant to bestow originality and singularity. No matter how many Emmas exist in history or in the same class, the name Emma, when called upon to name and refer to a specific person, as Derrida observes in *Glas*, "magnificent and classed, at once raised above all taxonomy, all nomenclature, and already identifiable in an order" (7). The proper name, therefore, represents an attempt of naming the unnamable—in the sense that it aspires to encapsulate existence in its entirety within a single name. Yet, what if the illusion of oneness falls apart? What happens when the name is called upon in an onomatopoeic manner, with some syllables swallowed, altered, or added? How shall one respond to a name that lacks the precision to trigger a spontaneous response while the person being addressed, on second thought, realizes nonetheless that it is meant to refer to him or her?

In his autobiography *Hunger of Memory: The Education of Richard Rodriguez*, Richard Rodriguez, a Chicano writer and intellectual, recalls his first day of school in Sacramento: "The nun said, in a friendly but oddly impersonal voice, 'Boys and girls, this is Richard Rodriguez.' (I heard her sound out: *Rich-heard Road-ree-guess*.) It was the first time I had heard anyone name me in English" (9). Unlike his original name, through which affection and love flow from the maternal voice and become coded in letters and sounds, *Rich-heard Road-ree-guess* crystalizes the moment where his existence is subject to translation, and where the name stops to invoke a bodily intimacy but refers back to itself as contrived and inauthentic. The basic units of the name become more or less composed of English words. Divisions and pauses are added according to the habits of the English tongue. The voice is impersonal, and the mode of address objective. Such moment of onomatopoeic renaming, occasionally accompanied with meaningful silence and well-intended clumsiness, preludes the beginning of a translated life. In Rodriguez's case, *-heard* and *-guess* highlight the instance of being hailed into a foreign language. "'Mr.?...' Rodriguez. The name on the door. The name on my passport. The name I carry from my parents—who are no longer my parents, in a cultural sense. This is how I pronounce it: *Rich-heard Road-ree-guess*. This is how I hear it most often" (2). No matter how unnatural and painful, Rodriguez suggests, in order to "exist," the person in a foreign language has to translate his life in a way that corresponds to the linguistic conventions and social expectations implicit in these onomatopoeic sounds. He has to leave unattended the nuances of his original name which fall out of the earshot, disregarding sounds and syllables which make his mother tongue singular and untranslatable.

In the context of cross-cultural encounters, the name can easily get mispronounced and displaced. A foreign name stands for a token of linguistic otherness and untranslatability. (In some cases, names are "translatable" in the sense that they have established equivalents in different languages. The Dutch name Andries, for example, is equivalent to the Italian Andrea and the English Andrew. However, there is always this uncanny moment of doubt and hesitation: What makes this middle-aged Dutch friend of mine Andrew? He is and simply should remain Andries.) The practice of onomatopoeic naming happens to Vladimir Nabokov's fictional character Pnin as well. As mentioned in the previous chapter, Pnin was a Russian-born professor who taught Russian at a college in the United States. When he was invited for a speech, the chair Judith Clyde introduced him in a way that made the audience aware of his foreignness: "Tonight we have here, I am proud to say, the Russian-born, and citizen of this country, Professor-now comes a difficult one, I am afraid—Professor Pun-neen" (23). If the juxtaposition of Pnin's national origin and current citizenship implies a rich background of migration and a potentially cosmopolitan mindset, Clyde's obvious struggle with the name and her mispronunciation unwittingly stages a reductive reading of Pnin's emigrant trajectory. Instead of being enriched by linguistic and cultural differences, Pun-neen summons a name that becomes stuck in between tongues and a life caught and lost in translation.

The name Pun-neen is an imaginative and imitative improvisation which aims to make the Russian sounds more compatible to the native tongue of English. Though absurd, this exclusive orientation is not without reason, especially when one considers how the native ears prepare the speaker to turn a deaf ear to foreign sounds. Knowing that Joan Clements and his husband were looking for a new lodger, Pnin made a phone call to them:

> "Here speaks Professor—" There followed a preposterous little explosion. "I conduct the classes in Russian. Mrs. Fire, who is now working at the library part time—"
>
> "Yes-Mrs. Thayer, I know. Well, do you want to see that room?"
>
> He did. Could he come to inspect it in approximately half an hour? Yes, she would be in. Untenderly she cradled the receiver.
>
> "What was it this time?" asked her husband, looking back, pudgy freckled hand on banister, on his way upstairs to the security of his study.
>
> "A cracked ping-pong ball. Russian." (27)

In terms of names, here we have a carnival of gibberish. Over the phone, Pnin's name does not reach Joan's ears as representing a language and a person, but purely as senseless noises—"a preposterous little explosion" and "a cracked ping-pong ball." Ironically, Pnin's speech appears both devoid of signification and saturated with the noise of meaning. Whereas Pnin is turned into a less-human by Joan and by other unsympathetic characters, he equally translates others into more-than-a-thing. Mrs. Thayer is caught under fire (Mrs. Fire) in Pnin's mouth, whereas Joan appears as a confusion of gender: on one occasion, Mr. Clements comments that Pnin "employs a nomenclature all his own. His verbal vagaries add a new thrill to life. His mispronunciations are mythopoetic. His slips of the tongue are oracular. He calls my wife John" (138). Pnin's verbal enigma, as Mr. Clements implies, has its appeal of being almost mythical and prophetic. However, as soon as such enigma casts its spell on a concrete person, who happens to be Mr. Clements's wife, the seemingly aesthetic and sublime dimension of Pnin's speech is reduced to a mere function of preparing for a rhetorical shift. The manufactured aura of myth and grace, after all, is meant to dramatize the moment of exposure where Pnin's demystified mispronunciation lapses into absurdity and indignity.

Like all foreigners who have challenging names, Pnin has to translate his name into English sensibility. On one occasion, Pnin explained to

Victor—the son of his ex-wife: "'My name is Timofey,' said Pnin, as they made themselves comfortable at a window table in the shabby old dinner, 'Second syllable pronounced as "muff," ahksent on last syllable, "ey" as in "prey" but a little more protracted'"(104). The surname Timofey, which in Russian refers to the honor shown to God, does the opposite when it meets the ears tuned by another language. It is dissected into a dead pile of "mutilated" syllables that fall flat upon the English tongue. As Pnin spends great effort making himself more verbally accessible, the words he employs insistently evoke the image of an incompetent speaker taken hostage by his tongue. The words "muff" and "prey," though meant to smooth out the pronunciation, consolidate the image of a clownish and impassive dupe. As if to add substance to this image, Pnin generously acts out the onomatopoeic tongue of mimicry and imprecision with the word "ahksent," making one wonder whether he means "accent" or "absent" and whether one should accentuate or leave out the last syllable. "Ahksent" is the tongue's misfired shot that makes Pnin's name alien and undecidable. The dramatic effect of onomatopoeic self-renaming reaches the climax when the uncanny pairing of "accent/absent" sets the speaker up; the absence of intention and subjectivity is accented as Pnin's surname is anatomized into bits and pieces to conform to an English sensibility.

To measure up to the native ears that remain resolutely inattentive to foreign sounds, Rodriguez and Pnin have to respond to the onomatopoeic imitation of their names, while sometimes dissecting their own names into a collage of foreign syllables. However, when it comes to the domestication of foreign names and sounds, the shortcut, it seems, is to replace them with their "doubles" or equivalents in another language. For instance, Eva Hoffman, a Polish American writer and academic, has recounted in her memoir *Lost in Translation: Life in a New Language* her struggle and reconciliation with an imposed condition of exile and translation. In particular, Hoffman traces the beginning of this painful process of translation to the moment where she and her sister acquired new names:

> This morning, in the rinky-dink wooden barracks where the classes are held, we've acquired new names. All it takes is a brief conference between Mr. Rosenberg and the teacher, a kindly looking woman who tried to give us reassuring glances, but who has seen too many people come and go to get sentimental about a name. Mine—"Ewa"—is easy to change into its near equivalent in English, "Eva." My sister's name—"Alina"—poses more of a problem, but after a moment's thought, Mr. Rosenberg and the teacher decide that "Elaine" is close enough. My sister and I hang our heads

wordlessly under this careless baptism. The teacher then introduces us to the class, mispronouncing our last name—"Wydra"—in a way we've never heard before. We make our way to a bench at the back of the room; nothing much has happened, except a small, seismic mental shift. The twist in our names takes them a tiny distance from us—but it's a gap into which the infinite hobgoblin of abstraction enters. Our Polish names didn't refer to us; they were as surely us as our eyes or hands. These new appellations, which we ourselves can't yet pronounce, are not us. They are identification tags, disembodied signs pointing to objects that happen to be my sister and myself. We walk to our seats, into a roomful of unknown faces, with names that make us strangers to ourselves. (105)

Drawing on a melancholic yet lucid tone, Hoffman reflects upon her and her family's experiences of emigration, which have tremendously reshaped her relation to languages. This book contains three parts—"Paradise," "Exile," and "The New World"—with each opening up to a specific linguistic sense of existence that revolves around and changes through emigration. The narrative begins with a nostalgic and retrospective evocation of Hoffman's once perfect unity with the Polish language. After she moved to Vancouver with her family, however, the intimacy with her native language became fragile. Hoffman experienced an initial dreadful loss of language and the painful disintegration of her psyche. Her sentimentality at this stage is understandable, since it was not her decision to leave Cracow, the place where she was born and spent her childhood. She was still a teenager when her parents, who had escaped the Holocaust and were frustrated by the antisemitic sentiment in the Communist state, decided to move to Canada in the 1950s. Exposed to the "harsh-sounding language" (105), Hoffman had to reconstruct her private and public lives in and through this new language. She consciously relinquished her Polish, forcing English to enter and inhabit her psychic interiority.

The painstaking process of having her existence translated into a new language, as seen from the quote earlier, is illustrated and epitomized at the event of being publicly assigned new "equivalent" names. Crucial to this "careless baptism" and onomatopoeic manner of translation is the name's precarious relation to the body. If Hoffman's Polish name truly radiates with bodily warmth—as she claims, "Our Polish names didn't refer to us; they were as surely us as our eyes or hands"—it is because it became attached to the primordial body through the repetition of intimate invocations in a safe familial setting. The name is, to some degree, an intangible extension of the infantile body. In general, the event of naming takes place before the stage of active remembrance and vocalization; the formality and sacredness of the original name resides partially in the fact that it lies beyond the knowledge and awareness of the person being named. The name is a given. Hoffman and her sister's experience of being renamed, however, stands as a stark contrast to this ritualized procedure. Their presence on the occasion, instead of making their new names more "real," rules out their potential bodily intimacy with these names. The transformative force of creation indicated in "Eva" (life) and "Elaine" (shining light) does not call their bodies into being; nor does it strive after the bodies as the absolute original. Moreover, the occasion seems embarrassingly hasty and inconsequential. It is "a brief conference," and even the more "challenging" name of her sister deserves only "a moment's thought." When it comes to the "untranslated" and untranslatable element—namely, their surname—the teacher mispronounces it, which, in a sense, "evidences" the necessity of onomatopoeic renaming and "justifies" the practice of nominal homogenization.

Whereas in the cases of Rodriguez and Pnin where the practice of onomatopoeic renaming is a matter of improvisation, Hoffman and her sister are renamed more or less based on a socially agreed-upon mechanism of nominal translation. Well intended, the occasion of renaming aims to smooth out their passage into a new linguistic environment by giving their symbolic source of origin a translatable equivalent. Yet, to what extent are proper names translatable? Jacques Derrida, in "Des Tours de Babel," notes that the proper name as such remains singular, even though its conceptual generality, as a common noun, is translatable:

> The noun *pierre* belongs to the French language, and its translation into a foreign language should in principle transport its meaning. This is no longer the case with "Pierre," whose belonging to the French language is not assured and is in any case not of the same type. "Peter" in this sense is not a *translation* of Pierre, any more than "Londres" is a translation of London, and so forth. (198)

It is arguable, as Derrida explains, whether a proper name belongs to any specific language, since it suggests a correlation between form and content and thus cannot be translated into another language without losing its sense of singularity. The French word *pierre* has "rock" or "stone" as its equivalent in English. Yet the name Pierre—although it is connected to *pierre* and "Peter" in the sense that they are all derived from the Greek word Πέτρος (*petros*, meaning "stone, rock," via Latin *petra*)—becomes a proper name by effacing its conceptual equivalents and by making the entity it refers to an indispensable part of its significance.

Likewise, Benjamin suggests that "in name appears the essential law of language, according to which to express oneself and to address everything else amounts to the same thing" ("On Language as Such" 65). The name is the coming together of language as an expression of the mental being of man and language as a communicable and receptive quality of any entity. Through it, language communicates itself purely and absolutely. The name is, perhaps, what comes closest to Benjamin's idea of pure word or pure language. Whereas it is through his essay "The Task of the Translator" (1921) that Benjamin's idea of pure language becomes well known—which refers to a totality of supplementing intentions enabled by translation—Benjamin already grapples with this idea of pure word in relation to names in his earlier article "On Language as Such and on the Language of Man." For Benjamin, as it is for Derrida, the proper name is not bound to one particular language; it is "the point where human language participates most intimately in the divine infinity of the pure word" ("On Language as Such" 69).

"My sister and I hang our heads wordlessly under this careless baptism," writes Hoffman. Here the word "wordlessly" is not only a metaphorical expression for shock and startle; wordlessness is the physical state of her body at that moment, a body that is imprisoned in translation and unable to respond to the subtle change of her name. It is not so much a matter of not speaking English as of possessing no language at all. "Polish is becoming a dead language, the language of the untranslatable past" (120), while English is the language that makes her existence petty and inauthentic. With the channel of articulation blocked, the body is weighed down by its unsettling translatability. From "Ewa" to "Eva," from "Alina" to "Elaine," the translation of names, in this scenario, cannot be an innocent onomatopoeic rendering of sounds in different languages; it constitutes the moment where a foreign body is hailed by a new language and where one begins to redefine and reinvent itself through translation.

Translation, however, does not come to Hoffman as a natural practice; neither does it bridge the languages in question nor reaffirm the image of the designated thing. Quite the opposite, the practice of translation seems to deepen the fissure of languages, bodies, and things:

> But mostly, the problem is that the signifier has become severed from the signified. The words I learn now don't stand for things in the same unquestioned way they did in my native tongue. "River" in Polish was a vital sound, energized with the essence of riverhood, of my rivers, of my being immersed in rivers. "River" in English is cold—a word without an

aura. It has no accumulated associations for me, and it does not give off the radiating haze of connotation. It does not evoke.

The process, alas, works in reverse as well. When I see a river now, it is not shaped, assimilated by the word that accommodates it to the psyche—a word that makes a body of water a river rather than an uncontained element. The river before me remains a thing, absolutely other, absolutely unbending to the grasp of my mind. (106)

The river, which is called *rzeka* in Polish, to Hoffman, is subject to a similar turbulence of onomatopoeic and nominal translation that Hoffman herself has undergone. To inhabit the new form of life that makes translation indispensable, one has to reconfigure the relation among bodies, languages, and things. At least at the initial stage of this translational rebirth, such relation is lived through as rupture, isolation, and alienation. In terms of language, words become frozen in abstraction and in what Hoffman calls "a Platonic stratosphere." Words are without objects or auras. For instance, the coldness of the English word "river," suggests Hoffman, comes from its lack of associations: the English word does not activate the memory of a particular landscape; the meek sound of it fails to correspond to the "vital sound, energized with the essence of riverhood" that characterizes her memory of the Polish river. "English words don't hook on to anything" (108), Hoffman observes. Words, transient and slippery, no longer stick to the things they refer to.

While words slip off the things they signify, things begin to gain an unsettling autonomy, growing into an uncontainable other. As things, thoughts, and feelings seem to skip over the communicating medium of language and bump into her psyche and perception directly, the immediate reaction of Hoffman is fear and rejection. Her existence is threatened and crushed by the immensity of their raw and unmediated presence. Deprived of a language to make sense of her new environment, Hoffman relives the pre-linguistic experience of alienation and anxiety—"the things threaten to crush me with their thinghood, with their inorganic proliferation, with their meaninglessness" (136). Worse still, unlike an infant who is under the protection of a maternal body, she cannot ward off the existential crisis of absolute isolation by burying her head in the familiar and comforting scent of a nursing mother. What she can do, instead, is to numb her psyche and sensation—no resonance, no penetration, no "spontaneity of response" (106). Confronted with a new language and an unworded world, Hoffman stands alone among things, insensitive and irresponsive to their language.

While language, as Bredin argues, imprints the impression of things on the psyche of the speaker via the shapes and sounds of corresponding words, for Hoffman, this process has to be done unconsciously and gradually. It can be painful to experience words tearing apart from the things they are "naturally" attached to, since to feel at home in a language means to narrow the gap between the word and the thing it refers to. The difficulty of reinventing a life via translation is that it makes one practical and disillusioned, too self-conscious to preserve a fetishized relation to language, "becoming a living avatar of structuralist wisdom" (107). The loss of psychic intimacy and comfort with her languages is the price she had to pay for the knowledge and experience of the arbitrariness of words in relation to things. The "double vision" (132) toward life, once installed through translation, cannot be dismantled easily:

> The tiny gap that opened when my sister and I were given new names can never be fully closed up; I can't have one name again. My sister has returned to her Polish name—Alina. It takes a while for me to switch back to it; Alina, in English, is a different word than it is in Polish: it has the stamp of the unusual, its syllables don't fall as easily on an English speaker's tongue. In order to transport a single word without distortion, one would have to transport the entire language around it. My sister no longer has one, authentic name, the name that is inseparable from her single essence. (272)

In retrospect, Hoffman attributes the beginning of her life in translation to the moment where she and her sister were onomatopoeically renamed. When names are caught in translation, the earlier belief in the unquestioned and fetishized unity between names and body becomes breached; and it is no longer possible to bypass the knowledge and awareness of language as unmotivated signs. A person that undergoes the onomatopoeic translation, as Hoffman suggests, inevitably becomes a disillusioned structuralist: no longer inhabiting a pre-Babel paradise where bodies and names are in perfect match, the person caught up in translation cannot help but become aware of the arbitrariness and reductiveness of language. It is an option to switch back to one's "original" name, of course, like what Alina did. Yet, it is unlikely to undo the sense of inauthenticity through this symbolic return. Even if the trace of a translated life is not left in the name, it shall be manifested in the portable melodrama of the native tongue and ears, considering the fact that the mother tongue often tricks the speaker into a certain habit of listening and speaking. *Road-ree-guess* or *Pun-neen*: these are examples of foreign names becoming an acrobatic improvisation of sounds. Either to be renamed through translation or to be heard in translation: this is how onomatopoeia becomes a cross-linguistic practice and a mode of existence.

If you happen to be a foreigner with a difficult name, you might have been amazed by the fresh and enriching imagination that people demonstrate with their attempts of reproducing your name. This intriguing phenomenon might even have led you to a philosophical inquiry into repetition and difference. The name is the prosthesis of the body. Or shall we say—language as such is the prosthesis of the body, which, as a virtual replacement that compensates for the loss of oneness with the external world, consoles and interacts with the human psyche by making it possible to conjure up the lost objects anytime? Whereas the concept of onomatopoeic translation, as an imitative device and a cultural practice, unfolds piecemeal and in line with the scene of speaking with an accent and naming, the body, with the tongue being an enigmatic embodiment of a translated life, stands out and sheds light on its intimate and incongruous relation to languages.

To speak is to translate; and to translate, one has to subject oneself to the regime of onomatopoeia.

5. The Little Girl, the Schizophrenic, and the Exophonic

Im/Expressing the Oral Regress of Literature

Abstract: This chapter investigates the relationship between orality and literary creativity, focusing on the interplay between speaking and eating, expressing and consuming. In *Logic of Sense*, Gilles Deleuze connects the act of speaking to eating in Lewis Carroll's works. This chapter explores how language functions both as a medium of expression and consumption. Through a close reading of Yoko Tawada's works *Where Europe Begins* and *Portrait of a Tongue*, it explores the metaphor of speaking as eating and the implications for literary creation. It introduces the concept of the "exophonic" voice, exploring how speaking a foreign language disrupts one's sense of self and fosters a new form of literary expression.

Keywords: orality; exophony; minor literature; bilingualism; Yoko Tawada

Queen Alice: Adapted from *Through the Looking Glass*

"She's all right again now," said the Red Queen. "Do you know Languages? What's the French for fiddle-de-dee?"

"Fiddle-de-dee's not English," Alice replied gravely.

"Who ever said it was?" said the Red Queen.

"That's not fair," Alice exclaimed. Feeling she had been wronged, Alice paused and added, "How am I supposed to know the French word for *fiddle-de-dee* if I speak neither of the languages?"

"But you did say *fiddle-de-dee*, didn't you? I saw it passing through your lips." The Red Queen looked rather puzzled and annoyed.

Well, Alice caught the sight of the word just before it landed in the mug in front of her. The word had a flashy green color, which, Alice thought to herself, was not unappetizing but she *surely* didn't want it with her tea.

Hui, Tingting. *Accented Speech in Literature, Art, and Theory: Melodramas of the Foreign Tongue.* Amsterdam: Amsterdam University Press, 2025.
DOI: 10.5117/9789048569007_CH05

Before the Red Queen had the time to protest, Alice hastily grabbed the word, put it back into her mouth, and started chewing on it. To her surprise, the word had a sandy taste that matched neither the garish color nor the tiptoe sound of *fiddle-de-dee*.

"What impertinence!" cried the Red Queen. "Didn't your parents teach you to use the cutlery?"

"Yes, they did, your majesty," Alice continued chewing loudly while speaking. "But they never mentioned I should follow the same manner with *words*."

"I order you to eat civilly, especially when it comes to words."

Alice picked up her fork and knife with great reluctance. As she was about to begin the meal, she was disappointed to find there was nothing on her plate, whereas the plate of the Red Queen was piled high with all sorts of delicacies which Alice could barely name.

"What shall I eat?" asked Alice.

"You mean how you shall speak," replied the Red Queen gravely. "*Bon appétit.*"

As soon as the Red Queen finished her sentence, the letters of "*Bon appétit*" dropped from her lips one after another. Slowly they gathered into the shape of spaghetti, floating leisurely right in front of the nose of Alice.

Hungry and curious, Alice waved her fork in the air to grab the words-spaghetti. "This is fun," thought Alice, "to play hide-and-seek with your food." But if she had been asked to give her opinion, she would have added that she didn't really appreciate the giggling sound the words made when her fork touched them. "Even if you are ticklish," spoke Alice to herself, "it is a bad manner to make that sound at the dining table."

At last, Alice managed to fix some of the words-spaghetti on her plate—but only to find that they were too elastic for her to bite off.

"If Peter Piper you pronounce with ease, then twist your tongue around these." The Red Queen looked at Alice triumphantly.

Impatient and humiliated, Alice decided to give up the cutlery. She grabbed the wordy mess from her plate and stuffed everything into her mouth.

Not long after, Alice started to burp so loudly that even she herself could no longer pretend to not hear it.

"Grrrrrr... Excuse me."

"Excuse me?" asked the Red Queen. "You mean *s'il vous plaît*?" More letters fell from her mouth and gathered into the shape of puddings and tarts.

Alice was curious how the other foreign words would taste.

"Grrrrrr... How do you say 'bread and butter' in French?" Alice attempted.

"You speak well, child." The Red Queen bit her tongue, as it became as slippery as an eel. "However, do not expect to feast on *my* mouth. Mind you."

Oral Regress: To Speak of Food or to Eat Words

In *Alice's Adventures in Wonderland* (1865/1998) and *Through the Looking-Glass* (1872/1998), Alice found a mirror world that appeared identical but in fact reversed the forward and backward axis. In her series of adventures (down the rabbit hole and through the looking-glass), Alice, being dreamy and chatty but always sensible in the beginning of the stories—complaining to her sister about the uselessness of books with no pictures or conversations, or scolding the black kitten for running after its own tail—little by little lost her good sense and common sense as her journeys led her to a world of the reversible. Gilles Deleuze succinctly summarizes, in *Logic of Sense* (1990/2015), Alice's adventures as those of reversals:

> Hence the reversals which constitute Alice's adventures: the reversal of becoming larger and becoming smaller—"which way, which way?" asks Alice, sensing that it is always in both directions at the same time, so that for once she stays the same, through an optical illusion; the reversal of the day before and the day after, the present always being eluded—"jam tomorrow and jam yesterday—but never jam *to-day*"; the reversal of more and less: five nights are five times hotter than a single one, "but they must be five times as cold for the same reason"; the reversal of active and passive: "do cats eat bats?" is as good as "do bats eat cats"; the reversal of cause of effect: to be punished before having committed a fault, to cry before having pricked oneself, to serve before having divided up the servings. (2)

A philosopher's mind, to some extent, is all too ready to succumb to the little girl (but *never* to the little boy, the image of which invokes nothing but the tyranny of ignorance), whose silly senseless babble, like a magic cure for the sickness of the rational mind, seems capable of igniting the passion of thought. In the case of Deleuze, the charm of the little girl was in full swing as she advanced into the reversible mirror world, where the *non*sense slid in no longer as a measure of and a revolt against good sense and common sense, but as a joker with no preexisting values and fixed identities, leading the game of language to an infinite regression into a paradoxical reference of itself. Whereas before her adventures, Alice had to behave prudishly, pretending to be concerned about good manners and sensible deeds—she talked to Kitty about the idea of living in the Looking-glass House: "that's just the same as our drawing-room, only the things go *the other way*," and "the books are something like our books, only the words go *the wrong way*" (*Logic of Sense* 125–26; emphasis added)—once she was through the glass, the play of sense and nonsense ceased being a matter of difference between good and bad, becoming instead that of perpetual sliding and reversing on the surface of words, which resulted in a series of paradoxes. In a world of the reversible, although Alice would still be caught in surprise or in awe, she dwelled no more upon a particular thought, happening, or word. She simply let it slide.

In *Logic of Sense*, Deleuze presents a philosophical inquiry into the structure of sense and the genesis of language by developing a series of paradoxes inspired by Lewis Carroll's fantastic literary world. Among all these thirty-four series of paradoxes, Deleuze points out that "the source of the alternative which runs through all the works of Carroll [is] to eat or to speak" (25). In general, speaking and eating are not to be confused with one another. To eat is—to use the Deleuzian terms—to reach down to the mixture of bodies in depth, whereas to speak is to slide at the surface of incorporeal events. Even though the act of eating and that of speaking do converge at certain occasions—for instance, if we were to excuse the impertinence of speaking with a mouthful of food, they are more often than not kept separate from each other. Each subscribes to its own sets of rules that divide the mouth into an inward passage for food and an outward channel for words. One ingests food but lets out words and emotions.

The adventures of Alice, in contrast, are carried out precisely through a mouth that *reversely* consumes the speakable and expresses the edible. When trying to make conversations with animals she met, Alice was constantly at the verge of placing them back to her consuming mouth. Upon hearing the Mock Turtle's song about a whiting and a snail, Alice blurted out, "I've often seen them at dinn—" (*Alice's Adventures in Wonderland* 89). Considerate and merciful as she was, Alice bit off the last part of the word "dinner," since it is impolite, I suppose, to emphasize that one's immediate relation to a (talking) animal is that of eating and consuming. Whereas civil manners demand one to distinguish the edible from the speakable—remember the Red Queen's teaching: "it isn't etiquette to cut any one you've been introduced to. Remove the joint!" (*Through the Looking-Glass* 229–30)—Alice's slippery tongue continuously betrayed her good intentions by suggesting that the proper place for a talking animal was the plate served at dinner. Speaking, on the other hand, can go awry to express the edible. For example, when Alice was conversing with the Mock Turtle and Gryphon, Alice noticed words sounded differently once she began to recite the poem called "'Tis the voice of the sluggard": "'Tis the voice of the Lobster: I heard him declare, 'You have baked me too brown, I must sugar my hair'" (*Alice's Adventures in Wonderland* 91). What a strange exchange between the Lobster and the inexperienced cook! Here the poem begins to speak in the voice of the other: no longer content with approximating the bodily sounds of chewing, grinding, and swallowing, the Lobster comes to reclaim the literary space through revolting against the supposed silence of the consumable other.

So how shall one refrain from speaking of food? How to rescue words from a consumptive mouth? "At Alice's coronation dinner," Deleuze notes, "you either eat what is presented to you, or you are presented to what you eat" (*Logic of Sense* 25). Here Alice was confronted with a paradox: the Red Queen deemed it proper for Alice and her food to be introduced to each other, the consequence of which was that the introduction transformed the food into a conversational partner that Alice would no longer be allowed to eat. To her dismay, Alice found out that the required table manner of conviviality precluded the possibility of eating, and the delightful ritual of small talk could only be pursued at the cost of starvation. "'I won't be introduced to the pudding, please,' Alice said rather hastily, 'or we shall get no dinner at all. May I give you some?'" (*Through the Looking-Glass* 230). The Red Queen would not budge; she introduced Alice and the pudding, nonetheless. Since her attempt of leaving the pudding mute and consumable had failed, Alice, hungry and annoyed, decided to break the rule that kept the manners of eating and speaking apart. She ordered the waiter to bring back the pudding and boldly cut a slice.

What follows this violation, as the literary scholar Sara Guyer mentions in her analysis of the coronation scene, "like all dramas of animation, is the speech of the other" (160). "'What impertinence!' said the Pudding. 'I wonder how you'd like it, if I were to cut a slice out of you, you creature!'" (*Through the Looking-Glass* 230). By cutting and eating a pudding that could speak, Alice risked eating up the voice as well—the voice that blended the oral and the literary, and that disarrayed the inward and outward passages of the body.

"What is more serious," asks Deleuze in *Logic of Sense*, "to speak of food or to eat words?" (25). Raised in a philosophical treatise on language, this question appears rather trivial, if not all together misleading, since neither of the options speaks to us as genuine or serious. Well, it is possible to speak of food—as Alice was inclined to do unconsciously—but to *eat* words? The peculiar phrasing demonstrates little concern for practicality and common sense, causing instead an untimely traffic jam inside the mouth. Is this question merely a philosopher's serious play with words? When words become edible and food becomes speakable, how should this bizarre reversibility of ingestion and expression clarify anything about the nature of language? What does it mean to have the weight of language measured in a situation where food and words switch identities, each pursuing a journey that is supposed to belong to the other?

Alice *could have* eaten words—after seeing the leg of mutton making a little bow on Alice's plate, very few things, I suppose, would strike us as false or impossible. The opening section of this chapter is exactly such a bold rewriting of Queen Alice on my part. It is meant, on the one hand, to be a literal rendering of Deleuze's formulation about eating words in the context of the little girl and, on the other hand, to achieve the effect of mirror writing with regard to Carroll's original depiction of the coronation dinner. The order of speaking (*of* food or *to* food), which largely concerned Alice in the original scene, is now reversed; the dinner becomes for Alice a feast on foreign words, and the manners of eating words are what the little girl is now encouraged to explore and rebel against. Whereas in the original Alice's slippery tongue operated at different levels of what was said, meant, and referred to, the current adaptation trains the looking-glass on the mouth, reversing the outbound passage of words while making the words consumable foodstuffs.

It is only natural that the protest of the pudding is replaced by the protest of Alice's stomach: the burping sound, due to the compulsive and fitful bouts of consumption, is how words sound and smell when the pure act of *expression* becomes *impressed* with the physicality of a body that is made open to oral regress. If the speech of the other—"'What impertinence!' said the Pudding. 'I wonder how you'd like it, if I were to cut a slice out of you, you creature!'" (*Through the Looking-Glass* 230)—speaks for literature its demand for empathy, the "grrrrrr" sound brings literature in earshot of the *other* of the literary voice. This chapter, therefore, picking up where Alice of the original and of the current adapted version left off, continues the bizarre feast on words while exploring the relation between literature and language via the speaking and consuming body. Whereas the literary voice is often deemed as pure and devoid of corporeality, which has to transform the eating impulse into metaphysical and verbal catharsis, this chapter asks instead: What if the literary language burdens itself with the weight of the speaking body—especially when the body is foreign and accented—and what if the literary voice is confronted with an oral regress?

Quite often, the Freudian term "oral regress" is invoked in clinical cases of neurotic fixation on the oral stage, the symptoms of which involve excessive eating and/or aggressive verbal behaviors. However, when Deleuze makes the observation that "*Alice* is the story of an oral *regress*," instead of aiming at a pathological reading of Alice, he foregrounds the adventures of Alice as a sliding across "two heterogeneous series of orality: to eat/to speak, consumable things/expressible senses" (*Logic of Sense* 39). Whereas the Freudian overtone of the term distinguishes the symbolic from the oral as a superior organization, Deleuze emphasizes the *serial* form of orality that, on the one hand, teases out a playful rule of regression intrinsic to the *mouth* and, on the other hand, enables the game of *language and literature* to be perceived in terms of a productive and creative relay between expression and ingestion, surface and depth, bodies and words. The oral regress, to Deleuze, is not only what happens to a speaking body inside the mouth but also what a speaking body can do to his or her languages and writings.

The oral duality of eating and speaking keeps coming back in different chapters of *Logic of Sense*, a book that showcases Deleuze's most sustained reflection on language. He uses the examples of Alice, Antonin Artaud, and Louis Wolfson to discuss the different ways in which their languages regress to the alimentary and consumptive oral impulse. Whereas, traditionally, philosophers such as Martin Heidegger, Ludwig Wittgenstein, and Giorgio Agamben, just to name a few, pitch language against *silence and death* in their reflections on language, Deleuze in this book suggests that the limits of language should be sought not only in the domain of the *ineffable* but also in relation to the *edible*. Deleuze interprets the genesis of language as a dynamic procedure in which language gradually differentiates itself from other bodily sounds and noises, ridding of a body that eats and consumes while constituting itself as an impersonal entity. "It is always a mouth which speaks," says Deleuze, "but the sound is no longer the noise of a body which eats—a pure orality—in order to become the manifestation of a subject expressing itself" (*Logic of Sense* 187). The oral regress of literature—whose prototype, as Deleuze implies, is Carroll's bewildered little girl—is therefore the oral regress of the literary language, which becomes impregnated with noise, voice, and speech, rediscovering the mouth, tongue, and teeth as what deterritorializes the articulation of sounds while, as Deleuze and Guattari argue at another occasion, "transform[ing] words into things capable of rivaling food" ("What Is a Minor Literature" 19).

This chapter, by juxtaposing three different literary figures (the little girl, the madman, and the exophonic), explores the two alternating series of orality—to eat and to speak, to express and to consume—in literature, while addressing the following questions: How to understand the event of language as opposed to other bodily sounds and oral activities? In what ways does the oral regress manifest itself in these literary figures? What if literature welcomes and embraces the oral regress of these figures, instead of glossing it over as a neurotic sign of psychic and literary fixation? In the context of the literary scene, what is more serious—to speak of food or to eat words?

Speaking of Food: The Little Girl and the Schizophrenic

The French poet and theater director Antonin Artaud apparently takes the trope of eating and speaking very seriously. His utter detestation of Carroll's slippery surface language made itself very much felt in a letter he wrote to Henri Parisot, regarding his translation of Carroll's poem "Jabberwocky":

> I have not produced a translation of "Jabberwocky." I tried to translate a fragment of it, but it bored me. I never liked this poem, which always struck me as an affected infantilism. ... *I do not like poems or languages of the surface* which smell of happy leisures and of intellectual success—as if the intellect relied on the anus, but without any heart or soul in it. The anus is always terror, and I will not admit that one loses an excrement without being torn from, thereby losing one's soul as well, and there is no soul in "Jabberwocky" [...]. One may invent one's language, and make pure language speak with an extra-grammatical or a-grammatical meaning, but this meaning must have value in itself, that is, must issue from torment [...]. "Jabberwocky" is the work of a profiteer who, satiated after a fine meal, seeks to indulge himself in the pain of others [...]. When one digs through the shit of being and its language, the poem necessarily smells badly, and "Jabberwocky" is a poem whose author took steps to keep himself from the uterine being of suffering into which every great poet has plunged, and having been born from it, smells badly. There are in "Jabberwocky" passages of fecality, but it is the fecality of an English snob, who curls the obscene within himself like ringlets of hair around a curling iron [...]. It is the work of a man who ate well—and this makes itself felt in his writing. (Artaud, qtd. in Deleuze, *Logic of Sense* 86–87)

Face to face—or should I say nose to anus—with the poem "Jabberwocky," Artaud is at once disoriented and annoyed, as if Carroll's language of the surface makes the act of reading and translating less a genuine art of diving and plunging but of an impossible acrobatics of skating and sliding. The surface language has no depth, no suffering, no heart and soul. It is nothing but a pure sense of being in and for itself. Artaud does not believe that such half-heartedness and self-indulgence can make literature a fine example of earthly torment. "It is the work of a man who ate well," writes Artaud, "and this makes itself felt in his writing." To Artaud, the oral drive for eating—at least in the case of Carroll—consumes and exhausts literary expressions, decomposing writings into feces and excrement. The "English snob" who eats well stands for Artaud as a stigma of literature's ethical regression. To translate the poem "Jabberwocky" and its light-hearted neologism, therefore, is no less than "dig[ging] through the shit of being and its language." The act of translation defeats him. I could imagine Artaud, in a sudden spasm of despair and insight, raising his head and wiping his nose with smelly fingers, crying, "Why should I feed on someone's shit?"

"To Artaud," comments Deleuze, "Carroll's games seem puerile, his food too worldly, and even his fecality hypocritical and too well-bred" (*Logic of Sense* 87). Artaud seems to suggest that if literature, like a mouth whose opening can deeply affect and transform the body, has to reconcile the oral duality of eating and speaking—if not to ward off incessantly the oral obsession with eating well. Carroll's neologism upsets Artaud: it is a deluxe rendezvous between words and food that happens in the erogenous zone of the anus. Neither food nor words—because of the lack of commensurability and resemblance—manage to transform into the other in totality. Food and words meet halfway, yielding to a comforting discharge that answers less to literary creativity than to a diarrheic impulse. As Deleuze explains, for example, the title of the poem "Jabberwocky" is a portmanteau word that "is formed from 'wocer' or 'wocor,' which means offspring or fruit, and 'jabber,' which expresses a voluble, animated, or chattering discussion" (48). Blending morsels of consumable objects with bits of expressible senses, the portmanteau words exemplify the instance of an incomplete transformation between food and words in Carroll's poem.

Insofar as Carroll's words are the result of food finishing its epic journey through the body, to Artaud, the poem is deprived of a starving body that is eager to ruminate and to lend depth to thoughts. The act of writing, in this scenario, equals to nothing but the outlet of excrement after a good meal. How does Artaud then, as a translator, deal with his overt aversion to the poem, "the fecality of an English snob"? Ros Murray, in her book *Antonin Artaud: The Scum of the Soul* (2014), observes that Artaud tends to substitute the portmanteau words in Carroll's original version with very different verbal forms that conjure up the bodily image of eating and digesting—a strategy that is mostly visible in Artaud's translation of the poem "Jabberwocky."[1] "[T]he body becomes integrated into the translation

---

[1] The first stanza of "Jabberwocky" reads as follows: "'Twas brillig, and the slithy toves. Did gyre and gimble in the wabe: All mimsy were the borogoves, And the mome raths outgrabe." In Artaud's translation, it says, "Il était Roparant, et les vliqueux tarands/Allaient en gilroyant et en brimbulkdriquant/Jusque-là où la rourghe est a rouarghe a rangmbde et rangmbde a rouarghambde :Tous les falomitards étaient les chats-huants/Et les Ghoré Uk'hatis dans le GRABÜG-EÛMENT." See Ros Murray 38–39.

process through guttural expulsions and sounds that mobilise the mouth," comments Murray, "as if the words were being chewed; the articulation of these sounds requires the throat ('r'), the nose ('m'), the lips ('b') and the teeth ('d'), but the sounds produced recall an intestinal rumbling as well as a throaty gurgling or a mastication" (39).

Likewise, Deleuze observes that in Artaud's translation of "Jabberwocky," although the first two verses still correspond to the syntax of Carroll's original version, a slippage occurs as we reach the end of the second line. The word *brimbulkdriquant*, whose tonic singularity decomposes words into irreducible phonetic units, begins the bleak and total collapse of the alternation between surface and depth, objects and expressions. Artaud obviously has no wish to be faithful to Carroll's digestive system: the portmanteau words are replaced with glossolalia of a disparate order. The alternating series that underline Carroll's portmanteau words have collapsed and disappeared in Artaud's translation. In Artaud's translation, words regress into chops of syllables and unpronounceable clusters of consonants that are intimate to the guttural and intestinal sounds of the body itself. "With horror," says Deleuze, "we recognize it easily: it is the language of schizophrenia" (*Logic of Sense* 86).

Although both Artaud and Carroll hold on to an alimentary and excremental vocabulary in their writings, Deleuze reminds us that the striking resemblance "does not at all justify the grotesque trinity of child, poet, and madman" (*Logic of Sense* 85). The little girl's confusion of food and words is an innocent play of sense and nonsense. Even though Alice's adventures can be disorienting sometimes—remember her anxious cry "Which way? Which way?" as she failed to predict and decide whether she was going to grow bigger or small—there is nothing profound or devastating in her voice that disfigures her open mouth. Through the looking-glass, Alice discovered her body as a smooth surface. To prevent the body from thickening into a corporeal entity, Alice had to flatten the mouth. Seldom did the starving little girl enjoy a meal without disturbance. She had to resist and defer the actualization of eating, for eating suggests a commitment to depth and penetration. Alice was speaking all the time—she recited poems, asked questions, and talked to herself when no one was around. A mouth without depth cannot register the taste, sensation, and gravity of bodily impression; it is rather a slippery surface for words to slide between sense and nonsense. In this sense, according to Deleuze, the opening scene *could not have happened*, since Alice shall never be absorbed into the activity of eating, no matter whether it comes to food or words. Artaud, on the other hand, lies at the other end of the spectrum:

> The revelation which enlivens Artaud's genius is known to any schizophrenic, who lives it as well in his or her own manner. For him, *there is not, there is no longer, any surface.* How could Carroll not strike him as an affected little girl, protected from all deep problems? The first schizophrenic evidence is that the surface has split open. Things and propositions have no longer any frontier between them, precisely because bodies have no surface. The primary aspect of the schizophrenic body is that it is a sort of body-sieve. (*Logic of Sense* 89)

Without accurate sense of surfaces and boundaries, the schizophrenic body does not emerge from the dialectics of interiority and exteriority, figure and background. Each encounter, no matter whether it is with food or with words, is singularly intense and wounding. "For the schizophrenic, then," says Deleuze, "it is less a question of recovering meaning than of destroying the word" (90). For example, as Deleuze explains further, Artaud's "creation of breath-words (*mots-souffles*) and howl-words (*mots-cris*), in which all literal, syllabic, and phonetic values have been replaced by *values which are exclusively tonic* and not written" (90–91), embodies the destructive and aggressive impulse of schizophrenic language. Speaking, thus, is turned inside out: it is no longer primarily an outbound journey of words but a defensive act of eating words.

Even though both the schizophrenic and the little girl mess with words and food, to Deleuze, their passions are of a different nature. With the schizophrenic, the act of speaking is burdened with consequences and shot through with the desire of consuming. The little girl, in contrast, whose tongue is unfledged and playful, confuses eating with speaking as she lets words go astray and food be introduced. Deleuze further translates the difference between these two figures into two types of literature: the literary language of surface and the schizophrenic language of depth:

> Artaud thrusts the child into an extremely violent alternative, an alternative of corporeal action and passion, which conforms to the two languages in depth [...] Carroll, on the contrary, awaits the child, in a manner conforming to his language of incorporeal sense: he waits at the point and at the moment in which the child has left the depth of the maternal body and has yet to discover the depth of her own body. (*Logic of Sense* 94–95)

Speaking of food, as Deleuze's reading of Alice shows, leads the writer back to the little girl, whose confusion is of an innocent and inspiring kind. Eating words, in contrast, gives away the madman, who devours words until there are only skeletons of sounds left. It is thus the serious business of the writer and the poet to speak of food, and to speak as if their words are in competition with food to occupy the mouth.

Eating Words: Translating the Mother Tongue

Artaud started the translation of *Through the Looking-Glass* when he was a patient in a psychiatric hospital in Rodez; his doctor Gaston Ferdière suggested Carroll's works to him as an exercise of art therapy (Murray 44). This might explain why Deleuze insists on reading Artaud as a clinical case. However, intended as a therapeutic exercise, the practice of translation did not fulfill its mission completely: Artaud's version, instead of resonating with Carroll's masterly play with language, wears the language out to the point of disarticulation, where words are dissolved into the pure voice that grunts, trembles, and undoes the original version. Worse still, as Deleuze indicates, it is a language that betrays itself as a symptom of schizophrenia. If Carroll plays with nonsense as an oversupply of sense, Artaud appeals to "the nonsense of the word devoid of sense, which is decomposed into phonetic elements; and the nonsense of tonic elements, which form a word incapable of being decomposed and no less devoid of sense" (*Logic of Sense* 92–93).

The translation therapy, it seems, led Artaud to the discovery of how words can and need to be destroyed and decomposed. Does the practice of translation, then, act as a mirror through which the schizophrenic language reveals its madness, fragility, and aggression? Deleuze mentions another case—"whose beauty and density remain clinical" (*Logic of Sense* 87), according to Deleuze—that may illustrate the consuming impulse of the schizophrenic language manifested via translation. In 1970 Louis Wolfson, who referred to himself as "a schizophrenic student of language," published a book titled *Le Schizo et les langues*, with a preface written by Deleuze. Wolfson wrote the book in French, a language that is not his mother tongue. This, however, does not align him with bilingual writers who craft their works in a foreign language for reasons of migration or exile. In fact, it is not French that matters. Any borrowed tongue would do as long as it could help Wolfson undo the mother tongue living inside of him. The sounds of his mother tongue English made him vulnerable and hysterical, especially when they reached him through his mother's voice. He tried all means to avoid hearing English. In his book *Le Schizo et les langues*, Wolfson introduced a method of spontaneous translation, a method that he invented and used systematically to survive his mother tongue:

> Nevertheless, since it was hardly possible not to listen to his mother tongue at all, he tried to develop ways to convert words almost instantly (especially those he found most troublesome) into foreign words each time, after they had penetrated his consciousness despite his efforts not to perceive them. So that he could somehow imagine that he was not being spoken to in that damned tongue, his mother tongue, English. Indeed, he experienced reactions that were at times acute and that made it even painful for him to hear the language without being able to convert the terms into words that were foreign to him, or without being able to destroy constructively, in his mind, the terms that he just heard in that bloody language, English! (Wolfson, qtd. in Heller-Roazen, *Echolalias* 181)

The mother tongue, whose sounds and senses come to envelop the infantile body from the very beginning, is irresistibly threatening and singularly wounding in Wolfson's case. When the mother tongue is not perceived to offer shelter, the body becomes porous and borderless, failing at distinguishing the figure from the background. The horror of a body with open borders is that it is at the mercy of the squeaking whims of others; undesirable sounds and voices can instantly claim and occupy the uninhabited territory without much resistance. Translation, therefore, becomes a defense mechanism for Wolfson. Upon hearing English, Wolfson would instantly translate the words into foreign expressions that resemble the original phonetic and semantic properties, as if his apprenticeship to a foreign tongue could either dull the sharp edge of his mother tongue or escort him to escape the persecution of the unbearable sounds.

As Wolfson rejects being wrapped under the skin of the mother tongue, his body, as if being turned inside out, repulses the idea of food coming in. In his essay "Louis Wolfson; Or, the Procedure," Deleuze describes Wolfson's aversion to food in the following manner:

> He feels as much guilt after eating as he does after hearing his mother speak English. To ward off this new form of danger, he takes great pains to "memorize" a foreign phrase he had already learned; better yet, he fixes in his mind, he invests with all his strength, a certain number of calories, or the chemical formulas that correspond to the desired food, intellectualized and purified—for example, the "long chains of unsaturated carbon atoms" of vegetable oil. (Deleuze, "Louis Wolfson; Or, the Procedure" 13–14)

Unprepared for the confrontation between interiority and exteriority, the schizophrenic body does not distinguish the different impressions that food and maternal words leave on the tongue. To Wolfson, they are equally immediate, concrete, and threatening. The intense taste of food and words has to be diluted and purified through a process of decomposition and abstraction, to the point where neither food nor words are entitled to the claim of being self-contained entities. Foreignness, therefore, is alluring for Wolfson because it makes meaning contingent and transient, unattached from the particular shapes and sounds of the mother tongue. To Wolfson, foreign words and atomic formulas are of the same structure, which decompose the original and translate the mouth into a channel for pure expressivity.

Unlike the translation therapy of Artaud, which stretches language as such to approximate bodily sounds, Wolfson's practice of translation discriminates the "bad" mother tongue from the "good" foreign languages. In *Logic of Sense*, Deleuze understands Wolfson's troubled relation to English words and food as a symptom of "the existence and disjunction of two series of orality: the duality of things/words, consumptions/expressions, consumable objects/expressible propositions":

> But in particular, this duality is transported to, and is recovered in, a duality of two sorts of words, propositions, or two kinds of language: namely, the mother tongue, English, which is essentially alimentary and excremental; and foreign languages, which are essentially expressive, and which the patient strives to acquire. (*Logic of Sense* 87)

Here Deleuze notices that the trope of eating and speaking acquires different articulations, as the mother tongue and foreign languages configure the mouth in different means. With the schizophrenic language of Wolfson, the tongue is bifurcated into tongues that are mothered and grafted, fated and learned. His aversion to the mother tongue is transferred to food, which is comparable to the mother tongue in the sense that both are, to use Deleuze's words, "essentially alimentary and excremental." The foreign words, on the other hand, are like atomic structures or dietary supplements, which satisfy the basic need for survival without dramatizing the distinction between inside and outside, self and other.

Foreignness Ingested: The In-Between Figure of the Exophonic

Whereas Deleuze uses the examples of Alice, Artaud, and Wolfson to distill a literary language of surface from a schizophrenic language of depth, I would like to ask: Is there an in-between figure that reconciles the child and the madman, emerging, perhaps, from the gap between the mother tongue and foreign languages? As the "forked" tongue makes the literary voice resound in a digestive manner and an uncanny style, what shall we make of the oral regress of literature? Can a "forked" tongue be something other than a clinical symptom, giving rise, instead, to literary inspiration and creativity?

In her interview with Yoko Tawada, Bettina Brandt asked her to elaborate on the metaphors she used in *Overseas-Tongues* (*Überseezungen*), in which Tawada compared her mother tongue to her "exterior skin," referring to a foreign tongue as something she "swallowed whole" and that "has been sitting in [her] stomach ever since" (4). Moreover, Tawada linked the experience of speaking a foreign language to that of eating and digesting food:

> Words in a foreign language are, to me, in a particular way, words that I am consuming. These words are outside of my body and I eat them, I consciously eat them. I can put them into my mouth and then they enter my body; but they are not part of my body. Sometimes these words turn out to be indigestible and then you easily can get a stomachache. These foreign words, though, can also slowly transform themselves and become meat and then, ultimately, they can become my flesh. Although sometimes this process does not work and then the foreign words remains something in between, in between my own body and the foreign body. But, in any case, foreign words are consciously consumed much later on: we are not born with these words. (Tawada and Brandt 4)

When her mouth is cracked open to foreign words, as Tawada phrases it, it fuses two types of oral activities: eating and speaking. Such a fusion is not simply a matter of borrowing the vocabulary related to eating to that of speaking. Figural and symbolic readings fail to comprehend the bleak rupture of the body and the wrinkled surface of the text. Here it is rather about words becoming flesh, about expressions being turned inside out, and bodies being impressed with shapes and sensations of foreign objects. Neither the speaker nor the language stands self-evident by each other. Words enter and accommodate themselves in the mouth, where they, with their voluptuous yet wild shapes, challenge the speaking tongue by refusing to have their traces of passage buried and smoothed out.

Tawada says, "In my own case, this bodily image is also quite concretely linked to the feeling that I get when I pronounce words in a foreign language. Then I am working with my tongue, just like when I am eating" (5). By taking on a concrete yet invisible body, the foreign language requires that the tongue "tastes" the curves and contours of words and adjusts itself to these particularities. Correspondingly, one has to move the mouth and the tongue, chew and swallow the words vigorously, so that the flesh of words can be transformed into the flesh of the body. Doesn't this intense contact and transformation between body and language invite us to reimagine the mouth not as a ready-made space where words are produced by vocal organs, but as a transformative space inhabited by these two bodies and constantly reshaped by their interaction?

This sensory impression of the tongue, Tawada seems to imply, pertains to any languages but one's mother tongue. For Tawada, one inhabits the mother tongue in the same way that one remains inside one's skin. This metaphor recognizes the mother tongue not only as an organic part of the body, which is by nature inedible and cannot be consumed, but also as a perspective through which the speaking body is able to be distinguished from its background. That being said, the mother tongue does not offer up the speaking body to the speaker as a visible and complete field of vision and comprehension. Fragmentary in sight and undivided in imagination, it constitutes the surface of the body and remains unchallenged until the moment that foreign languages parade through the body, unearthing what is beneath the skin and what can be otherwise. Foreignness is to be digested, consumed, and incorporated. Sometimes, however, as Tawada suggests, it may sit inside, alien and still, like a pebble, reinforcing the division and incompatibility from within. Even worse, this odd sensation is contagious; on such occasions, the body undoes its surface image of familiarity and begins to taste its own bittersweet uncanniness.

This image of someone who begins to take in a foreign tongue and lets it bloom into literary sensibility constitutes another figure whose force and creativity, while deriving from the same trope of eating and speaking, cannot be completely mapped into the images of the schizophrenic and the child. This figure has literature look into the primitive opening of the mouth head-on: how it chews, smells, digests, and fails to digest, before words salute the bottomless depth of the body and are sublimated to the misty surface of the page. It is important to note that, with this figure, the trope of eating and speaking ceases to gain currency from language as such but finds its distinctive metaphors and manifestations in foreign tongues. At issue is foreignness: language is alien to the speaking body, as orality is to literature; consumption and absorption are barely imagined in relation to expression, as literary creativity is rarely thought to be crafted from a foreign tongue. If the metaphor of swallowed words and ingested foreignness affirms a linguistic apprenticeship (if not indecency and primitivity), how could this figure convey the authenticity and originality of the author? Is the disorder of "I am to be devoured and expressed" compatible with the law of "I eat, I express, I create"?

This figure, I propose—taking the cue from Chantal Wright—can be named *the exophonic*. "Yoko Tawada is an example of a type of writer I will label 'exophonic'," writes Wright in the introduction of her experimental translation of Tawada's *Portrait of a Tongue*.[2] Wright continues to describe "exophony" as "the phenomenon where a writer adopts a literary language other than his or her mother tongue, entirely replacing or complementing his or her native language as a vehicle of literary expression" (2). Defined in a way that emphasizes the linguistic and literary non-nativeness of a writer, exophonic literature, as it implies here, overlaps with migrant and bilingual writings on the grounds that its narrators and authors often journey through languages and move back and forth among cultures in a quest for literary voice.

As a critical concept, the term "exophonic" has been widely used and vigorously theorized by scholars after the publication of Tawada's book of essays *Exusophoni: bogo no soto e deru tabi* (*Exophony: Traveling Outward from One's Mother Tongue*) (2003).[3] For Tawada, "exophony" is a concept that crystallizes the metamorphosis of a speaking tongue when confronted with a foreign language: how the speaker divests a mother-tongued body and becomes re-imprinted with the contour of a foreign language, searching for daily and artistic expressions in the gap between body and language, between thoughts and words, and between the mother tongue and a foreign language. Whereas Wright's definition emphasizes the matter-of-fact status of the author being a non-native speaker and the creative act of writing

---

2   In an earlier article, Wright examined the limits of the terms such as "axial," "postnational," "postcolonial," "hyphenated," and "non-native," terms that are being used to categorize writers whose literary languages are not their mother tongues. Wright proposed that "exophonic" is a more appropriate term, at least in the German context, to discuss the linguistic status and the stylistic features of non-native writers. See Wright, "Writing in the 'Grey Zone,'" 26–42.

3   Chantal Wright writes that "Tawada first heard the term 'exophony' at a conference held in Senegal in 2002 entitled 'Afrika-Europa. Transporte des Literarischen' (personal correspondence). Tawada reports that the non-native-speaker French writers at the conference were given the well-known label 'francophone', the German writers 'germanophone', and that the collective label used for the various non-native-speaker writers from different countries were 'exophone'. Tawada's collection of essays bearing the title Exophonie was published the year after the conference and in 2007 the co-organizers of the Senegal conference brought out an edited volume, also entitled Exophonie (Arndt et al. 2007), the proceedings of a 2005 colloquium of the same name" ("Writing in the 'Grey Zone'" 39).

in a foreign tongue, I propose that the exophonic, especially in the case of Yoko Tawada, be understood as a literary concept that nourishes the image of a speaking body and of an eating tongue in writing and, therefore, advances the return of a redoubled orality in literature. I understand the exophonic primarily in terms of a literary style instead of as a plain fact. The foreigner status is not necessary for a writer to be qualified as exophonic. Writers such as Proust and Kafka, for example, would be considered, in this definition, to be exophonic insofar as they are able, according to Deleuze and Guattari, "[t]o be a foreigner, but in one's own language, and not simply as someone who speaks in a language other than his or her own. To be bilingual, multilingual, but in a single and same language, without even dialect or patois" (*A Thousand Plateaus* 98). Foreignness, in this sense, refers to a state of mind and an approach to language. It requires that the speaker is ready to give up a ready-made approach to language that lacks reflection and contestation, to wrestle with the tyranny of meaning, and to move beyond an imagined unity and consistency. In short, in order to write, one has to be exophonic even in one's mother tongue.

Tawada writes, "Literary language is in any case never the mother tongue. The way I write in Japanese never equates to the Japanese which I speak, or the Japanese language which I learnt as a child. When one has separated from the language of daily use, this is the moment at which literary language arises, and this is in any case a foreign language" (Tawada, qtd. in "'Von der Muttersprache zur Sprachmutter'"). To Tawada, literature does not speak through a mother tongue. One has to consciously unsettle one's relation to his or her language and text, insistently searching for the odd vision and revelation of a foreigner who fails to recognize the obvious and cannot take things for granted. To be exophonic entails that one speak to literature in an untamed voice and with an unsatiated appetite, re-invoking the ghostly other of literature—be it the original opening of the mouth or the doomed return of the oral instinct. The question follows: How to understand this third figure of the exophonic in relation to the little girl and the schizophrenic? How does it mobilize the interplay of eating and speaking, consumption and expression, surface and depth, in the very domain of literature?

There is a very thin line, as Deleuze observes, between a madman and a poet. What keeps them apart is neither sanity nor reason; it is the child that differentiates them. The schizophrenic is anything but childish; he is without childhood and innocence. Like a poet, he messes up with words, looking for the liberty of *un*doing language and getting closer to things themselves. Yet, unlike a poet, he does not play with his materials. He either survives his language or becomes devastated. Between the schizophrenic and his languages, there is the void of the mouth. The exophonic, in a similar vein, checks the spontaneous outflow of thoughts with a foreign tongue. The exophonic devours words with similar passion and doggedness that borders madness.

"We wrote down what we ate every day; I used the same notebook for food and conjugations," writes Kaplan in *French Lessons: A Memoir*. "Wednesday. Breakfast: two crusts and coffee. And so on. I wrote 'Force de volonté' (force of will) across my notebook, the way other girls wrote 'Susie loves Ralph' [...]. For each bar of chocolate I didn't eat I learned a verb. I grew thinner and thinner. I ate French" (52–53). The Alice that craves to be fed on foreign words in the opening scene of this chapter, strangely, is not altogether fictional. Kaplan, in her memoir, confesses her insatiable appetite for French: words, more words, and many more. She would buy a round trip ticket to Genève just to taste the delicious French phrase *aller et retour* and let it roll off her tongue in grace and in power (53). She whipped the American "r," which was, according to Kaplan, "like a big lump in throat" (54), into a French fashion. She finally learned to have the air caress her vocal chords with a combined force of tenderness and roughness, and the "r" dropped off her lips like "the sound cat makes when she wants to go out: between a purr and a meouw, a gurgling deep in the throat" (55). Whenever French words floated in the air, she pricked her ears and tidied her tongue, ready to make words transform into food. She fell in love with the French language and the French man—both were, for Kaplan, one and the same. "It was the rhythm and pulse of his French I wanted, the body of it, and he refused me, he told me I could never get that. I had to get it another way" (94). The lips she kissed were the promise to get closer to the type of French she desired. She leaped over the physical barrier like what a horse did to the fence, lured by the horizon, faraway but shimmering—that is, the call to life.

Possessed by a mania for words as food, the exophonic writers chew and consume words in voracity and naivety. However, unlike the schizophrenic, there is no end in view in terms of the gesture of swallowing and devouring. Words ingested are to be re-transformed into a sensibility to language and an expressivity tinted with the memory of eating. Tawada, for instance, speaks of pain and delight, confusion and creativity, as the foreign tongue consumes words as if they were food (*"Ein Wort"* 4–5). Her literary style is a natural extension of a foreigner's situation that is marked by ignorance and innocence: as Wright observes, the foreign gaze is ubiquitous in Tawada's texts; it is a vision that blends the anthropological with the fictitious, which leads to a narrative tone that is both curious and factual, hesitating and poised (Wright, "Introduction" 5). Wright further points out that "[c]entral features of Tawada's style in this broader sense are the defamiliarizing techniques that the reader encounters in her texts and the texts' tendency to foreground structures and properties of language itself, achieved via metalinguistic reflection" (4). Tawada implants in her writings a powerful image of someone who is possessed by a mania for words as food and one who chews and consumes words in voracity and naivety.

Tawada's narrators and characters are often hyperaware of the visual and acoustic qualities of language, especially since the sustainability of their bodies seems to rely on how well they have digested the language in question. In "Canned Foreign," the narrator arrived in Hamburg without knowing the letters of the alphabet. The city was as unintelligible and veiled as the letters that "lacked both moisture and flesh" (*Where Europe Begins* 86). People were uneasy because the language of her face was not readable for them. She bought a little can with the image of a Japanese woman on the wrapping paper but found a piece of tuna fish inside. The image and the content were completely mismatched. "Every foreign sound, every foreign glance, every foreign taste struck my body as disagreeable until my body changed. The Ö sounds, for example, stabbed too deeply into my ears and the R sounds scratched my throat" (87). Masked and unveiled, the enigma of being outside the protective skin of the mother tongue is embodied in sound, glance, taste. The art of vanishing (to be as invisible as the skin) is the privilege of the ordinary; the foreign stands out in its entirety, leaving intense and even overwhelming sensations on the speaking body.

At the same time, the narrator could not bear the idea of being wrapped up seamlessly in one language: "Often it sickened me to hear people speak their native tongues fluently. It was as if they were unable to think and feel anything but what their language so readily served up to them" (*Where Europe Begins* 87–88). Listen, what a horror: with the native tongue, thoughts are poured out, smooth and bare, as if the language had no need of the speaking body, but mastered it, or bypassed it. Does the narrator exile her tongue to a state of inexpressivity and alienness so as to avoid the horror of being numb and unreflective with one's language? The narrators of Tawada's other stories—like the one in "A Guest" who was haunted by a voice from the tape recorder, or the one in "The Bath" who was a translator but later lost her tongue and voice during a meal—they all have to deal with the penetration of words into the body. "The narrator of Tawada's essay is but one of many possessed by words and driven to the edge of madness" (6), comments Douglas Slaymaker. The clash between language and body is concrete and curious, real and fantastic. The literary style of Tawada captures the fleeting sparks of such a clash; the unfolding of various events, strange and unjustified as they might appear, is done by a narrator who is constantly suspended in the process of speaking and lost in the mixture of words and bodies, and thus is incapable of comprehending the events in a language of logics and causality. The beauty of Tawada's stumbling and struggling tongue is that it is so simple that it leaves intact the strangeness of things and events, whose relation to language remains mysterious and unfathomable.

Because of their apprenticeship to the foreign tongue, the narrators of Tawada's stories seem protected from common sense. Their narrative tones are shot through with the innocence of being, the mystery of otherness, and the self-assurance of interpretation—all of which are further dramatized by the anonymity of the narrators and their obviously contestable relation to the linguistic and cultural situations they are in. For example, in Tawada's short story "The Talisman," the narrator was searching for meanings of different symbols sincerely, but always in wrong, or at least uninvited, places. "In this city there are a great many women who wear bits of metal on their ears" (*Where Europe Begins* 91), we read very early in the story. This everyday scene, ordinary and invisible, becomes obtrusive and hilarious when being pondered as if it were a great mystery and taboo. Intuitively, the narrator interpreted those bits of metal as talismans of some sort. When her friend Gilda explained to her that the earring was a piece of jewelry and had no meaning at all, she interpreted it as reluctance to reveal a secret. What could it be? She thought of the rite of circumcision. Could it be that the sexual organ was substituted by the ears? Fissures of interpretations slipped in, which underlined the fragility of signs and symbols. At the end of the story, the narrator said, "The piece of metal on her ear was heavier and colder than before. I swallowed the words I'd meant to say to her, for she seemed to me, all at once, like a stranger who—although I lived in her language—couldn't have understood me" (95–96). So, she swallowed the words; they were too private to provoke any kind of resonance.

Partially digested and poured onto pages, Tawada's exophonic writings point to a literary expressivity that congeals and clashes with reality instead of illuminating and representing it. Words are like mad stones flung against named things. "At a flea market," says the narrator in Tawada's short story "A Guest," "no one tries to hide the traces hidden in an object. The stuffed animals with their somewhat squashed faces observed me ironically, furiously or disdainfully. Paperback novelettes with faded covers still bore coffee stains and greasy fingerprints from their first readers" (*Where Europe Begins* 152). Likewise, the exophonic writer speaks and writes in a language found in the flea market. Words are indexed with intimate and unsettling memories of the previous owners. However, this is not yet madness—since no words are without the traces of other speakers. Curiosity gives way to madness only when the proximity of things is translated into an imperative that forces one to guess at their relations. "An iron and a candlestick stood side by side, as though there were some relation between them," says the narrator. "I was even able to think how this proximity might be deciphered: the iron produces heat and the candlestick light. Each takes the place of the sun, which from the underground passage is never visible" (152–53). Aren't the foreign words initially bundles of objects traded at the flea market, whose relations are not at all obvious? Tawada, like the narrator in her story, half playfully and half sincerely, lavishes superficial structures upon these words, which—as she makes herself believe—measures up to the weird arrangements of these words. Mad, mad, mad. Later the narrator goes to see the ear doctor because she suspects that there is a flea in her ear. "You are pregnant," the doctor says to her after checking the ear. "Please look again to be sure if I'm really pregnant; it really isn't possible. Could you have confused a flea with an embryo?" (157–58) What is the relation between a flea and an embryo? The solution to this puzzle is hard to contrive—or, at least not obvious. Yet, if we think that foreignness is the embryo of madness, maybe there is indeed a flea living in the ears of the narrator, who mishears the tone and confuses a doctor's routine question with a statement.

In fact, the chaotic world of the flea market was what Tawada discovered when she first tried out her German tongue. In the essay titled "From Mother Tongue to Linguistic Mother," Tawada recounts that the gender system of German, which has neither explicit bearing on the referred objects nor well-ordered rules among the words themselves, does not constitute a natural way of perceiving for her. "Whenever I saw a fountain pen, for instance," says Tawada, "I really tried to perceive it as a male object—not in my head, but with my senses. I would take it in my hand and stare it for a long time, murmuring all the while, 'Masculine, masculine, masculine.' The magic words gradually gave me a new way of looking at things" (141). At such moments, Tawada as a writer becomes the narrator of her story, standing in front of the flea market, pondering the possible connections of the objects lying bewilderingly and curiously close-by. As the relations between objects and words are rediscovered and redefined, Tawada begins to experience herself anew in relation to the German language. What she has discovered is a female object—the typewriter, *die Schreibmaschine*—that has "a large, broad body tattooed with all the letters of the alphabet." For Tawada, from the Mother Tongue to the Linguistic Mother is a passage from language as a natural encapsulation of the body to language as a symbolized mechanical body of a typewriter, whose keys, when tapped correctly, can change the letters of the alphabet into the inky life of words.

Tawada suggests that being adopted by the Linguistic Mother entails that one accepts and repeats its terms and principles, toying with them insofar as one complies with this superimposed condition. If such a formulation reminds one of what Lacan says about the symbolic order, there is a major difference: whereas the symbolic order speaks of the otherness of language in the name of the Father that subjects the speaker to a primary linguistic vulnerability, Tawada's typewriter, while promising a second childhood that is primarily associated with playfulness and creativity, mobilizes the imagination of the relation between language and body by shifting the related vocabulary and metaphor from an organic one to a mechanical one.[4]

Übersetzungen/Überseezungen: Writing with Tongue in Cheek

Becoming mad, becoming the child. "But it is at the same time that one becomes larger than one was and smaller than one becomes" (*Logic of Sense* 1), observes Deleuze in his reading of Alice. The exophonic does not become mad without growing childlike. Inhabiting the border between languages, Tawada stretches the art of writing in multiple directions: perversion and naivety, real passions and light-hearted blunders, pain and pleasure, suffering and indulgence. Such is the in-betweenness of the exophonic: it is torn between madness and innocence; it bespeaks the pleasure of eating as well as the primitivity of speaking. The foreign tongue makes the division between expression and consumption a very thin one; and literary creativity, as the exophonic comes to testify, may spring from the mouth where the desire of speaking is mediated and meliorated in relation to the eating impulse. Words are taken in as if they are food: chewed, consumed, some are indigestible and may cause a stomachache ("*Ein Wort*" 4). Meanwhile, to prevent literature from falling into the schizophrenic depth, the oral regress has to be compensated by the reterritorialization of words in sense.

---

[4] For Tawada, the experience of learning to speak a foreign language may bring back the bygone childhood, providing the speaker insights into how a child perceives and relates to a language. Tawada writes, "Whenever I typed a character, it stood out on the paper straightaway: black on white and, at the same time, full of mystery. If you have a new linguistic mother, you can experience a second childhood. As a child, you take language literally. Consequently, every word acquires a life that is independent of its meaning within a sentence. There are even words that are so alive that, like mythical figures, they can develop biographies" ("From Mother Tongue to Linguistic Mother" 141).

For the exophonic, words are not only like food; they *are* food. "Are there some words that have wombs in their bodies" (55), asks Tawada in her essay "Speech Police and Polyglot Play." In this essay, with determined obstinacy, Tawada continues confusing words with food and things until these questions tie her tongue into a knot:

> Is there a particular taste when I place a woman-word on my own tongue? How does a chocolate bar (*eine Tafel Schokolade*) taste as a word? You say you'd like to have a chocolate bar. Do you actually want to have a bar or a chocolate? [...] Things get forced into a box so that they can be counted and controlled. One bar of chocolate is allowed, two might cause tooth decay, three chocolate bars will already be called a sin by some. Nevertheless the appetite knows no end. Most edible things are uncountable: honey, noodles, vegetables. They will be measured with a spoon, a cup, or a scale. ("Speech Police and Polyglot Play" 55)

Here the conflation of words and food can easily slide into the paranoid and phantasmatic life of the schizophrenic. A chocolate bar: the economy of words is organized in terms of taste and appetite. A spoon of honey or a long piece of spaghetti: conversely, the disordered integrity of food is measured by chunks of words that sit close to one another. Don't words exhibit a sort of oral regress? Isn't the act of speaking a way of biting into the organless body of food? "A word waits secretly to be taken apart," says Tawada, "Not only when the line ends, but when, for example, one remembers a certain woman. If someone thinks of Monica, a Monica jumps out of his *Mundharmonica* ("mouth-harmonica"), and the word is divided in two: *Mundhar* (mouth-hair) and Monica" (56–57). If a word is too long, it is better to do it one bite after another. *Mundharmonica*: first bite from the bottom, a beautiful woman is named; another bite with good intention—ugh, gross, where does the mouth-hair come from?

This manner of eating words is not without risk. Tawada is well aware of it: "What is separated and what must stay together is decreed by particular decrees. 'Rules must exist,' declare, not the policemen but your friends" ("Speech Police and Polyglot Play" 57). However, the problem is the tongue, which is used to defy good intentions and sensible rules. "If you have a short tongue and say the word *Spielregel* ("rule of the game") very fast," Tawada continues, "it sounds like *Spiegel* ('mirror')." What can you do with a short tongue? Can you eat words decently without stretching your tongue too much to observe the rules? Indeed, if you have a short tongue, you may turn the rule of the game into a mirror. As the short tongue is physically unable to match the length of *Spielregel*, the image of the speaking body, which is largely forgotten in the mother tongue, is intruded into the foreign language. Speaking and writing, therefore, become dramas of the tongue, whose paradoxes are unresolvable but provoking, problematic yet laughable.

Tawada, as an exophonic writer, is undoubtedly under the spell of the tongue. She once sketched a textual portrait of a tongue that belongs to her friend called P, who lives in the US but speaks German as a foreign language. "P pronounced the word *erklären* in a heavy, dragging fashion not typical of her," writes Tawada. "The word bore regret and tears under its skin. '*Ich erkläre Dir das.*' Because it sounded unexpectedly guilty, I reacted quickly: 'No, no, you don't have to explain anything'" (*Portrait of a Tongue* 74). On closer inspection, the foreign tongue becomes for Tawada the place where the body is closely and incongruously knit to a language. While the meaning of a word becomes tangible via divorce from a singular vocalizing mouth and through a process of historical sediment, Tawada turns to the tongue to see how the speaking body might add a *style* to language. This corporeal style, whose register in language is manifested by virtue of what we usually call the accent, is not only something that intensifies or distorts prescribed meanings; it is also, for Tawada, the thing that helps one to survive the foreign tongue:

> P said to me that she could never reach the same level she had in English in another language. But whereas in English she had an accent, she had no accent in French. Her French friends confirmed this. In French she didn't need to speak with an accent. An accent preserves the memories of one's mother tongue. Without an accent you could be swallowed up by the present of a foreign tongue. (*Portrait of a Tongue* 91)

If the intrusion of the tongue into language opens up a schizophrenic abyss, the presence of an accent, as Tawada implies, checks the consuming impulse of language; and the very rhetoric of the exophonic—"I am to be expressed, I am to be eaten"—relies on the accent to release and survive the oral regress of literature.

The essay mentioned above is called "Porträt einer Zunge" ("Portrait of a Tongue"), which originally appears in a collection of essays by Tawada entitled *Überseezungen*. As Wright observes,

> The word *Übersetzungen* in German means "translation." *Überseezungen*, however, is a neologism, a compound noun meaning "overseas tongues" [...]. *Seezunge*, which occurs in the middle of *Überseezungen*, literally

translates as "sea-tongue" and refers to the type of fish known as sole in English. *Seezunge* accurately describes the appearance of the fish, which is flat and wide, rather like a swimming tongue, and which suggests the ability to cross the oceans, both physically and linguistically. ("Introduction" 18)

This neologism *Überseezungen*, when read against the backdrop of Tawada's literary fascination with the body of language, can be seen as a textual manifestation of accent rendered by an inept short tongue, stuck in between the linguistic and bodily translation of the mother tongue into a foreign language. Although the correlation among translation, tongue, and sole is accidental in this case, it is not without consequence. By introducing a fallible tongue into translation, the meaning of the word *Übersetzungen* is mobilized, displaced, and extended all at once. Aren't the tongue and the fish ideal metaphors for the practice of translation, which entails the traveling of meaning from one language to another, from one tongue to another? Isn't meaning a fragile thing that can be altered or destroyed by the whims of the tongue? If the act of speaking is equivalent to the translation of body into language, no original, as Tawada suggests in another essay titled "Storytellers without Souls," can be properly and unequivocally traced to render any tongues essentially delinquent:

> The lip movements and gestures of each interpreter and the way each of them glances about as she speaks are so various it's difficult to believe they are all translating a single, shared text. And perhaps it isn't really a single, shared text after all, perhaps the translators, by translating, demonstrate that his text is really many texts at once. The human body, too, contains many booths in which translations are made. I suspect that these are all translations for which no original exists. (*Where Europe Begins* 104)

Listening to *Überseezungen* with overtones of *Übersetzungen*, Tawada appears to be democratizing or leveling up all foreign tongues to the point where the very idea of the original is deflated into one among many. However, the drama of speaking, for Tawada, is fully displayed when the corporeal translation brings about the primitive and regressive impulse of eating, capturing the speaking tongue in a paradox of excess and lack.

Tawada's short story "The Bath" can be read allegorically as an elaborated version of her wordplay with *Überseezungen/Übersetzungen*, in which Tawada extensively engages with the implications of translation and tongue in relation to speaking. The narrator of the story is a Japanese woman who has been learning to speak German. Throughout the story, the narrator retells the story several times and keeps revising her profession (model, interpreter, typist) and the profession of her lover, Xander (photographer, German teacher, carpenter). In one of the typical moments of rephrasing, she says, "I wasn't really a model, I was only a simultaneous interpreter who was uncertified and thus got very few assignments" (*Where Europe Begins* 13). This sentence structure "…wasn't… was…" is very characteristic in this story and serves to push forward a leap of the narrative. Another example comes after the narrator loses her tongue and falls mute: "Xander wasn't really a photographer at all, he was my German teacher" (27). Here the loss of her tongue leads to an incredible revision of the story that intensifies the sense of anxiety; because of the change of his profession, her inability to speak becomes a betrayal of his language. In a broader sense, I interpret the oscillation suggested in the sentence pattern "was/wasn't" as an embodiment of the narrator's paradoxical relation to the tongue, which exists hauntingly with a past that is under revision from time to time, whose metamorphoses depend on newly found situations and circumstances.

In the scenario of the narrator being an interpreter, the story takes place at a restaurant where she is supposed to do interpretation for a group of Japanese businessmen and their German clients. The narrator says that she always orders sole when she goes to a restaurant because the word reminds her of "soul, sol, solid, delicious sole of my soul; the *sole* reason I don't *lose* my *soul*, and my *soles* stand on a *solid* footing still …" "When I eat sole, I'm never at a loss for words with which to translate" (*Where Europe Begins* 14), comments the narrator. Sole, *Seezunge* in German, whose literal translation is "sea-tongue," is consumed to moisten and nourish the tongue before it has to twist itself to find the right words in translation. The proliferation of words is dependent on the metonymic digestion of the tongue beforehand. However, that day she could not order sole because a large fish is already ordered for the whole group. The chef comes with his assistant to cut the fish in front of them. "The open mouth had no tongue in it" (16), the narrator notices. Later, the luncheon begins and her mouth starts to be stuffed with smelly words mixed with undigested chunks of fish:

> When jaw muscles relax, the atmosphere becomes relaxed as well. People's mouths fell open like trash bags, and garbage spilled out. I had to chew the garbage, swallow it, and spit it back out in different words. Some of the words stank of nicotine. Some smelled like hair tonic. The conversation became animated. Everyone began to talk, using my mouth. Their words bolted into my stomach and then back out again, footsteps resounding

up to my brain. The chunk of fish in my stomach was having a bad time of it and began to protest. My stomach muscles clenched up and I began to stutter. It felt good to stutter. "Tha, tha, tha, that," I said. The skin of my stomach grew taut like a bagpipe and I bellowed, "That ha, ha, ha, has, has." I didn't know myself whether I was laughing or stuttering, but it felt agreeable. The words scattered and rose fluttering into the air. (*Where Europe Begins* 17)

This scene of translation gives off a bad smell of food. The linguistic metamorphosis of words is obviously corrupted by the unchecked opening of the mouth. *Übersetzungen* is haunted by its illegitimate double, the *Überseezungen*. Translation regresses into an open rehearsal of the dancing tongue ("Tha, tha, tha, that"), orchestrated by the clenched stomach that drowns words in depth. Words are dizzy. She stutters.

The juggling of the tongue ends abruptly, however. The narrator recounts, "Something wet and soft was touching my lips from the outside. The sole came slipping into my mouth and played with my tongue, gently at first, then with more force. Finally the sole gripped my tongue between its teeth and ate it up" (29). Here the intrusion of the overseas-tongue (*Überseezungen*) in the order of translation (*Übersetzungen*) suggests an oversupply of corporeality in speaking a foreign language; and the metaphor of the swimming sole (*seezunge*) points to the danger of translation. Since the foreign language is a tongueless fish and a soulful flesh-eater, the tongue in translation would either craft a style of cohabitation for language and body or become lost and swallowed, sealed in silence.

Tawada's wordplay with *Überseezungen/Übersetzungen* is, without doubt, largely unnatural and contrived. So are the jumping plots that characterize her stories. Words are usually not invoked to fill in the gap between thoughts and language; instead, her narratives are meant to enrich the chance encounters among words across different languages. Tawada's literary playground is essentially a flea market of words, where the accent is overheard as an unwitting comment on the largely contrived connection of words created by their accidental proximity:

People say my sentences in German are very clear and easy to hear, but still they are "not ordinary" and deviant in some ways. No wonder, because they are the results of the sound that I as an individual body have absorbed and accumulated by living through this multilingual world. It is of no use if I tried to delete my accents or remove my habits in utterance. Today a human subject is a place where different languages coexist by mutually transforming each other and it is meaningless to cancel their cohabitation and suppress the resulting distortion. Rather, to pursue one's accents and what they bring about may begin to matter for one's literary creation. (Tawada, qtd. in Suga 28)

The accent, for Tawada, can be a corporeal translation of a language, a literary style mobilized by the speaking tongue, a defense mechanism against the eating impulse of language. It is the accent that brings forth the oral regress of exophonic writings, whose fallible tongue stands out unexpectedly with an uncommon choice of words or a chunk of ungrammatical thought. Yet it is also the accent that enables the figure of the exophonic to speak like the little girl while eating like the schizophrenic. If the order of expression and consumption is stretched to all directions with exophonic writings, the accent, at least, makes sure that the monster of the language machine spits out bones of the devoured flesh, which, when nourished with care, can bloom into what we might not object to call literature.

Conclusion: For the Love of Literature

Abstract: The conclusion begins with an analysis of Lawrence Abu Hamdan's *The Freedom of Speech Itself,* which critiques the accent test used by the UK government to determine asylum seekers' countries of origin. The accent test, resembling a modern version of the biblical shibboleth, treats accent as a performative act that determines identity and citizenship. The chapter links this practice to the Derrida-Searle debate on performative speech, contrasting the linguistic approach to the artistic perspective presented in Hamdan's work. While linguists seek to formalize accent's performativity, Hamdan's exhibition challenges the reduction of accent to a political or legal act, urging us to listen to accents as expressions of passion and desire rather than as markers of truth or falsity.

Keywords: accent test; border; linguistics and literature

To speak of the love of literature—

I am being reminded of an absurd man who tries to lodge a square of desire in the infinite flow of words. The image comes from a performance, in which the artist Song Dong sat in the Lhasa River in Tibet, repeatedly stamping the water with a wooden seal inscribed with the Chinese character 水 (water). A writer's infatuation (flirtation? love affair?) with literature is mad, hopeless, and futile. Indeed, a petite tragedy. "One Always Fails in Speaking of What One Loves": this is, sadly and ironically, the last sentence that Roland Barthes had typed before he met his end on the streets of Paris (Léger xx). The futility is not just about the enigma of desire, the evanescence of words, but also the mortality of the speaking body.

No matter how impossible the claim of love may sound in the matter of literature, still, the urge to put a finger on what one loves is real. What if, but what if—

> If a man could pass through Paradise in a dream, and have a flower presented to him as a pledge that his soul had really been there, and

he found that flower in his hand when he awoke—Ay! and what then? (Coleridge 282)

What if one woke up from the floral dream of literature, holding a strange and beautiful flower in the hand? Would the flower, which Jorge Luis Borges, in his short essay "Coleridge's Flower," understands as "the nexus between the real and the imaginary" (241), then stand for the *real* object of an ineffable desire?

The flower, the language: it is what literature offers one to pluck, to hold close, to admire, to scrunch up, to tread upon... It is the reminder of a whirlwind romance, the shiver that follows a sensation of touch, and the fortuitous body that animates the shadow of desire. Language is what the writer performs, in the name of love for literature.

* * *

These two images often come to my mind when I ask myself what literature does and why my passion about writing is not waning as this study, which is really about my love of language and my love of other writers' love of language, comes to an end. Which one do you believe in: the image of the writer being a madman trying to stage a spectacular scene of imprinting the ever-changing flow of language with his style, or the other image of the writer being a reaper of dreams who takes language as the reality of a fantasy?

I choose to be convinced by the second image and be swept off my feet by the inky scent of the flower, because I love literature *when it is a delicate art of crafting language*. In the introduction, I pursued the question of why the figure of the accent is important to literature. In the conclusion, I want to reverse the question: So, why literature? What is so special and illuminating about the literary approach to language? What consequence does the writer's love of language have for all the other lovers and traders of language—for instance, for linguists?

In his first solo exhibition *The Freedom of Speech Itself* (2012), Lawrence Abu Hamdan, a contemporary artist based in Beirut, invites one to contemplate the two different approaches—with one being linguistic, the other artistic—to language, or to be precise, to accent.[1] The central piece

---

1   This discussion draws in part from my previous work "Cosmopolitan Hospitality and Accented Crossing," published in the edited volume *New Cosmopolitanisms, Race, and Ethnicity*, which provides a more detailed analysis of the performance (Hui).

of this exhibition features an audio documentary, which brings attention to the practice of language analysis, often loosely referred to as the accent test, used by the UK government in asylum procedures to determine the applicant's country of origin. Since the 1990s, in response to the concern that asylum applicants might make false claims, many countries, including the Netherlands, Germany, Australia, etc., have implemented the method to evaluate language profiles of applicants who present no documentary proofs of their origins. While the specific operating methods vary from country to country, language analysis, in general, consists of two stages. In the beginning, an interview is carried out and tape-recorded in the presence of the applicant, an interpreter, and an immigration official. The recording is then sent to analysts and linguists, who compile the results of the evaluation into a written report, which is later presented to the immigration department.

Ever since the method of language analysis was introduced, there have been heated debates over its theoretical assumptions and operating conditions. Linguists and practitioners of language analysis have to address questions such as: Can the borderlines of language varieties be unequivocally mapped, overlapping with the territorial borders of nations and regions? How reliable is speech and accent in verifying a speaker's national origin in a multilingual context? Central to these debates is the question of whether or not the intuitive knowledge of the native speaker should be incorporated to judge the authenticity of the accent in question. The linguists who are in favor of the proposal argue that native speakers are better at judging whether certain speech features are genuine or fake and should be appropriated as a valid and complementary form of knowledge (Neuhauser and Simpson; Cambier-Langeveld). Helen Fraser, whose expertise lies in phonetics and forensic linguistics, holds the opposite position, arguing that native speakers tend to be overconfident about their folk knowledge and beliefs, which, when admitted in the practice, may end up discrediting linguistics as a positive science:

> It is well known that people without extended training in academic linguistics are often ignorant not just about many aspects of language, but about their own ignorance, and so tend to put unjustified faith in their own 'folk knowledge'. Linguists of all persuasions have been engaged for many years in fostering appreciation of linguistics as a discipline among other professions and in society at large (Hudson 1981), promoting the view that a 'linguist' is not someone who can speak several languages or knows 'good grammar', but someone with advanced academic qualifications and professional expertise in the science of language –equivalent to a chemist, psychologist or engineer. (114)

The possibility of having native speakers "transcend" their position of being merely research objects clearly touches a nerve. Fraser thinks that linguistic studies have had a hard time being accepted as a valid branch of science; and the promoted differentiation between linguists and native or competent speakers marks a watershed in this debate. If native speakers were to be permitted to interpret the data, this is the equivalent of saying that the knowledge and expertise of linguists is not original and specialized. Whereas a chemist, psychologist, or engineer would seem to have acquired his or her scientific status rightfully, a linguist only becomes one of them after proving that a linguist knows more with regard to language, or at least knows it in a different way than a native speaker does.

While linguists within the field are concerned with regulating the practice, as an artist, Hamdan responds to the issue from a different angle. His audio documentary brings together interviews and testimonies of lawyers, phonetic linguists and linguistic anthropologists, asylum seekers, Home Office officials, and the artist himself. There are no visuals to enhance the audience's identification of the people who are speaking in the audio. To make it more complicated, words and voices continuously interweave with and interrupt one another, to the point that different strands of thoughts and observations are fragmented into sonic clues to identify who is speaking and whose voice it is. Whereas the voices of the experts, officials, and the artist himself—no matter whether accented or not—usually sound calm and even, the asylum seekers can easily be distinguished by their marked English accents, "excited" voices, or "unfamiliar" languages. The anxious and stirring emotions of the asylum seekers can, to the audience's ears, also be intensified, owing to the rough and loud background noise, which is not there in most expert interviews. The background sound becomes a prominent medium that registers different levels of precarity and senses of security in terms of the living and working environments of asylum seekers, experts, and officials.

At one point, following a brief moment of chirpy and carefree background music, one hears only a constant and squeaking repetition of the /a/ sound, as if the cassette tape were jammed. As the sound gradually fades away, a male voice (very likely that of the artist) impassively explains,

> This syllable is the sound that provides the UK border agency with the alleged certainty of Muhammad's Syrian origin. They designate this vowel as a Syrian national, and imply that its use in the word 'tomato' is coterminous with Syria's borders. But locating this Syrian vowel in the speech of a Palestinian surely proves nothing more than the displacement

of the Palestinians themselves. In other words, the instability of an accent, its borrowed and hybridized phonetical form, is testimonial not to someone's origins, but only to an unstable and migratory lifestyle, which is of course common in those fleeing from conflict and seeking asylum. Is it not more likely then that a genuine asylum seeker's accent would be an irregular and an itinerary concoction of voices, a set of a biography of a journey, rather than an immediately distinguishable voice that vows its unshakable roots to a single place?

Throughout this segment of analysis, the repetitive utterance of the phoneme /a/ stubbornly stays in the background, while the male voice evenly performs itself. Because of its irregular frequencies and amplitudes, it haunts the narrating voice—sometimes like a malfunctioning machine, and sometimes like a wounded and grunting animal. While the male voice remains neutral and nonchalant, as the rate of repetition slows down, the background sound seems to add an emotional tone of desperation and sympathy to the voice's plea for justice. In contrast, when the sound suddenly accelerates and overtakes the voice, the shrieking sound constitutes a striking contrast to the calm voice, making one wonder whether the knowledge that arises from these two different forms of voicing will ever be compatible.

* * *

The accent test resembles, to some extent, a modernized version of the biblical shibboleth with the old technique of *catch*words replaced by an assumingly more scientific method conducted by forensic linguists. Whereas the linguists are called upon to make the accented speech a performative act of border and citizenship, Hamdan's audio documentary does the opposite: it is meant to *suspend* the performativity of the accented speech, and to sharpen the awareness of the listening conditions that influence how speech acts. The linguists' interest lies in formalizing and delimiting a "total speech situation" (Austin 147) for the accent test. The artist, instead, focuses on the possibility and necessity of listening to accents as expressions of passion and desire, which should not be buried and trivialized by the institutional discourse that makes a claim on worthiness and unworthiness based on a scientific evaluation of truth and falsity.

So, between the linguists and the artist, the border and the borderless, law and desire, which position shall one side with? The answer varies. But what if one decided to resist the temptation of taking sides, or simply found both positions tenable in their own ways? What if the debates demonstrated nothing but, to use Shoshana Felman's words from a different context, "the basic nonconfrontation, the intrinsically missed encounter or the inherent misunderstanding" (62) between two disciplines and two approaches?

In *The Scandal of the Speaking Body*, Felman argues that behind what she calls the "theoretical coincidences" between Lacanian psychoanalysis and Austinian performative theory there lies an unbridgeable gap of knowledge, brought forth by the impenetrable linguistic mentalities of French and Anglo-Saxon thought:

> In fact, if Lacan and Austin—with the same taste for paradox and the same self-subverting consciousness of a breach, at every point, in knowledge—are concerned with the same thing, they explore this object only within the respective—and divergent—geniuses of their own language: the (ironically empirical and pragmatic) genius of English, or the (sophisticated, allusive, speculative) genius of French. This means that they say (more or less, on certain points) the same thing, but they say it in the specific ways in which English and French are nevertheless destined to *miss each other*, not to meet. (62–63)

Felman thinks that even though Lacanian psychoanalysis is inspired by the muse of language, whose discovery is largely owed to Austin, the coincidental relation between these two disciplines demonstrates nothing but a nonrelation between French and English, and a nonconfrontation between fields whose languages are, by nature, foreign to each other.

The accent test also testifies the missed encounter, but this time between linguistics and literature (or the arts in general), both of which, instead of bonding over their shared passion for language, are divided because of it. A linguist loves language insofar as it offers the experience of science, and a writer the experience of art. This differentiation—generalized as it is—is not so much an essential quality as a way of explaining how linguists and writers fail and are doomed to fail to speak the same language. And the failure is precisely the hope: even when we desire the same thing, we desire it in different ways.

In fact, history has more than once witnessed the quarrel between linguistics and literature over the guardianship of language. A well-known head-on clash took place at the end of the 1970s between Jacques Derrida and John Searle, triggered by Derrida's criticism of Austin's speech act theory in "Signature Event Context." In this essay, Derrida put forth a theory of communication modeled on writing, which "must be repeatable—iterable—in the absolute absence of the receiver or of any empirically determinable collectivity of receivers" (7). Derrida proposed that communication, qua writing, is a singular and pure event that arises from an original context; however, such context is neither fixed or determinable, since the logic of writing presupposes that it has to circulate beyond the original context delimited by the conscious intent of the writer. The "force of rupture" (9) from the original context or a general iterability is what characterizes writing per se and is what, to Derrida, problematizes Austin's speech acts theory.

Indeed, literature poses a conundrum for Austin. As literary critic J. Hillis Miller observed in *Speech Acts in Literature*, "Literature is the ghost that haunts *How to Do Things with Words*. It keeps creeping back in and vitiating the attempt to establish the conditions of a felicitous performative and so constitutes another kind of failure" (18). On the one hand, Austin often quoted from literary works and plays to illustrate various speech situations and different types of speech acts. On the other hand, Austin was at a loss to explain why a speech act—for instance, a marriage proposal—that happens on stage does not produce the same performative effect as it does off stage. Austin, therefore, claimed that "a performative utterance will, for example, be *in a peculiar way* hollow or void if said by an actor on the stage, or if introduced in a poem, or spoken in soliloquy," disregarding literary examples as being out of the norm, "used not seriously, but in ways *parasitic* upon its normal use" (Austin 22). Derrida interpreted Austin's systematic exclusion of fictional speech from the speech acts theory as a telling case of mistaking the essential for the accidental: what Austin tried to do was to limit an original context—a felicitous and total speech situation—for the performative, by means of precluding what Austin considered as being the abnormal and the parasitic, which, for Derrida, constitutes the most basic and exemplary form of communication as iterable.

In his reply, Searle stated that Derrida had profoundly misinterpreted Austin's theory, which made Searle hesitate to see the debate as a confrontation between the analytical and continental philosophical traditions (198). Searle explained that Austin's exclusion of the fictional discourse is a "research strategy" instead of a "metaphysical exclusion" (205). It is thus unwarranted to criticize Austin for limiting the scope of his theory, since the validity of any science is, as Ann Banfield commented in a different context regarding linguistics as a scientific field, "dependent on its refusal to comment on all *uses* of language" (6). Searle, moreover, clarified that Austin's use of the term "parasitic" does not imply an ethical judgment; it is meant to say that the effect of the fictional discourse is dependent upon the ordinary use and is able to be conveyed only through a prior exposure to the speech outside fiction.

Reading through the articles from the exchange between Derrida and Searle—some of which were collected in a volume entitled *Limited Inc* (1988)—many readers would immediately pick up the frustration and annoyance that both sides felt and showed toward each other. In his reply, Searle wrote, "The problem is rather that Derrida's Austin is unrecognizable. He bears almost no relation to the original" (204). Searle refused to have his response reprinted in the book, because "he does not feel that the kind of work Derrida does is legitimate (or, for the most part, intelligible)" (Alfino 143). Derrida, being no less irritated, wrote an afterword to criticize Searle's apparent lack of ethical discussion, for Searle quoted from a private conversation with Foucault to tease Derrida's obscure writing style. Derrida claimed that Searle did not even try—and perhaps was incapable of—understanding him (Derrida 29).

The exchange overall was, to use a Chinese idiom, like a chicken talking to a duck: both sides felt that the other had missed his point, failing, on purpose, at taking his criticism and response seriously. The missed encounter between, for Searle, two philosophical traditions and, for Felman, two languages, nonetheless and at least, confronts one with the broader question of what literature is for linguistics: Is it exceptional or exemplary? Is it merely an archive of speech samples or an indispensable field for understanding what language is and what it does?

"Listen, this is what I can say," said Gilles Deleuze in *L'Abécédaire de Gilles Deleuze*, an eight-hour series of interviews recorded around 1990 but published posthumously at Deleuze's request. "To understand what style is, one must know nothing about linguistics. *Linguistics has done a lot of harm.* Why is this the case? Because there is an opposition—Foucault said it well—and it's even their complementarity, between linguistics and literature. As opposed to what many say, they do not fit each other at all." Speaking from beyond his grave, Deleuze did not need to worry about making a scene. His seemingly sweeping statement about linguistics is, in fact, a condensed version of his and Guattari's critique of linguistics dating back to the 1980s in their collaborative work *A Thousand Plateaus*. In this book, they attacked what they perceived to be the four "postulates of linguistics":

I. Language is informational and communicational.
II. There is an abstract machine of language that does not appeal to any "extrinsic" factor.
III. There are constants or universals of language that enable us to define it as a homogeneous system.
IV. Language can be scientifically studied only under the conditions of a standard or major language. (75–100)

CONCLUSION: FOR THE LOVE OF LITERATURE

So, indeed, *la linguistique a fait beaucoup de mal*. Deleuze and Guattari had no sympathy for linguists' failed project of constructing a science of language. Their criticism of linguistics is indeed more targeted at structural and generative linguistics, which were made popular after Saussure and Chomsky, respectively, and have largely contributed to the general impression of linguistics in its entirety as a scientific field. Deleuze and Guattari's primary concern is that linguists make language lose its vitality by forcing it to conform to rules and orders. Grammaticality, according to them, "is a power marker before it is a syntactical marker" (101). The ordinary scene of a schoolmistress instructing students in language lessons becomes to them the typical instance of language becoming a word-order assemblage, installing a hierarchy between the standard and the deviant, the major and the minor, the universal and the atypical. Saussure's privilege of *la langue* over *la parole* says less about what language is than about the linguist's ambition of making language a scientific research object and an invariable constant. Contrary to what Saussure believed, in terms of language, Deleuze and Guattari explained, "[i]t is the variation itself that is systematic, in the sense in which musicians say that 'the theme is the variation'" (93). In the hands of linguists, the life of language withers; it is abstracted into a homogeneous sign system, which needs neither speakers nor referents to breathe life into expressions. "Linguistics treats language as if no living being would speak it, as *no-body*'s language, language without body" (127), wrote Boštjan Nedoh in *Lacan and Deleuze: A Disjunctive Synthesis* (2017). It is, therefore, the concrete and individual experiences of language that become overlooked and trivialized.

Deleuze and Guattari's explicit and determined renunciation of linguistics is not an individual case. It reflects a prevailing sentiment of mistrust toward linguistics that some non-linguists of the time—who had once been inspired by Saussure's linguistic model and transplanted it to their own fields—came to harbor. Two years before the publication of *A Thousand Plateaus*, Jean-Claude Milner, a French linguist and philosopher, wrote a little book *For the Love of Language* (1980), which, as the title readily hints, this conclusion aims to show respect to and enter into dialogue with. In the opening of the introduction, Ann Banfield, who is also the English translator of Milner's book, observed that the relation between linguists and non-linguists was perplexing and non-reciprocal (2). On the one hand, the way that other disciplines, such as poetics and psychoanalysis, employed the linguistic model appeared, for linguists, largely unrecognizable and enigmatic. On the other hand, linguistics, as a self-sufficient field of science, did not need other disciplines as much as the other way around—which finally became a bother for non-linguists. "The death of linguistics was hence repeatedly proclaimed, for now that non-linguists had ceased to think about linguistics, how could its continued existence be anything but an anachronism?" (Banfield 3).

This was exactly the question that Milner attempted to address from the viewpoint of himself as a linguist. His approach, however, was psychoanalytical: How come, when preparing for a strictly syntactic work, contrary to what was often expected, he did not feel boredom and languor? "So the suspicion sometimes came to me: could it be possible that linguistics interested me?" (52). Milner thus undertook a reevaluation of principles and assumptions that uphold linguistics' claim to science, with the focus emphatically shifted from the falsifiability of linguistic methodologies to a linguist's experience of language as prone to a formalized and mathematical writing. It is unclear whether or not Deleuze and Guattari had gotten acquainted with Milner's book, which, written earlier than *A Thousand Plateaus*, strangely, reads like a thought-out response to a criticism that it foresees.[2]

Central to Milner's argument is that in order to experience a science of language, linguists have to mark the boundary of their knowledge, which will inevitably separate them from other lovers of language. For Milner, this limit is calculability. But how shall one make language calculable? Milner explained that to make language a proper object of science—and proper in the sense of being calculable—it has to meet four requirements, which, for the sake of brevity, I summarize as follows:

> I. Language has to be made its own cause by means of the arbitrariness of the sign.
> II. The distinctiveness of the sign forms a basic principle from which all the operations are deduced.
> III. The speaking being is retained as "the dimension of pure enunciation," which is "thought of as a point without division or extension, with neither past nor future, neither a consciousness nor an unconscious, without a body—and without any other desire except to articulate."
> IV. The multiplicity of speaking beings is understood in terms of two symmetrical points: that of emission and that of reception. (51–52)

---

2   It is more logical, of course, to assume that Deleuze and Guattari's critique of linguistics is a response to Milner's formulation. However, it does not read like so because, for one, Deleuze and Guattari do not explicitly cite or argue against Milner in their writings and for another, they leave untouched the central thesis of Milner's book, which is that a science of language is possible because language gives linguists the possibility to formalize the empirical.

CONCLUSION: FOR THE LOVE OF LITERATURE

Milner held that these conditions are what enable a linguist's work. "I was in fact called upon by circumstances to turn to the very area of language where something presenting itself as a scientifically expressible rule interested me" (54), wrote Milner. As a linguist, Milner's passion for language submits to the order of science, which entails language being expressed in terms of internal criteria rather than external realities.

This is—I have to admit—not my preferred way of loving language. Yet I can relate to Milner's thrill as a linguist. The risk of Milner's psychoanalytical approach to linguistics, in foregrounding his partiality and his role as a linguist, is that people seem not to know what to do with it: a scholarship founded on an experiencing and feeling subject seems to prevent critical engagements from the outset. Who would want to openly judge what is the correct form of love, passion, and experience—who else but a despot, a religious fanatic, a fascist? However, it is one thing to comment on the form of love *in itself*; it is another to discuss and criticize the *implications, interpretations, and consequences* of one's love. The strength of Deleuze and Guattari's critique of linguistics—let us assume that they had read Milner's book—lies not in whether language can be experienced as science, but in the consequences that linguistic practices of language have led to: that is, the construction and stratification of a major and a minor language, of a standard and an accented speech, and of a perfect and an atypical expression. Whereas Milner proposes that linguists have to dismiss the speaking being and the state of things as irrelevant and external to the well-defined limits of the linguistic field, Deleuze and Guattari are more concerned with language and the speaker being made under the yoke of linguistics. Linguistics is not performed in a vacuum. It bears consequences and is called upon—as it is in the case of the accent test—to take responsibility for what is happening outside its disciplinary constraints.

* * *

Deleuze and Guattari's critique of linguistics, as what happened in the Derrida-Searle debate, does not confront the theoretical framework that Milner initially laid out. To start with, there is no evidence showing that they read Milner's book. However, on a theoretical level, this is perhaps what criticism is about: a missed encounter *par excellence*, an infinite shifting of grounds, an illusion of a common language... Then, what is the point of criticism? What if the interdisciplinary borrowing and poaching is nothing but a self-righteous misreading in the end?

I would propose to address these questions through the concept of a *critical* machine, which I borrow from Deleuze's formulation of "a literary machine" in his book *Proust & Signs* (1964/2000). In his discussion of the French novelist Marcel Proust's work, Deleuze argues that the modern work of art offers the occasion to talk about a machinic functionary of art, which has its focus on the use of the work instead of the meaning. "The modern work of art is anything it may seem; it is even its very property of being whatever we like, from the moment *it works*: the modern work of art is a machine and functions as such" (145). Likewise, the critical machine does not steer through various disciplines to harvest ripe ideas; meaning is at best an effect and a by-product. The sole requirement for the crossbreeding of concepts and paradigms is that it has to be productive. It can be anything provided that it adds momentum to the critical machine, "provided we make the whole thing work, and 'it works, believe me'" (146). The point of criticism, therefore, is neither to outsmart the other nor to take sides, but to make the machine work and to take care of what it produces, displaces, and mobilizes.

The imagery of the machine has always been part of Deleuze's philosophical sign system. However, it was not until the publication of Deleuze and Guattari's collaborative work *A Thousand Plateaus* that the imagery of the machine ripened into a philosophical concept. There the machinic becomes more than a unique feature of the modern work: it is a mode of thinking in which the literary machine becomes part of a machinic assemblage by conjoining with multiple other machines (for instance, a war machine, love machine, desiring machine, etc.). Considering how much Deleuze and Guattari champion the concept of the machine, it seems counterintuitive to note that one of their critiques of the four postulates of linguistics is about there being "an abstract machine of language that does not appeal to any 'extrinsic' factor" (85). What exactly do they mean when they associate the object and scope of linguistics with "an abstract machine of language"? Deleuze and Guattari explain it well in the introduction:

> Our criticism of these linguistic models is not that they are too abstract but, on the contrary, that they are not abstract enough, that they do not reach the *abstract machine* that connects a language to the semantic and pragmatic contents of statements, to collective assemblages of enunciation, to a whole micropolitics of the social field. (7)

So, the accent of their criticism is not on the machine part but rather on the degree of abstraction. The linguistic perception and construction of language makes the machinic quality a matter of language, which results in a "naïve" or even "bad" machine that does not entail being plugged into other machines in order to function. "It is language that depends on the abstract machine, not the reverse" (91), say Deleuze and Guattari. What linguists assemble is thus a pseudo machine, in the sense that it is a machine that fails to promise and realize what I would call the machinic potentials. What I mean is that the critical potentiality of the concept of the machine is, for Deleuze and Guattari, maximized when the machine becomes the nexus of several other concepts—namely, productivity, assemblage, heterogeneity and multiplicity, deterritorialization and reterritorialization. In other words, an ideal machine should be an aggregation of heterogeneous components, giving rise to products that are not deducible to the machinic structure. Meanwhile, the logic of the combination of the components is not that of a linear ordering but of a fortuitous emergence that remains open to changes. All these concepts central to the machinic potentials can find their counteragents in linguistics: meaning as opposed to productivity, structure to assemblage, homogeneity to heterogeneity, and representation to deterritorialization. Because these concepts, which serve as pillars for the postulates of linguistics, are fundamentally antithetical to the machinic potentials, the linguists' abstract machine of language is at best a pseudo machine that, instead of contributing to a bigger assemblage, runs on the internal criteria generated by the sign system of language itself.

I would say that Deleuze and Guattari's diagnosis of the problematic of linguistics is not so much about curing linguists of their infatuation with science as about assembling a critical machine that emancipates language from the constraints of linguistics. The engine that they plug in is the literary machine. In his book *Deleuze and Language* (2002), Jean-Jacques Lecercle makes a comment on Deleuze's statement about style and linguistics:

> Literature is not one of the regions providing texts from which the empirical linguist will democratically choose his examples, on a par with the language of advertising or cookery. It is not even a specific region of language, often called poetic language, the object of a specific sub-part of linguistics, called stylistics. Literature is conceived here as the other of linguistics, its opponent, that which puts it in its place (which is no place at all). (64)

Literature, no longer merely a subfield of linguistics that consists of an archive of linguistic examples, is perceived by Deleuze as the opponent, the alternative, and the utopia: it is what intensifies the aura of language, making it glimmer with projections, memories, and echoes. It is what brings about the return of the speaking body; and more crucially, as Deleuze and Guattari write in *A Thousand Plateaus*, this speaking body is gifted with the stammering but creative tongue of a foreigner. Deleuze and Guattari envision that literature should obstruct the routine flow of words, emancipating language from a state of being as-if-perfect and as-if-unbound: "It was Proust who said that 'masterpieces are written in a kind of foreign language.' That is the same as stammering, making language stammer rather than stammering in speech. To be a foreigner, but in one's own tongue, not only when speaking a language other than one's own" (98).

The image of the foreigner, for Deleuze and Guattari, is nothing but a convenient metaphor, which stands for their perspective about a writer's optimal relation to language. In a way, the metaphor of the foreigner is not very different from what poets, children, and lunatics mean for them: these are all figures of the "atypical expression [which] constitutes a cutting edge of deterritorialization of language" (99). It is also not very different from, for instance, what Caroline Bergvall calls to "speak with a cat in the throat" (*Meddle English* 157) or what Roland Barthes says about playing with the mother's body, "to take bliss in a disfiguration of the language" (*The Pleasure of the Text* 37).

However, to unpack the metaphor of the foreigner, it suggests a plethora of interpretations in terms of Deleuze and Guattari's understanding of literary style. First of all, the foreigner is the one who cannot take his or her language for granted. His or her relation to language is not that of mastery but of apprenticeship, experiment, and exploration. There are always signs that need to be deciphered and boxes to be unpacked, since the foreigner's love of words is incongruous, fragile, and unreliable. Secondly, the foreigner does not merely do things *with* language but also does something *to* language. The strangeness of his or her tongue—sometimes charming and sometimes disturbing—comes from the fact that the foreigner, being innocently ignorant, is protected from clichés and common sense. Even when the foreigner states something obvious and common—for example, the idiom "on edge"—he or she says it as if it were fresh and original. Thirdly, the foreigner re-embodies language. The breath, tone, pitch, hiccup, stammer, silence, clearing of the throat—everything that happens alongside language is now an essential part of the event of speaking. Words are traces of the speaking body—intimidating in a way as they are impressed with full-bodied personality, and blissful, on the other hand, as they are imbued with linguistic sensuality. There is something perverse about taking pleasure in the foreigner's language. One is never completely sure what one is celebrating: is it audacity or stupidity, transgression or innocence, love or indifference?

CONCLUSION: FOR THE LOVE OF LITERATURE

Still, what about the foreigner's problems? Unlike Deleuze and Guattari, who abstract the foreigner into a metaphorical machine, this study lays bare and theorizes the language issues that a foreigner may face and deal with. Besides accent, one prominent problem that the foreigner may encounter while learning a new language is the metaphor. Literalism is the cult of the foreigner: so a babysitter is someone who makes the baby *sit* while the parents are away—no standing, no crawling, no lying down; to wait a second means you are welcome to lose patience after counting from one to two; and when someone tiptoes gingerly, the spicy aroma must make you want to cry... In a way, this study is not only about the accented tongue of the foreigner but also about *becoming* the foreigner by looking for ideas that have been hidden in plain sight.

Literalism is a reading strategy of mine that runs through all the chapters. Chapter 1, for example, comes from a *literal* reading of Bergvall's observation that "variations in accent and deviations from a broad English pronunciation still frequently entail degrees of harassment and verbal, sometimes, physical, abuse" (*Fig* 51). So, what makes a linguistic phenomenon impinge on the bodily domain? Could it be that speech itself is already bodily in some way? Chapter 2 is a *superficial* interpretation of mishearing a foreigner's language as an instance of face and speech becoming unsynched. Chapter 3 *investigates*—here this big word has to be understood trivially, so not as a real detective's adventure, but as what a mother would ask about a broken vase: "Who did it? Maggie, John, or Kitten?"—Vladimir Nabokov's charge of Pnin's English being murderous. So, murder of what and whom? Chapter 4 *takes* the lyrics of John Prine's song "onomatopoeia: I don't want to see ya speaking in a foreign tongue" *at face value*. What if a foreign tongue is indeed derivative and onomatopoeic, in the same way that a cat is forced to say "meow meow" in English but "*nyā nyā*" in Japanese? Chapter 5, inspired by Yoko Tawada's testimonial that the "German language, on the other hand, I swallowed whole and it has been sitting in my stomach ever since" ("*Ein Wort*" 4), presents a culinary journey *word-for-word*. The guest list for word tasting is drafted by Deleuze, which includes children, poets, and madmen. Inspired by Tawada's writing, I revise Deleuze's list by adding the figure of "the exophonic," whose literary expressions proceed from the consumption of foreign words.

All these chapters are written in the rigor of Deleuze and Guattari's proposal about being "a foreigner, but in one's own tongue" (98). However, when they made the claim, Deleuze and Guattari were less interested in the foreigner's problems than in a landscape of creative eccentricity that surrounds the image of the foreigner. Hence the qualifier: "but in one's own tongue." It suggests that the-writer-as-the-foreigner stammers in a conscious and contrived way, and he or she shall be able to speak perfectly if he or she wishes. It means that the ease of speaking and the ability of being at home with one's language not only should remain a suppressed and unrealized potentiality but also is the basic requirement for what they perceived to be the creative stammering of the writer. The literalism of this study thus offers a way of "deterritorializing" Deleuze and Guattari's metaphor. It leads, on the one hand, to a pure play of thoughts—*nonsense*, as some people see it—that I have learned *not* to be apologetic for after hearing Barthes say "pleasure is a critical principle" (*The Pleasure of the Text* 52) and, on the other hand, to *complexities and nuances*. How, indeed, does the foreigner relate to different languages? What is one's own tongue—the mother tongue, the stepmother tongue, or the real tongue inside one's mouth? Is it a given, or could one make a tongue one's own?

Even though the language learner is not a novel subject—since everyone was once a learner of his or her mother tongue—the recent years have witnessed a proliferation of foreign language learners, who acquire new languages in a circumstance of mental and physical displacements and enchantments, who are intellectually mature to reflect on the process of language learning and to narrate these experiences. A key observation, brought forth by writers who are also practitioners of foreign languages, is precisely the varying images of the speaking body in different languages. Whereas the native speaker is able to enjoy the state of anonymity (with the mother tongue being the skin, the mask, the shelter), the foreigner, whose attachment to the new language is too fragile and singular to make his or her speech merge with the smooth and homogenous background noise of the native speaker, cannot help but stand out. Writers have drawn upon a whole repertoire of similes and metaphors to understand the nature of the pacts they are making with their languages. Wang Ping, for instance, when commenting on her English poems in the essay "Writing in Two Tongues," compares herself to an innocent daredevil "who knows no fear or inhibition, who never hesitates to point and shout, 'The emperor has no clothes!'" (12). Tawada, likewise, says that a foreign language offers one the chance to become a playful child again, who is free to toy with his or her language without being weighed down by taboos and conventions ("*Ein Wort*" 7–8). Dorfman, on the contrary, suggests that it is innocence that he has lost because of living in two tongues:

> It is as a resident of this dual existence, married to two tongues, inhabited by both English and Spanish in equal measures, in love with them both

now that they have called off the war for my throat, it is as an adulterer of language that I presently trust that the distress of being double and somewhat homeless is overshadowed by the glory of being hybrid and open. (33)

Besides adulterer, Dorfman also calls himself "a fluid bigamist of language" (33) and a smuggler of foreign syntax (34). The strong vocabulary implies an intense emotional distress for being disloyal to the mother tongue and for being carried away by another language. Moreover, the sexual undertone implies a desiring body that lay dormant in the hands of the mother tongue, testifying to Judith Butler's claim that "speaking itself is a bodily act" ("On Linguistic Vulnerability" 10). Hence Isabelle de Courtivron's confession: "I have always felt like a linguistic transvestite" (163), and Nancy Huston's concern: "to my dismay, my voice has turned into the same loose woman" (62). The linguistic adventure leads to a rediscovery and reimagination of one's own body in terms of age, sexuality, gender, etc.

The list of metaphors is longer than I could possibly accommodate here. Yet, in general, the image of the foreign language learner oscillates between a celebration of freedom and an agony of betrayal. The uncertain linguistic metamorphosis of the foreigner, imbued with dramatic tensions and struggles, thus contributes to the rise of language-related writings. In her essay "On Language Memoir," Kaplan observes that when she started to work on her book *French Lessons: A Memoir*, she noticed that there was an emerging genre of twentieth-century autobiographical literature inspired by the experience of second language acquisition, which she termed "language memoir":

> When I began, I read as many scholarly disquisitions as I could find on second language acquisition—linguistics, sociology, education—and I found methods and statistics and the occasional anecdote, but nothing, really, about what is going on inside the head of the person who suddenly finds herself passionately engaged in new sounds and a new voice, who discovers that *"chat"* is not a cat at all, but a new creature in new surroundings. I wanted to see the "cat," then the *"chat."* I wanted the differences between languages to come alive in a dialogue and characterization. What I was looking for was not theory, but fiction. When I turned to fiction I found, to my delight, that there is an entire genre of twentieth century autobiographical writing which is in essence about language learning. But it has never been categorized or named as such, either because it is discussed in terms of the history of a specific ethnic or national literature,

or because language is understood in these books as mere décor in a drama of upward mobility or exile. (59)

What the science of language failed or did not bother to offer Kaplan found in literature: that is, the story of an enchanted encounter with a new language that resonated with her experience of learning French. French fascinated her not only as an object to be mastered but, more crucially, as an emerging horizon that would lead her to a subjective and singular experience of language colored by emotional intensity and psychological insight. Kaplan wanted to create a labyrinth of words where the cat and the *chat* were neither chained to English nor French, but became mixed and contrasted with each other, affording the cat in reality a fresh, mysterious aura. Learning a new language offered her the occasion to regain the *aura* of words, re-experiencing language as a stylization of reality that bore with itself the signature of the speaker. Kaplan's love of French as a foreign language was, in fact, translatable to her love of literature, which, to quote Barthes from a different context, "by exposing the subject's place and energy, even his deficiency (which is not his absence), focuses on the very reality of language, acknowledging that language is an immense halo of implications, of effects, of echoes, of turns, returns, and degrees" ("Lecture" 35).

* * *

As a final thought—

It *strikes* me—a strange English word, isn't it? It invokes a fierce physical sensation that often makes me pause and wonder if I have not overstated my case—it strikes me that there is a ready-made figure that answers *literally* Deleuze and Guattari's description of what it is "to be a foreigner, but in one's own tongue."

In the ballroom scene of the film *Pygmalion*, Henry Higgins, a professor of phonetics, presents Eliza Doolittle—who was an ordinary flower girl speaking with a thick Cockney accent but had been receiving strict speech training from him—to the upper classes gathered at the embassy, in order to test if he can indeed successfully pass her off as a duchess. The unexpected presence of a former pupil of Professor Higgins, whose name is Aristid Karpathy, makes the plan likely to misfire, since Karpathy, being "the best and the greatest" of Higgins's students, claims that he can place a man anywhere in Europe once he opens his mouth. Karpathy soon busies himself with finding out the true origin of Doolittle, who mesmerizes everyone at the ball with her perfect English, elegant moves, and proper manners.

"She is a fraud!" says Karpathy in the end. "She cannot deceive me. Her name cannot be Doolittle, because Doolittle is an English name and she is not English."

"But she speaks it perfectly," says the Queen.

"*Too perfectly.* Can you show me any Englishwoman *who speaks English as it should be*? The English do not know how to speak their own language. Only foreigners who have been taught to speak it speak it well," Karpathy assures the crowd gathered around him.

"But if she is not English, what is she?" the Queen asks, perplexed.

So, this is Karpathy's verdict: "Hungarian. Yes, Hungarian, and of royal blood."

It is, as we know from the story, a far cry from what Doolittle actually is. The verdict is simply wrong and absurd.

But, is Karpathy utterly wrong? What do you become when you speak *too perfectly*?

A foreigner, according to Karpathy. And a foreigner who is less a speaking body than a language automaton, who is *native* to linguistics but *foreign* to the kind of languages that literature has taught one to believe in.

Works Cited

"Accent." *Oxford English Dictionary*, 2019, www.oed.com/dictionary/accent_n?tl=true. Accessed 10 Mar. 2025.

Achebe, Chinua. "English and the African Writer." *Transition*, no. 75/76, 1997, pp. 342–49.

Alfino, Mark. "Another Look at the Derrida-Searle Debate." *Philosophy & Rhetoric*, vol. 24, no. 2, 1991, pp. 143–52.

Ang, Ien. *On Not Speaking Chinese: Living between Asia and the West*. 2001. Routledge, 2004.

Austin, John Langshaw. *How to Do Things with Words*. The Clarendon Press, 1962.

Bakhtin, Mikhail Mikhailovich. *The Dialogic Imagination: Four Essays*. Translated by Caryl Emerson and Michael Holquist, edited by Michael Holquist, University of Texas Press, 1981.

Bal, Mieke. "Narrative Inside Out: Louise Bourgeois' Spider as Theoretical Object." *Oxford Art Journal*, vol. 22, no. 2, 1999, pp. 101–26.

Bal, Mieke. *Quoting Caravaggio: Contemporary Art, Preposterous History*. University of Chicago Press, 2001.

Baldwin, James. "If Black English isn't a Language, Then Tell Me, What Is?" *The Black Scholar*, vol. 27, no. 1, 1997, pp. 5–6.

Banfield, Ann. "Introduction: What do Linguists Want?" *For the Love of Language*, by Jean-Claude Milner, translated by Ann Banfield, Palgrave Macmillan, 1990, pp. 1–49.

Barthes, Roland. *Camera Lucida: Reflections on Photography*. 1980. Translated by Richard Howard, Hill and Wang, 2010.

Barthes, Roland. "The Death of the Author." *Image Music Text*, translated by Stephen Heath, Fontana Press, 1977, pp. 142–148.

Barthes, Roland. *Empire of Signs*. 1970. Translated by Richard Howard, Hill and Wang, 1983.

Barthes, Roland. "The Grain of the Voice." *Image Music Text*, translated by Stephen Heath, Fontana Press, 1977, pp. 179–89.

Barthes, Roland. "Lecture in Inauguration of the Chair of Literary Semiology, College de France, January 7, 1977." *The Oxford Literary Review*, vol. 4, autumn 1979, pp. 31–44.

Barthes, Roland. *The Pleasure of the Text*. 1973. Translated by Richard Miller, Hill and Wang, 1975.

Barthes, Roland. *The Preparation of the Novel: Lecture Courses and Seminars at the Collège de France, 1978–1979 and 1979–1980*. Translated by Kate Briggs, Columbia University Press, 2011.

Baudrillard, Jean. "The Precession of Simulacra." Translated by Paul Foss and Paul Patton. 1983. *Norton Anthology of Theory and Criticism*, edited by Vincent B. Leitch, Norton, 2010, pp. 1732–41.

Bauman, Carina. "Social Evaluation of Asian Accented English in the United States." *University of Pennsylvania Working Papers in Linguistics*, vol. 19, no. 2, 2013, pp. 10–20.

Beaujour, Elizabeth Klosty. *Alien Tongues: Bilingual Russian Writers of the "First" Emigration*. Cornell University Press, 1989.

Beckett, Samuel. *Not I*. Faber, 1973.

Beckett, Samuel. "A Piece of Monologue." *The Kenyon Review*, vol. 1, no. 3, 1979, pp. 1–4.

Benjamin, Walter. "Children's Literature." *Walter Benjamin: Selected Writings, Volume 2: 1927–1930*, edited by Michael W. Jennings, Howard Eiland, and Gary Smith, Harvard University Press, 2005, pp. 250–56.

Benjamin, Walter. "Doctrine of the Similar." *New German Critique*, vol. 17, spring, 1979, pp. 65–69.

Benjamin, Walter. "On Language as Such and on the Language of Man." *Walter Benjamin: Selected Writings, Volume 1: 1913–1926*, edited by Marcus Bullock and Michael W. Jennings, Harvard University Press, 1997, pp. 62–74.

Benjamin, Walter. "The Task of the Translator." *One-Way Street and Other Writings*, translated by J. A. Underwood, Penguin Books, 2009, pp. 29–45.
Bentley, Eric. *The Life of the Drama*. 1964. Applause Theatre Books, 1991.
Benveniste, Émile. *Problems in General Linguistics*. University of Miami Press, 1971.
Bergvall, Caroline. *Meddle English*. Nightboat Books Callicoon, 2011.
Bergvall, Caroline. "Say: 'Parsley.'" *Fig*, Salt Publishing, 2005, pp. 49–62.
Blanchot, Maurice. "Literature and the Right to Death." *The Work of Fire*, 1949, translated by Charlotte Mandell, Stanford University Press, 1995, pp. 300–344.
Boletsi, Maria, and Christian Moser. *Barbarism Revisited: New Perspectives on an Old Concept*. Brill, 2015.
Borges, Jorge Luis. "Coleridge's Flower." *Selected Non-Fictions*, edited by Eliot Weinberger, Viking Penguin, 1999, pp. 240–42.
Braine, Goerge, editor. *Non-Native Educators in English Language Teaching*. Lawrence Erlbaum Associates, 1999.
Bredin, Hugh. "Onomatopoeia as a Figure and a Linguistic Principle." *New Literary History*, vol. 27, no. 3, 1996, pp. 555–69.
Briggs, Kate. *This Little Art*. Fitzcarraldo Editions, 2017.
Brooks, Peter. *The Melodramatic Imagination: Balzac, Henry James, Melodrama, and the Mode of Excess*. Yale University Press, 1976.
Butler, Judith. Afterword. *The Scandal of the Speaking Body: Don Juan with J. L. Austin, or Seduction in Two Languages*, by Shoshana Felman, Stanford University Press, 2003, pp. 113–23.
Butler, Judith. "On Linguistic Vulnerability." *Excitable Speech: A Politics of the Performative*, Routledge, 1997, pp. 1–41.
Cambier-Langeveld, Tina. "The Role of Linguists and Native Speakers in Language Analysis for the Determination of Speaker Origin." *International Journal of Speech, Language & the Law*, vol. 17, no. 1, 2010, pp. 67–93.
Cameron, Deborah, and Don Kulick. *Language and Sexuality*. Cambridge University Press, 2003.
Carroll, Lewis. *Alice's Adventures in Wonderland and Through the Looking-Glass*. 1865, 1872. Penguin Books, 1998.
Cha, Theresa Hak Kyung. *Dictee*. 1982. University of California Press, 2009.
Cheung, King-Kok. *Articulate Silences: Hisaye Yamamoto, Maxine Hong Kingston, Joy Kogawa*. Cornell University Press, 1993.
Ch'ien, Evelyn Nien-Ming. *Weird English*. Harvard University Press, 2004.
Chion, Michel. *Audio-Vision: Sound on Screen*. Edited and translated by Claudia Gorbman, Columbia University Press, 1994.
Chion, Michel. *The Voice in Cinema*. Edited and translated by Claudia Gorbman, Columbia University Press, 1999.
Chow, Rey. *Not Like a Native Speaker*. Columbia University Press, 2014.
Coleridge, Samuel Taylor. *Anima Poetae: From the Unpublished Note-Books of Samuel Taylor Coleridge*, edited by Ernest Hartley Coleridge, William Heinemann, 1895.
Davies, Alan. *The Native Speaker: Myth and Reality*. Multilingual Matters Ltd., 2003.
De Certeau, Michel. *The Practice of Everyday Life*. Translated by Steven Rendall, University of California Press, 1984.
De Courtivron, Isabelle. "Memoirs of a Bilingual Daughter." *Lives in Translation: Bilingual Writers on Identity and Creativity*, edited by Isabelle de Courtivron, Palgrave Macmillan, 2003, pp. 157–66.
Deleuze, Gilles. *L'Abécédaire de Gilles Deleuze*. Interview with Claire Parnet, 1988–89.

Deleuze, Gilles. *Logic of Sense*. 1990. Translated by Constantin V. Boundas, Mark Lester, and Charles J. Stivale, Bloomsbury, 2015.

Deleuze, Gilles. "Louis Wolfson; Or, the Procedure." *Essays Critical and Clinical*, translated by Daniel W. Smith and Michael A. Greco, Verso, 1998, pp. 7–20.

Deleuze, Gilles. *Proust & Signs*. Translated by Richard Howard, University of Minnesota Press, 2000.

Deleuze, Gilles, and Félix Guattari. *A Thousand Plateaus: Capitalism and Schizophrenia*. 1980. Translated by Brian Massumi, University of Minnesota Press, 1987.

Deleuze, Gilles, and Félix Guattari. "What Is a Minor Literature?" *Mississippi Review*, vol. 11, no. 3, Essays Literary Criticism, winter/spring, 1983, pp. 13–33.

Deleuze, Gilles, and Félix Guattari. *What Is Philosophy?* 1991. Translated by Graham Burchell and Hugh Tomlinson, Verso, 1994.

De Nooy, Juliana. *Derrida, Kristeva, and the Dividing Line: An Articulation of Two Theories of Difference*. Routledge, 2013.

Derrida, Jacques. "Des tours de Babel." *Psyche: Invention of the Other, Volume I*, edited by Peggy Kamuf and Elizabeth G. Rottenberg, Stanford University Press, 2007, pp. 191–225. 2 vols.

Derrida, Jacques. "Foreigner Question: Coming from Abroad/ from the Foreigner." *Of Hospitality*, translated by Rachel Bowlby, Stanford University Press, 2000, pp. 3–73.

Derrida, Jacques. *Glas*. 1974. Translated by John P. Leavey, Jr. and Richard Rand, University of Nebraska Press, 1986.

Derrida, Jacques. *Monolingualism of the Other, or, the Prosthesis of Origin*. 1996. Translated by Patrick Mensah, Stanford University Press, 1998.

Derrida, Jacques. *Of Grammatology*. 1967. Translated by Gayatri Chakravorty Spivak, The Johns Hopkins University Press, 1997.

Derrida, Jacques. "Signature Event Context." *Limited Inc*, Northwestern University Press, 1988, pp. 1–24.

Derrida, Jacques. "Shibboleth: For Paul Celan." *Sovereignties in Question: The Poetics of Paul Celan*, edited by Thomas Dutoit and Outi Pasanen, Fordham University Press, 2005, pp. 1–64.

Derrida, Jacques. *Speech and Phenomena, and Other Essays on Husserl's Theory of Signs*. Translated by David B. Allison and Newton Garver, Northwestern University Press, 1973.

De Saussure, Ferdinand. *Course in General Linguistics*. Translated by Wade Baskin, McGraw-Hill Book Company, 1915.

Dolar, Mladen. *A Voice and Nothing More*. MIT Press, 2006.

Dong, Li. "English in China." *English Today*, vol. 11, no. 1, 1995, pp. 53–56.

Dorfman, Ariel. "The Wandering Bigamists of Language." *Lives in Translation: Bilingual Writers on Identity and Creativity*, edited by Isabelle de Courtivron, Palgrave Macmillan, 2003, pp. 29–38.

Elsaesser, Thomas. "Tales of Sound and Fury: Observation on the Family Melodrama." *Imitation of Life: A Reader on Film and Television Melodrama*, edited by Marcia Landy, Wayne State University Press, 1991.

Fanon, Frantz. *Black Skin, White Masks*. 1952. Translated by Charles Lam Markmann, Pluto Press, 2008.

Felman, Shoshana. *The Scandal of the Speaking Body: Don Juan with J. L. Austin, or Seduction in Two Languages*. 1983. Translated by Catherine Porter, Stanford University Press, 2003.

Ferguson, Charles. Foreword. *The Other Tongue: English across Cultures*, edited by Braj B. Kachru, University of Illinois Press, 1992, pp. xiii–xvii.

Fraser, Helen. "The Role of 'Educated Native Speakers' in Providing Language Analysis for the Determination of the Origin of Asylum Seekers." *International Journal of Speech: Language & the Law*, vol. 16, no. 1, 2009, pp. 113–38.

Frumkin, Lara. "Influences of Accent and Ethnic Background on Perceptions of Eyewitness Testimony." *Psychology, Crime & Law*, vol. 13, no. 3, 2007, pp. 317–31.

Graham, Robert Somerville. "The Music of Language and the Foreign Accent." *The French Review*, vol. 42, no. 3, 1969, pp. 445–51.

Guattari, Félix. *The Machinic Unconscious: Essays in Schizoanalysis*. 1979. Translated by Taylor Adkins, Semiotext(e), 2011.

Guyer, Sara. "The Girl with the Open Mouth: Through the Looking Glass." *Angelaki: Journal of the Theoretical Humanities*, vol. 9, no. 1, 2004, pp. 159–63.

Hamdan, Lawrence Abu. *Contra Diction: Speech Against Itself*, 2016, Haus der Kulturen der Welt, Berlin.

Hamdan, Lawrence Abu. *The Freedom of Speech Itself*. 2012, SoundCloud, soundcloud.com/forensic-architecture-1/the-freedom-of-speech-itself. Accessed 6 Mar. 2025.

Han, Shaogong. *A Dictionary of Maqiao*. 1996. Translated by Julia Lovell, Dial Press Trade Paperbacks, 2005.

Hartman, Geoffrey H. "Monsieur Texte: On Jacques Derrida, His *Glas*." *The Georgia Review*, vol. 29, no. 4, 1975, pp. 759–97.

Hegel, Georg Wilhelm Friedrich. *System of Ethical Life and First Philosophy of Spirit*. Translated by H. S. Harris and T. M. Knox, State University of New York Press, 1979.

Heller-Roazen, Daniel. *Dark Tongues: The Art of Rogues and Riddlers*. Zone Books, 2013.

Heller-Roazen, Daniel. *Echolalias: On the Forgetting of Language*. Zone Books, 2005.

Hiroshima Mon Amour. Directed by Alain Resnais, written by Marguerite Duras, Pathé Films, 1959.

Hoffman, Eva. *Lost in Translation: Life in a New Language*. Penguin Books, 1989.

Hui, Tingting. "Cosmopolitan Hospitality and Accented Crossing: Forging an Ethics of Listening with Lawrence Abu Hamdan's Artworks." *New Cosmopolitanisms, Race, and Ethnicity: Cultural Perspectives*, De Gruyter, 2018, pp. 328–43.

Hui, Tingting. "Performing Failure: Rethinking the Strategic Value of Translation." *Third Text*, vol. 33, no. 2, 2019, 235–46.

Huston, Nancy. "The Mask and the Pen." *Lives in Translation: Bilingual Writers on Identity and Creativity*, edited by Isabelle de Courtivron, Palgrave Macmillan, 2003, pp. 55–68.

Jakobson, Roman, and Linda R. Waugh. *The Sound Shape of Language*. 1979. Mouton de Gruyter, 2011.

Kaplan, Alice. *French Lessons: A Memoir*. University of Chicago Press, 1993.

Khlebnikov, Velimir. "To the Artists of the World." *The King of Time: Selected Writings of the Russian Futurian*, translated by Paul Schmidt, edited by Charlotte Douglas, Harvard University Press, 1985, pp. 146–51.

Kingston, Maxine Hong. *The Woman Warrior: Memoirs of a Girlhood among Ghosts*. Random House, 1976.

Kittler, Friedrich A. *Discourse Networks 1800/1900*. 1985. Translated by Michael Metteer, Stanford University Press, 1990.

Kristeva, Julia. *Strangers to Ourselves*. Translated by Leon S. Roudiez, Columbia University Press, 1991.

Kristiansen, Gitte. "Social and Linguistic Stereotyping: A Cognitive Approach to Accents." *Estudios ingleses de la Universidad Complutense*, vol. 9, 2001, pp. 129–45.

Krivosheeva, Elena. "Iconicity and Its Representation in Japanese Onomatopoeia." The Japanese Studies Association of Australia, the 18th Biennial Conference, 8–11 July 2013, the Australian National University.

Lacan, Jacques. *The Seminar of Jacques Lacan, Book XI: The Four Fundamental Concepts of Psychoanalysis, 1964*. Hogarth Press and Institute of Psycho-Analysis, 1977.

WORKS CITED

Lady and the Tramp. Directed by Clyde Geronimi, Wilfred Jackson, and Hamilton Luske, Walt Disney Productions, 1955.

Lee, Chang-Rae. *Native Speaker.* Penguin Books, 1995.

Lee, Sang-Oak. "The Korean Alphabet: An Optimal Featural System with Graphical Ingenuity." *Written Language & Literacy*, vol. 12, no. 2, 2009, pp. 202–12.

Lecercle, Jean-Jacques. *Deleuze and Language.* Springer, 2002.

Léger, Nathalie. Editor's Preface. *The Preparation of the Novel*, by Roland Barthes, 2003, translated by Kate Briggs, Columbia University Press, 2011, pp. xvii–xxiii.

Lippi-Green, Rosina. *English with an Accent: Language, Ideology, and Discrimination in the United States.* Routledge, 1997.

Lispector, Clarice. *Água Viva.* 1973. Translated by Stefan Tobler, A New Directions Book, 2012.

Lispector, Clarice. *The Hour of the Star.* 1977. Translated by Benjamin Moser, A New Directions Book, 2011.

MacKinnon, Catharine. *Only Words.* Harvard University Press, 1993.

Magnus, Margaret. *Gods in the Word: Archetypes in the Consonants.* CreateSpace Independent Publishing Platform, 2010.

Magnus, Margaret. *What's in a Word? Studies in Phonosemantics.* 2001. Norwegian University of Science and Technology, PhD dissertation.

Matsuda, Mari J. "Voices of America: Accent, Antidiscrimination Law, and a Jurisprudence for the Last Reconstruction." *The Yale Law Journal*, vol. 100, no. 5, 1991, pp. 1329–407.

Marinetti, Filippo Tommaso. "Words-in-Freedom War." *Futurism: An Anthology*, edited by Lawrence Rainey, Christine Poggi, and Laura Wittman, Yale University Press, 2009, pp. 431–36.

McLaren, Anne. "Women's Voices and Textuality: Chastity and Abduction in Chinese Nüshu Writing." *Modern China*, vol. 22, no. 4, 1996, pp. 382–416.

Meltzer, Donald. "Concerning the Perception of One's Own Attributes and Its Relation to Language Development." *Studies in Extended Metapsychology: Clinical Applications of Bion's Ideas*, Clunie Press, 1986, pp. 175–86.

Miller, J. Hillis. *Speech Acts in Literature.* Stanford University Press, 2001.

Milner, Jean-Claude. *For the Love of Language.* Translated by Ann Banfield, Palgrave Macmillan, 1990.

Moser, Benjamin. "Breathing Together." *Água Viva*, by Clarice Lispector, A New Directions Book, 2012, pp. vii–xiv.

Mugglestone, Lynda. *Talking Proper: The Rise of Accent as Social Symbol.* Clarendon Press, 1995.

Murray, Ros. *Antonin Artaud: The Scum of the Soul.* Springer, 2014.

Nabokov, Vladimir. *Pnin.* Avon Publications, 1957.

Nabokov, Vladimir. *The Real Life of Sebastian Knight.* 1941. New Directions, 1959.

Nedoh, Boštjan. *Lacan and Deleuze: A Disjunctive Synthesis.* Edinburgh University Press, 2016.

Neuhauser, S., and Simpson, A. P. "Imitated or Authentic? Listeners' Judgements of Foreign Accents." *ICPhS XVI Proceedings*, 2007, pp. 1805–8.

Ngan, Lucille Lok-Sun, and Chan Kwok-Bun. *The Chinese Face in Australia: Multi-Generational Ethnicity among Australian-Born Chinese.* Springer Science and Business Media, 2012.

Nietzsche, Friedrich. "On Truth and Lying in a Non-Moral Sense." *The Norton Anthology of Theory and Criticism*, edited by Vincent B. Leitch, Norton, 2010, pp. 874–84.

Nolan, Francis. "Degrees of Freedom in Speech Production: an Argument for Native Speakers in LADO." *International Journal of Speech, Language & the Law*, vol. 19, no. 2, 2012, pp. 263–89.

Paikeday, Thomas M. *The Native Speaker is Dead!* Paikeday Publishing Inc., 1985.

Parry, Richard Lloyd. "Koreans Take a Short Cut on the Road to English." *The Independent*, 9 Apr. 2002, www.independent.co.uk/news/world/asia/koreans-take-a-short-cut-on-the-road-to-english-5361932.html. Accessed 10 Mar. 2025.

Patel, Hetain. *It's Growing on Me*. 2008, video installation.
Patel, Hetain. *Who Am I? Think Again*. TED, 2013, recorded live performance, www.ted.com/talks/hetain_patel_who_am_i_think_again. Accessed 10 Mar. 2025.
Pearson, Barbara Zurer. "Learning Two (or More) Languages." *Raising a Bilingual Child*, Living Language, 2008, pp. 81–98.
"A Piece of Monologue." Wikipedia, Wikimedia Foundation, 15 Apr. 2020, en.wikipedia.org/wiki/A_Piece_of_Monologue#cite_note-13. Accessed 10 Mar. 2025.
Plato, et al. *Cratylus: Parmenides; Greater Hippias; Lesser Hippias*. Harvard University Press; W. Heinemann, 2015.
Prine, John. "Onomatopoeia." *Sweet Revenge*, Atlantic Records, 1973.
Pygmalion. Directed by Anthony Asquith and Leslie Howard, 1938.
Ram, Harsha. "Spatializing the Sign: The Futurist Eurasianism of Roman Jakobson and Velimir Khlebnikov." *Between Europe and Asia: The Origins, Theories, and Legacies of Russian Eurasianism*, edited by Mark Bassin et al., University of Pittsburgh Press, 2015, pp. 137–49.
Rangan, Pooja. "In Defense of Voicelessness." *Feminist Media Histories*, vol. 1, no. 3, 2015, pp. 95–126.
Rhode, Maria. "The Physicality of Words: Some Implications of Donald Meltzer's Writings on Language." *Infant Observation*, vol. 16, no. 3, 2013, pp. 270–85.
Rhode, Maria. "Sensory Aspects of Language Development in Relation to Primitive Anxieties." *Infant Observation*, vol. 6, no. 2, 2003, pp. 12–32.
Rodriguez, Richard. *Hunger of Memory: The Education of Richard Rodriguez*. 1982. The Dial Press, 2005.
Rosen, Michael, Helen Oxenbury, and Sophie Aldred. *We're Going on a Bear Hunt*. Walker, 1989.
Rubin, Donald L. "Nonlanguage Factors Affecting Undergraduates' Judgments of Nonnative English-speaking Teaching Assistants." *Research in Higher Education*, vol. 33, no. 4, 1992, pp. 511–31.
Schwenger, Peter. "Words and the Murder of the Thing." *Critical Inquiry*, vol. 28, no. 1, 2001, pp. 99–113.
Searle, John R. "Reiterating the Differences: A Reply to Derrida." *Glyph*, vol. 1, 1977, pp. 198–208.
Sedgwick, Eve Kosofsky. "Paranoid Reading and Reparative Reading, or, You're So Paranoid, You Probably Think This Introduction Is about You." *Touching Feeling: Affect, Pedagogy, Performativity*, Duke University Press, 2003, pp. 123–51.
Simpson, Lorna. *Easy for Who to Say*. 1989, Sean Kelly Gallery, New York.
Simpson, Lorna. *Twenty Questions (A Sampler)*. 1986, Tate Modern Art Gallery, London.
Slaymaker, Douglas. "Introduction: Yōko Tawada: Voices from Everywhere." *Yōko Tawada: Voices from Everywhere*, edited by Douglas Slaymaker, Lexington Books, 2007, pp. 1–12.
Solaris. Directed by Andrei Tarkovsky, written by Fridrikh Gorenshtein and Andrei Tarkovsky, 1972.
Song, Dong. *Stamping the Water*. 1996, Metropolitan Museum of Art, New York.
Speedy Gonzales. Directed by I. Freleng, Warner Bros, 1955.
Speiser, Ephraim Avigdor. "The Shibboleth Incident (Judges 12:6)." *Bulletin of the American Schools of Oriental Research*, vol. 85, 1942, pp. 10–13.
Steffensen, Kenn Nakata. "BBC English with an Accent: 'African' and 'Asian' Accents and the Translation of Culture in British Broadcasting." *Meta*, vol. 57, no. 2, 2012, pp. 510–27.
Still, Judith. *Derrida and Hospitality: Theory and Practice: Theory and Practice*. Edinburgh University Press, 2010.
Straub, Julia. "Melodrama and Narrative Fiction: Towards a Typology." *Anglia*, vol. 132, no. 2, 2014, pp. 225–41.
Suga, Keijirō. "Translation, Exophony, Omniphony." *Yōko Tawada: Voices from Everywhere*, edited by Douglas Slaymaker, Lexington Books, 2007, pp. 21–34.

WORKS CITED

Swift, Jonathan. *Gulliver's Travels*. Palgrave Macmillan, 1995.
Tan, Amy. "Mother Tongue." *Mother*, edited by Claudia O'Keefe, Simon and Schuster Inc., 1996, pp. 320–28.
Tawada, Yoko. *Exusophoni: bogo no soto e deru tabi* (*Exophony: Traveling Outward from One's Mother Tongue*). Iwanami Shoten, 2003.
Tawada, Yoko. "From Mother Tongue to Linguistic Mother." *Manoa*, vol. 18, no. 1, 2006, pp. 139–43.
Tawada, Yoko. *Portrait of a Tongue*. Translated by Chantal Wright, University of Ottawa Press, 2013.
Tawada, Yoko. "Speech Police and Polyglot Play." *Lyric Poetry Review*, vol. 9, 2006, pp. 55–63.
Tawada, Yoko. *Where Europe Begins*. Translated by Susan Bernofsky and Yumi Selden, A New Directions Book, 2007.
Tawada, Yoko, and Bettina Brandt. "*Ein Wort, ein Ort*, or How Words Create Places: Interview with Yoko Tawada." *Women in German Yearbook*, vol. 21, 2005, pp. 1–15.
Twain, Mark. *The Adventures of Huckleberry Finn*. 1884. Penguin Books, 2014.
Van Alphen, Ernst. "Exoticism or the Translation of Cultural Difference." *Literature, Aesthetics and History: Forum of Cultural Exchange between China and the Netherlands*, edited by Lu Jiande and Ernst van Alphen, Chinese Academy of Social Sciences, 2015, pp. 1–11.
Van Alphen, Ernst. "Legible Affects: The Melodramatic Imagination in Painting." *Legibility in the Age of Signs and Machines*, edited by Pepita Hesselberth, Janna Houwen, Esther Peeren, and Ruby de Vos, Brill, 2018, pp. 21–34.
"'Von der Muttersprache zur Sprachmutter': Yoko Tawada's Creative Multilingualism." *Taylor Institution Library*, 15 Feb. 2017, blogs.bodleian.ox.ac.uk/taylorian/2017/02/15/von-der-muttersprache-zur-sprachmutter-yoko-tawadas-creative-multilingualism/. Accessed 22 May 2019.
Wang, Ping. "Writing in Two Tongues." *Manoa*, vol. 18, no. 1, 2006, pp. 12–16.
Wikipedia contributors. "A Piece of Monologue." *Wikipedia, The Free Encyclopedia*, 16 Oct. 2018, en.wikipedia.org/wiki/A_Piece_of_Monologue. Accessed 10 Mar. 2025.
Wolfson, Louis. *Le Schizo et les langues; ou, La Phonétique chez le psychotique* (*Esquisses d'un étudiant de langues schizophrénique*). Gallimard, 1970.
Woolf, Virginia. *The Waves*. The Hogarth Press, 1931.
Wright, Chantal. "Introduction: Yoko Tawada's Exophonic Texts." *Portrait of a Tongue*, by Yoko Tawada, translated by Chantal Wright, University of Ottawa Press, 2013, pp. 1–33.
Wright, Chantal. "Writing in the 'Grey Zone': Exophonic Literature in Contemporary Germany." *German as a Foreign Language*, vol. 3, 2008, pp. 26–42.
Yildiz, Yasemin. *Beyond the Mother Tongue. The Postmonolingual Condition*. Fordham University Press, 2012.
Zhao, Liming. "Nüshu: Chinese Women's Characters." *International Journal of the Sociology of Language*, vol. 129, no. 1, 1998, pp. 127–38.

Index

accent
    as betrayal of one's origin   13
    as critical concept   21
    as foregrounding the music of language   16
    as incompatible with literature   14
    as manner of speaking and pronunciation   16
    as social marker   16
accents, foreign   14, 16, 19, 20, 26, 55, 56, 69, 73, 74, 131, 133
accents, native   16, 92
accents, non-native
    as onomatopoeic imitation   130, 142, 147
    dramatize encounter of language and body   100
accents, non-native   20, 26, 42, 43
accents, visualized   19
accent test   130, 187, 189, 190, 195
agency, linguistic   43, 44, 48
Ang, Ien   73, 74, 75
anthropomorphism   108, 110
appropriation   17, 30, 58, 71, 86, 171
Artaud, Antonin   161, 162, 163, 164, 165, 166, 168
assemblage   193, 196, 197
Austin, J. L.   24, 25, 46, 144, 189, 190, 191, 192
author, death of   9, 10, 11, 12
author, return of   10, 11
avant-gardes   107, 139

Babel   111, 128, 149, 152
Bal, Mieke   34
Barthes, Roland   9, 10, 11, 12, 13, 34, 35, 36, 107, 185, 198, 200, 202
Beckett, Samuel   36, 124
Benjamin, Walter   132, 135, 140, 141, 142, 150
Bergvall, Caroline   33, 43, 49, 198
bliss, text of   10, 12
bodies, foreign   14, 20, 150, 169
bodies, maternal   18, 60, 198
bodies, native   26, 117
bodies, non-native   26
bodies, stylized   45
bodies, textual   12
bodies, unconscious   26, 46, 48
bodies, voicing   12
Butler, Judith   24, 25, 29, 30, 43, 44, 45, 46, 47, 48, 55, 56, 57, 58, 201

camouflage   13, 31, 32, 96
care, affective   59
Carroll, Lewis   158, 162, 164, 165, 166
Cha, Hak Kyung   101, 102
Ch'ien, Evelyn Nien-Ming   106, 119
Chion, Michel   70, 72, 87

Chow, Rey   20, 88
consciousness   17, 24, 25, 46, 80, 100, 115, 116, 143, 167, 190, 194
convention   25, 58, 138
counterpoint, audiovisual   21, 70, 87, 88, 89, 92, 96
creativity, literary   28, 163, 170, 177

de Certeau, Michel   30
deconstruction   14
Deleuze, Gilles   35, 36, 76, 77, 78, 79, 80, 81, 82, 83, 84, 89, 157, 158, 159, 160, 161, 162, 163, 164, 165, 166, 167, 168, 172, 177, 192, 193, 194, 195, 196, 197, 198, 199, 202
Derrida, Jacques   13, 14, 24, 25, 31, 41, 49, 57, 136, 137, 138, 144, 149, 150, 190, 191, 192, 195
deterritorialization   197, 198
deviation, linguistic   17
différance   13, 49, 83
discrimination   17, 30, 43, 72, 84
diversity, linguistic   20

ears   5, 11, 15, 20, 27, 33, 34, 60, 68, 82, 85, 96, 116, 118, 127, 128, 130, 146, 147, 152, 173, 174, 175, 176, 188
ethnicities   20, 32, 42, 43, 73, 74, 75, 92, 96
exophony   34, 36, 37, 161, 171, 172, 173, 175, 177, 178, 179, 183, 199

face
    and speech   21, 69, 71, 72, 74, 75, 81, 85, 87, 88, 89, 91, 95, 96, 199
    as sustained by speech   84
    as visual percept   76
face-occurrences   80
face-types   80, 104
faciality   76, 77, 79, 80, 83, 85, 89, 93
Fanon, Frantz   73, 84, 85, 86
felicity   33, 47, 58
Felman, Shoshana   23, 24, 25, 26, 28, 29, 46, 190, 192
figuration   12, 13, 15, 36
figure of accent   15, 23, 186
foreigners   15, 23, 29, 31, 32, 36, 41, 42, 57, 81, 91, 95, 99, 102, 111, 146, 153, 172, 198, 199, 200, 201, 202, 203
foreignness   15, 20, 21, 31, 42, 50, 54, 55, 73, 75, 92, 95, 96, 101, 104, 118, 130, 145, 168, 170, 172, 176
frenectomy, lingual   29

globalization   21
Guattari, Félix   35, 76, 77, 78, 79, 80, 81, 82, 83, 84, 89, 104, 172, 193, 194, 195, 196, 197, 198, 199

habitus 45
Hamdan, Lawrence Abu 33, 186, 188
hate speech 21, 44, 45, 46, 47, 48, 54, 55, 56, 58
heteroglossia 78
Hoffman, Eva 15, 25, 28, 81, 82, 83, 100, 101, 147, 148, 149, 150, 151, 152
hostility 20, 21, 30, 43, 85
hybridity 69

image
    and sound 70, 90, 96
    and word 89, 90
imitation 16, 21, 97, 121, 123, 124, 125, 128, 130, 131, 132, 133, 134, 135, 138
immigrants 42, 50, 54, 62, 64, 95, 127
imperfection 15, 54
incongruity, between language and body 24, 34, 46, 49, 51, 117, 153, 179, 198
injurious speech 29
injury, linguistic 44, 55
insiders 15, 18, 19, 42
intentionality 24, 99
iterability 24, 25, 191
iteration 25

Jakobson, Roman 130, 140
jargons 17

Kaplan, Alice 23, 28, 173, 201, 202
Kingston, Maxine Hong 50, 51, 52, 53, 54
Kittler, Friedrich 18, 60, 61
Kristeva, Julia 5, 31, 99, 101, 138

language
    and body 13, 14, 21, 23, 24, 26, 27, 28, 44, 117, 134, 170, 171, 174, 177, 182
    as condition of existence 44
    materiality of 110
    murder of 15
    music of 16, 22
    seduction of 23
language analysis 187
language standardization 17, 18, 58, 61
Lee, Chang-Rae 28, 116
linguistic purism 14
linguistics 12, 27, 79, 140, 187, 188, 190, 191, 192, 193, 194, 195, 196, 197, 201, 203
linguistic turn 78
Lispector, Clarice 36
literalism 199
literary machine 196, 197
literary studies 13, 33
literary voice 13, 14, 15, 23, 28, 160, 169, 171
    as embodied 15
    as free of accent 13, 14
literature
    as distinct from mother tongue 172
    as favoring mother tongue 14
    in relation to linguistics 192
    in relation to oral regress 161
literature, exophonic 36, 37, 171
logocentrism 13, 137
loyalty, linguistic 26

Magnus, Margret 140, 142
melodramas 21, 22, 104, 152
melody 5, 14, 16, 22, 100
Meltzer, Donald 29, 119, 121, 122, 123, 124, 125
metaphors 18, 61, 76, 107, 108, 109, 119, 121, 125, 128, 137, 169, 170, 177, 180, 182, 198, 199, 200, 201
migration 21, 64, 129, 133, 145, 166
Milner, Jean-Claude 193, 194, 195
mise-en-scène 22
mispronunciation 40, 106, 145, 146
Mladen Dolar 99, 102
monolingualism 19, 43, 64, 94
monolingualism of the other 13, 31
mother tongue 14, 16, 18, 19, 21, 26, 27, 29, 36, 40, 41, 42, 44, 51, 58, 59, 60, 61, 62, 64, 65, 91, 94, 96, 97, 98, 100, 103, 114, 115, 116, 129, 130, 131, 133, 145, 152, 166, 167, 168, 169, 170, 171, 172, 174, 179, 180, 200, 201
mouth
    as buccal theater 119, 122, 124
    as buccal theatre 122
    as buccal tribunal 115, 116, 119
mouthing, exploratory 123, 124
Mugglestone, Lynda 17, 18, 20, 58
multilingualism 21
myth 18, 22, 24, 25, 26, 27, 29, 85, 86, 146

Nabokov, Vladimir 15, 36, 106, 110, 111, 114, 119, 145, 199
naming 109, 110, 111, 143, 144, 145, 148, 153
nation, and language 59

onomatopoeia 129, 130, 134, 135, 136, 137, 138, 140, 142, 143, 153, 199
orality 86, 160, 161, 168, 170, 172
organs, speech 25, 26, 27, 61, 100, 116
otherness 14, 43, 79, 133, 138, 145, 175, 177
outsiders 15, 19, 20, 42
ownership 33, 42, 56, 96, 102

passing, linguistic 78
Patel, Hetain 32, 90, 91, 92, 94, 95, 96, 97, 98, 99, 103, 104
performative contradiction 56
performativity 24, 25, 28, 33, 35, 46, 47, 48, 56, 58, 123, 124, 125, 144, 189, 190, 191
phonosemantics 140
pleasure, text of 10, 12
politics
    of performativity 43, 48, 56
polyglot 111, 135, 178

INDEX

race 20, 32, 86, 92
racism 45, 79, 84, 86, 88
regress, oral 160, 161, 169, 177, 178, 179, 183
representation 10, 12, 47, 87, 92, 107, 110, 125, 133, 135, 144, 197
resignification 29, 47, 48, 55, 57
Rhode, Maria 123, 124, 125
rhythm 5, 16, 22, 35, 36, 55, 64, 102, 173
Rodriguez, Richard 15, 44, 62, 63, 64, 65, 144, 147, 149

Saussure, Ferdinand de 136, 137, 138, 142, 193
schizophrenia 165, 166, 167, 168, 170, 172, 173, 177, 178, 179, 183
Schwenger, Peter 109, 110, 119
Searle, John 190, 191, 192, 195
shibboleth 21, 49, 50, 54, 189
silence
  as absence of meaning 52
  as pregnant with possibilities 52
  as self-marginalization 52
similarity, non-sensuous 141, 142
Simpson, Lorna 82, 84
slangs 17
sociolinguistics 18
sound symbolism 139
sovereignty 25, 26, 46, 48, 111
speakers, native 18, 19, 20, 21, 26, 27, 32, 40, 41, 42, 44, 58, 64, 73, 91, 104, 116, 118, 119, 129, 187, 188, 200
speakers, non-native 19, 42, 91, 92, 95, 171
speaking, and eating 158, 159, 161, 162, 163, 168, 169, 170, 172, 177, 183
spectacles, audiovisual 20, 71, 84, 86, 88, 95, 104
speech
  as bodily 21, 27, 46
  facial treatment of 81
speech, accented 21, 28, 30, 34, 43, 48, 50, 54, 55, 189, 195
speech act 24, 25, 29, 33, 45, 46, 48, 54, 55, 189, 190, 191
speech, broken 56
speech, intimate 65
speech, visualized 71, 72, 74, 86
stereotypes 17, 72, 92
structuralism 79, 80, 143, 152
stuttering 34, 50, 56, 182
subjects, postsovereign 48
survivability, linguistic 43, 44

tactics
  by accented speakers 13, 30, 31, 32, 33
  versus strategies 30, 33, 134
Tan, Amy 54, 57, 58, 62, 65
Tawada, Yoko 15, 36, 135, 169, 170, 171, 172, 173, 174, 176, 177, 178, 179, 180, 183, 199, 200
texts
  as bodily forms 12
theater, buccal 122, 124
theatre, buccal 119, 122
timbre 11, 16, 99
tongue, accented 42, 199
tongue-cutting 50, 51
tongue, foreign 42, 43, 54, 129, 130, 132, 143, 167, 169, 170, 172, 173, 175, 177, 179, 180, 199
tongue, onomatopoeic 147
translatability 131, 133, 150
translation 14, 15, 18, 20, 25, 28, 32, 33, 57, 70, 81, 90, 91, 93, 95, 96, 97, 108, 111, 113, 124, 127, 129, 131, 132, 133, 138, 141, 143, 145, 146, 147, 148, 149, 150, 151, 152, 162, 163, 164, 165, 166, 167, 168, 171, 179, 180, 181, 182, 183
translation, onomatopoeic 32, 132, 133, 152, 153
translation therapy 166, 168
translator 10, 32, 90, 91, 92, 96, 97, 121, 163, 174, 193
Triolet, Elsa 26

untranslatability 32, 130, 145, 149, 150
utterance, performative 24, 25, 46, 191

van Alphen, Ernst 22, 93
vocal writing 11
voice, accented 102, 104
voice, grain of 11, 102
vulnerability, linguistic 29, 43, 44, 54, 56, 57, 177

Wolfson, Louis 161, 166, 167, 168
Woolf, Virginia 5, 9, 15, 33
words, and things 108, 109, 110, 111, 121, 124, 133, 143
words, onomatopoeic 134, 135, 136, 140, 142
words, portmanteau 163, 164
writers, bilingual 111, 166
writers, exophonic 36, 173, 175, 179
writing aloud 11

xenophobia 21

Yildiz, Yasemin 59, 60, 61, 64

Printed in the United States
by Baker & Taylor Publisher Services